SPARKS FROM THE ANVIL OF OPPRESSION

PHILADELPHIA'S
African Methodists and
Southern Migrants, 1890–1940

South Street, South Philadelphia, 1930.
Courtesy Philadelphia City Archives

SPARKS
FROM THE ANVIL
OF
OPPRESSION

PHILADELPHIA'S
African Methodists and
Southern Migrants, 1890–1940

ROBERT GREGG

TEMPLE UNIVERSITY PRESS
PHILADELPHIA

Temple University Press, Philadelphia 19122
Copyright © 1993 by Temple University. All rights reserved
Published 1993
Printed in the United States of America

The paper used in this publication meets the minimum requirements of
American National Standard for Information Sciences—Permanence of Paper
for Printed Library Materials, ANSI Z39.48-1984 ⊚

Library of Congress Cataloging-in-Publication Data

Gregg, Robert, 1958–
    Sparks from the anvil of oppression : Philadelphia's African
    Methodists and Southern migrants, 1890–1940 / Robert Gregg.
    p.   cm.
    Includes bibliographical references and index.
    ISBN 1-56639-063-X (hard)
    1. African Methodist Episcopal Church—Pennsylvania—Philadelphia—
History—20th century.   2. Methodist Church—Pennsylvania—
Philadelphia—History—20th century.   3. Afro-American churches—
Pennsylvania—Philadelphia—History—20th century.   4. Philadelphia
(Pa.)—Church history—20th century.   5. Philadelphia (Pa.)—Race
relations.   6. Race relations—Religious aspects—Methodist Church.
I. Title.
BX8445.P5G74   1993   92-34589
287′.874811—dc20   CIP

To Madhavi

Contents

Maps and Tables   ix
Acknowledgments   xi

1 Introduction 1

PART I
Churches and Ghettos

2 "Drowned by a Torrent of Migration"   21
3 Evangelism and Social Service   45

PART II
"In the Pulpit and the Pew"

4 Uplifting "Backward Peoples"   69
5 "Pulpit Extension"   87
6 Service and Prestige   105
7 "Flaming Torches"   129

PART III
The "Great Migration"

8 Many "Promised Lands"   147
9 The Earnest Pastor's Heated Term   175
10 "Let This Be Your Home"   193
11 Conclusion   217

Notes   223
Index   262

Maps and Tables

Map 1 Concentration of African American Population in Philadelphia's Wards, 1900   22

Map 2 Concentration of African American Population in Philadelphia's Wards, 1930   26

Table 2.1 Black Laborers Employed in Industrial Plants in 1917   34

Table 2.2 Businesses Employing Blacks ca. 1923   35

Table 2.3 Black Professionals in 1908 and 1935   41

Table 7.1 Place of Birth of A.M.E. Ministers, 1880–1940   133

Table 7.2 Origins of Pastors by Region for Each Decade, 1880–1950   133

Table 7.3 Ministers' Membership in Orders by Licensing Date   137

Table 7.4 Mean Number of Years Served by Pastors at Churches to Which They Were Appointed between 1870 and 1949   143

Table 8.1 Reasons for Moving North by Rural and Urban Groupings   152

Table 8.2 Date of Arrival of Head of Household by Rural and Urban Groupings   153

Table 8.3 Mean Number of Children per Family by Age Groups and Rural and Urban Groupings   154

Table 8.4 Mean Wage of Household Head by Age Groups and Rural and Urban Groupings   156

Table 8.5 Type of Place of Origin of Letter-Bearers from Florida, Georgia, and South Carolina   162

Table 10.1 Distribution of Migrants among the Denominations, 1923   212

Acknowledgments

Because this book started out as a dissertation I would like first to thank the teachers who inspired me to embark on the project, encouraged me to stick to it, and helped me to finish it. Among these I owe a special debt to Owen Dudley Edwards, Kenneth Fielden, and John Dwyer of Edinburgh University, and Laurence Dickey, Walter Licht, Michael Zuckerman, Lee Cassanelli, David Ludden, Drew Faust, Antoine Joseph, Stan Vittoz, Michael Katz, Evelyn Higginbotham, and particularly Robert Engs at the University of Pennsylvania. I would also like to acknowledge a debt to Ken Kusmer, who guided me through the literature on ghettoization. Many of my ideas have been shaped by his interpretation of the literature and by his reflections on the responses to his own book, which, in my estimation, remains a classic study of ghettoization.

Fellow graduate students at the University of Pennsylvania also helped me immeasurably with their comments, inspirational work, and friendship. In particular, I would like to thank Rick Halpern, Andy Feffer, Ken Straus, Libby Smith, Karen Mittelman, Shan Holt, and Steve Cameron. I am also indebted to the Charlotte W. Newcombe Fellowship Foundation, which supported me during the research stages of my dissertation.

Since finishing graduate school I have acquired a number of other debts. At Princeton University, Gyan Prakash, Liz Lunbeck, Gary Gerstle, Alan Brinkley, and Carl Nightingale provided many perceptive comments and in their own work gave me a high standard to aim for. At Mount Holyoke College, I was fortunate that my colleagues Amy Kaplan, Lynda Morgan, Dan Czitrom, Joe Ellis, Jon Lipman, and Harold Garrett-Goodyear showed such great interest in my work. Their insights and encouragement helped me to make my revisions more quickly than would otherwise have been possible.

Other people have contributed to this study in important ways. Special thanks must go to Rev. Jeane B. Williams and Rev. Matthew H. Jones. The former has been extremely generous with her time, her insights about the A.M.E. Church, and her resources. She helped me unearth bits of information that might otherwise have been neglected. The Rev. Jones, a very energetic octogenarian, provided a view of the 1920s from both the pulpit and the pew that was invaluable.

I have benefited greatly from being a member of the Northeastern Seminar on Black Religion. Attendance at its meetings and the presentation of a paper enabled me to hear and respond to the ideas of Milton Sernett, David Wills, Randall Burkett, Peter Paris, and Jualynne Dodson. I am also grateful to Milton Sernett, Emma Lapsansky, and Randall Miller for their very helpful comments on an article I published on the Earnest Pastor. But I am even more grateful to Julie Winch for her extensive reader's comments. Many improvements to my original manuscript resulted from her very careful reading. Everyone should be so lucky as to have someone like Julie Winch as a reader.

I am also indebted to the people at the Afro-American Historical and Cultural Museum. Working on the exhibit, "Let This Be Your Home," helped me to refine a number of my views on the Great Migration. While much of the work on this exhibit was more stressful than I care to remember, my colleagues on the project, Director Rowena Stewart, Irene Ursula Burnham, Allen Ballard, Nannette Clark, Richard Watson, and Donna DeVore were a pleasure to work alongside. Thank you also to George Brightbill of the Temple University Urban Archives for his assistance over the last four years.

I chose Temple University Press for this work in part because of the nature of the topic. More important, however, Janet Francendese seemed to represent the best that one could hope for in an editor. My judgment turned out to be correct. Janet has always been ready with insightful and imaginative suggestions, as well as enthusiastic encouragement. Mary Capouya has shepherded the manuscript through production with equal care and professionalism, and Terry Schutz showed great skill with her copyediting pencil.

I have thanked family members before for their help with my dissertation. I want to add additional thanks to my mother, Mary Gregg, for helping to proofread the manuscript. I dedicate this work to Madhavi Kale to whom I owe a considerable intellectual debt. Besides this, she and our son, Nikhil, bring a joy to my life that I will not attempt to describe.

SPARKS FROM THE ANVIL OF OPPRESSION

PHILADELPHIA'S
*African Methodists and
Southern Migrants, 1890–1940*

CHAPTER 1

Introduction

The attitude of historians toward African American churches can be likened to that of a physician–friend of Bishop Richard R. Wright, Jr., who complained that black people wasted their money on "useless church buildings." When asked whether he actually knew how much money black people put into churches and whether he had even investigated the subject, the doctor responded in the negative. "But," he argued, "the subject does not need investigation."[1] Like this physician, historians have often made assumptions about the role of religion in black communities without studying churches directly. Many sociologists, anthropologists, and theologians have analyzed black churches from their own disciplinary perspectives, but relatively few social historians have focused directly on the way the churches operated and how they functioned within the larger community.[2]

Churches were the largest and most elaborate economic, social, and political institutions organized by African Americans, at least until the Second World War. The historians' omission is thus a serious hindrance to an understanding of the changing positions of black Americans in the United States. The purpose of this study is to focus on black churches and churchgoers in Philadelphia during a crucial period in the development of the black community's religious institutions, from 1890 to 1940.

I have confined my study to African Methodist churches[3] and their members because, in the words of W.E.B. Du Bois, black churches are "differentiating."[4] Because they divide people in many ways, socially, culturally, and ideologically, to make the assumption that they constitute a single group (the "Black Church") is erroneous. The historian needs to be aware of a particular denomination's structure, the nature of its theology, its internal divisions, and the way these changed over time as the society in which the denomination was embedded also changed. By treating the denominations as a single unit, historians have failed to do justice to the variety and richness of African American culture. They have also downplayed the ways in which churches helped shape class divisions within the black community and ignored the important changes within these institutions during the twentieth century.

As the leading black denomination in Philadelphia, the African Methodist Episcopal Church played a pivotal role in the city's black communities, a role that changed as a result of migration and ghettoization. The African Methodist Episcopal denomination had been established in Philadelphia in 1816, almost thirty years after Richard Allen, Absalom Jones and other black worshipers left Olde St. George's Methodist Episcopal Church in protest against their confinement to the balconies by the white congregation.[5] In forming a church in which African Americans would not have to face such discrimination, Allen and Jones disagreed over whether the new congregation should become Protestant Episcopal or remain within the Methodist fold, and two new churches emerged. St. Thomas's Protestant Episcopal Church soon attracted the more elite element within Philadelphia's black community, and it remained a small congregation within a very large white denomination. Bethel Methodist Church, in contrast, grew from a single congregation into a large denomination by spawning new churches around the city and in the free states. With the establishment of an episcopacy, the African Methodist Church acquired an entire hierarchical structure with bishops appointed to the different sections of the country.[6] It even made inroads into the slave South, but these were limited by southern whites who linked African Methodism to slave conspiracies.[7]

The A.M.E. Zion Church had a similar background, though its initial separation from a Methodist congregation occurred in 1792 in New York City.[8] While the A.M.E. Church was organized from Philadelphia and established only a small number of churches in New York, the Zion denomination was centered in New York and had just a few congregations in Philadelphia.[9] There also existed a Union African Methodist Episcopal Church, which had its origins in Wilmington, Delaware, and some Colored Methodist Episcopal churches, which were congregations affiliated with the white-controlled Methodist Episcopal Church.[10] Compared with the A.M.E. Church, these denominations were small. In general, they followed A.M.E. leadership in Philadelphia, where they all spoke for the same kinds of people.

The main differences among Methodist denominations in turn-of-the-century Philadelphia related not to differences in the social groups from which the particular denominations drew their members but rather to differences in the states from which many of their congregants had migrated. As the different denominations had expanded into the southern states after the Civil War, spheres of influence had been tacitly recognized.[11] Consequently, most black Methodists from Georgia and South Carolina were to be found at A.M.E. churches, those from North Carolina at A.M.E. Zion chuches, and those from Maryland at Colored Methodist Episcopal churches. As might be expected, these differences became more pronounced during the Great Migration. Yet "African Methodist" can be used to refer to these churches collectively because they attracted similar kinds of people, even if they were from different states. Moreover, the churches shared a Methodist theology and liturgy, and they generally played the same role in African American communities.

Their common role was to represent and provide spiritual sustenance for a middling group in the community, made up of people that W.E.B. Du Bois referred to as "the best of the great laboring class."[12] This group included the vast majority of black Philadelphians prior to the end of the nineteenth century: people working in building trades and other occupations traditionally labeled as working class and servants employed by the white elite. It did not include the leading caterers, barbers, and other black businessmen; such people gravitated toward Protestant Episcopal and Presbyterian denominations. Nor did it include the poorest blacks, the unemployed, and those eking out an existence in day labor. These people remained outside the churches or attended small storefront congregations, sometimes Baptist but usually not connected to any recognized denomination. Much of the story of this book concerns the fate of this "middling group." By the 1920s, and particularly during the depression years of the 1930s, it was diminishing in importance as the numbers of both professionals and unskilled, underemployed laborers increased.

The way in which African Methodists spoke for this middling group can be understood by looking closely at the philosophy of "uplift," the dominant ideology in turn-of-the-century Philadelphia. Bishop George W. Clinton of the A.M.E. Zion Church reflected the commitment to this philosophy among African Methodists when he asserted that the mission of Methodism was to provide "patient, loving, Christ-like leadership towards all that make for the salvation and uplifting to complete manhood of the backward peoples."[13] The concern that African Americans reach the level of "manhood," often expressed by white and black intellectuals alike, was derived from this philosophy of "uplift." The appeal of "uplift" was great because it could mean different things to different people. For social elites it meant accommodation to mainstream "American" culture; for the lower classes it meant the possibility and promise of full equality.[14]

Members of the white elite believed that if the great republican experiment was to survive, then European immigrants and blacks would have to be elevated to their own level through a process of accommodation. For this elite, the notion of "uplift" was comforting and conservative because it promised integration and equality only after people lower on the "scale of civilization" had undergone a transformation and had proved themselves worthy. For members of the lower classes, the idea of "uplift" held out the possibility that they could ascend the Social Darwinist ladder and the promise that when they reached the top they would benefit from the same rights as other Americans to define and shape their world according to their own needs. In addition, the notion of "uplift" prescribed certain rules to which all people, not just black people, were supposed to conform.[15] On the one hand, social elites had to undertake to assist their less fortunate brethren—even if only to maintain the fiction that they could better articulate the interests of the lower classes. On the other hand, the lower classes were required to espouse capitalist principles and to eschew revolutionary change. Transgressions against this code would be deplored as the failure of the other party to live up to the social compact.

"Uplift," then, incorporated within its meaning both accommodation and protest or, in historian Edward L. Wheeler's words, "a rich interplay of accommodation and possibility."[16] In African American historiography these two concepts have been torn asunder in the effort to create a neat dichotomy between the accommodationist forces of Booker T. Washington, on the one hand, and the radical supporters of W.E.B. Du Bois, on the other.[17] For the majority of black Philadelphians, at least, there was no contradiction between the two, and African Methodist ministers felt comfortable inviting both Washingtonians and Du Boisians to speak at their churches. But as Philadelphia became increasingly ghettoized, characterized by conflict between competing ethnic groups rather than by master–servant dynamics, the notion of "uplift" ceased to be relevant. Those who continued to talk in such terms would be progressives, idealists, Social Gospelers, and the like—people who wanted social harmony when the reality for many was social conflict. Accommodation and protest were separated in the ghetto, leaving propagandists of "uplift" like the African Methodists without many listeners.

The concept of "uplift" is even more complex than this. If the master and servant, colonizer and colonized, oppressor and oppressed had different roles to play in the quest for "uplift," then African Methodists played both roles. Sometimes they talked about uplifting the race as a whole to the level of white society. In this case they used the language of possibility articulated by the oppressed as they endeavored to push beyond the limits imposed on them. At other times they talked about uplifting other African Americans to their own level; this meaning, akin to that found among members of the white elite, represented the language of accommodation articulated by African Methodists attempting to uplift their poorer brethren. This language was one of prescription to African Methodist ideas rather than one of open-ended commitment to oppressed people and any cultural or religious expression they might want. And as African Methodists began to lose their dominant position in the community, their commitment to the denomination's "method" became more prescriptive and exclusive; the less able they were to appeal to the whole African American community, the less willing they were to try.

Recognizing the nature and importance of the concept of "uplift" enables us to understand James Porter's address to the African Methodist Episcopal Church's Philadelphia District Conference of 1890. "Methodists like sparks come out of the anvil of oppression," the pastor of the Germantown A.M.E. Church proclaimed. He continued, "The more you oppress or persecute a child of God the closer he adheres to Christ; and when he turns away, ten chances to one is he is a full-fledged Methodist. Remember always that Jesus said . . . , 'Marvel not that the world hates you; it hated me before it hated you; but I have overcome the world, and so shall you.'"[18] Rev. Porter recognized the appeal of Methodism for African Americans. He also knew, however, that it was able to attract to its banners those who had suffered oppression without advocating worldly liberation and political radicalism. For African Methodists, as for other Methodists, overcoming the world did not mean physically overthrowing offensive regimes; the sparks were not intended to ignite revolutionary fires. Indeed, while Porter and his ministerial colleagues fought discrimination vigorously, they shared a Social Gospel theology with many whom they might have considered their oppressors.

Nevertheless, African Methodists did not merely imitate white Americans. For one thing, their experiences were markedly different from those of other Philadelphians; an unfriendly environment necessitated creative responses on both individual and institutional levels. Sparks flew from the anvil of oppression. In Philadelphia, between 1890 and 1940, the anvils of oppression were the newly forming ghettos, while the sparks were the efforts of black people, in this case African Methodists, to create communities and to respond to their depressed living and working environments. While these communities were not always able to help their members "overcome the world" and escape the ghetto, they did provide them with support and outlets for cultural, economic, political, and religious expression.

As is apparent from the layout of the chapters that follow, I do not feel that the most obvious narrative approach is necessarily the most appropriate for understanding African Methodists and the Great Migration. Nearly all studies of northbound migration start with the conditions for African Americans in the South, turn to the problems faced in the movement north, and end with adjustment to life in the urban metropolis. In some ways, this narrative has been responsible for entrenching the "field-to-factory" model in the historiography, with the "rural" South giving up its labor to the "urban" North.[19] But the interconnectedness of capitalist markets, the industrialization of the "New South," and the ability of the new cities to shape their surrounding areas mean that such a narrative is too divorced from changes occurring throughout southern states and tends to exaggerate the "backwardness" of that region. This approach is particularly lacking with regard to the African Methodists involved in the migration. Because Philadelphia was the cradle of the A.M.E. Church and New York the cradle of the A.M.E. Zion Church, the physical migration of members of these denominations northward had been preceded by a cultural migration of the denominations southward.

In this work, I concentrate on the nature of and conditions within the northern African Methodist churches and the Philadelphia African American community before turning to the travails of southern migrants and refugees. The first part of the book focuses on the problems faced by the black community and black churches as a result of socioeconomic changes occurring in Philadelphia prior to and during the Great Migration. My analysis here uses the "ghetto" as its fundamental conceptual and theoretical framework. This framework has recently been brought into question by historians using an alternative "proletarianization" framework and hence requires some explanation.[20]

The ghettoization thesis was developed in the work of St. Clair Drake and Horace Cayton in the 1930s, popularized in the 1960s by Gilbert Osofsky and Allan H. Spear, and refined during the 1970s in the work of Kenneth L. Kusmer and James Borchert.[21] It emphasizes racial discrimination, in particular, the segregation of black people into impoverished urban areas where little or no work is available, educational opportunities and health facilities are poor, and the population is "demographically weak" (with high infant mortality and low life expectancy, for example), in determining the life chances of African Americans.

Joe William Trotter, Jr., has argued that, by itself, the ghettoization focus is insufficient: it "systematically fails to highlight the process of black transition to an urban-industrial working class." Further, " 'The ghetto' as a racial-spatial phenomenon is stretched beyond its limits . . . in efforts to employ it to describe the persistence of socioeconomic inequality between blacks and whites." He continues, "By its nearly singular focus on blacks and whites, the ghetto synthesis has also camouflaged the dynamics of class divisions within the black population. True, these studies have documented the importance of cleavages between black elites, but the division between the black bourgeois elite and the Afro-American urban-industrial proletariat has gained insufficient comment."[22]

The first weakness of the ghetto thesis, then, has been its tendency to describe African Americans as victims rather than as agents. The black community has been described as merely the product of white racism, rather than as being active in its own making in the Thompsonian manner. Quite rightly, historians who have employed the ghetto thesis in this way (Gilbert Osofsky in particular) can be accused of not giving their subjects the same respect that is given to white lower classes.

Meanwhile, those historians, like Kusmer and Borchert, who have managed to move beyond this pathological characterization of blacks have, Trotter argues, fallen afoul of the second weakness of the ghetto thesis—insufficiently differentiating among the various classes in the community.[23] Kusmer's study of Cleveland, however, shows clearly not only that the ghetto thesis does not necessitate a pathological interpretation of the ghetto but also that the black community in the ghetto was not an undifferentiated mass of people. Yet Trotter's criticism is somewhat justified. Kusmer ends his work by suggesting that the "paradox" of the ghetto was that it allowed for solidarity in the struggle for civil rights. It was, Kusmer argued, "isolation, and the sense of unique goals and needs that it fostered, that helped unify the black community and provided the basis for the future struggle against racism in all its manifestations."[24]

However, Kusmer's exaggeration of the potential for solidarity in this instance is not a weakness of the ghetto thesis itself. Rather, it is a problem with the way the thesis has been used and, in particular, a problem arising from the assumption that the racial–spatial pressures leading to the ghettoization of the black community would also lead to the development of black solidarity. In fact, the increasing separation of the black community from the rest of American society during the twentieth century has exacerbated divisions in that community. What I argue here is that black institutions became battlegrounds over power and prestige for people who could not look outside their community for these things.[25] According to Rev. Matthew H. Jones, a Philadelphia pastor during the 1920s, institutions like churches and secret orders or fraternities were extremely important to "destitute people starved of outlets to gain prestige."[26] Such institutions, like most of those in the ghetto, necessarily differentiated people.

Moreover, the fact that cultural institutions have been crucial in the definition of class within African American communities means that an overreliance on a "proletarianization" framework, which makes its "central concern" economic and class relations, may not be as fruitful as has been imagined.[27] First, defining and locating the black proletariat is extremely difficult without an appreciation of the nature of ghettoization. Whites and blacks doing the same jobs in the same workplaces should perhaps be characterized in different class terms. The white person may be one of the "true" proletarians, while the black person, because he or she is holding down a steady job, may have a more elevated status among African Americans. In defining black class position, cultural factors are clearly very important and these can often be determined by reference to the ghetto rather than to the means of production. A black person can intuitively recognize that he or she has "escaped from the ghetto" or remains "trapped" within the ghetto, while proletarianization remains more obscure.

Second, emphasis on proletarianization has, in its own way, led to a

monolithic understanding of African American history, particularly in analyses of the Great Migration, which has been described in terms of a
transformation from rural peasantry to urban proletariat, despite the fact
that the large majority of migrants never made the move from field to
factory. One of the problems they faced was making inroads into factory
jobs. When there were labor shortages men were able to get factory
work, but otherwise they found themselves pushed into a "reserve army
of labor."[28] Women seldom found such opportunities and remained stuck
in service occupations. Moreover, the failure of black men to become
fully proletarianized (because they were excluded from gender-specific,
"male" occupations) made institutions in the ghetto even more compen-
satory than they otherwise might have been; they witnessed battles for
status, not just between men but also between men and women. The
inclusion of gender analysis in African American history must surely
bring our attention back to the institutions of the ghetto.

The other way in which proletarianization has led to a monolithic
portrayal of black communities has been in its failure to focus sufficiently on churches. Ghettoization studies paid lip service to the centrality of black churches, but seldom described churches in detail; by focusing mainly on the workplace, proletarianization studies have replicated
this practice. This narrow focus is an irony, given that the roots of the
proletarianization thesis are attributed to ideas derived from *The Making
of the English Working Class*, wherein E. P. Thompson placed considerable
emphasis on the significance of Methodism.[29]

An understanding of the workplace needs to inform an analysis of
ghettoization, as Trotter suggests; but the analysis cannot focus on economic and class relations aside from racial relations, which are integral,
especially from the perspective of black people, whose divisions we are
trying to explain.[30] The need of capitalists for cheap labor and efforts by
mainstream society to marginalize some citizens both fit neatly into
ghettoization. The fact that black people have been so clearly divided
from the rest of American society means that they can neither unite
easily into a single community nor unite with working groups outside the
ghetto to combat discrimination.

In this study, members of ghettoized communities create their own
institutions, and they do so not in the pathological manner usually described in ghetto studies. Nevertheless, the ghetto is crucial as a locus of
this development. No community "made itself" (neither the English
working class nor the American) without reacting in some way to particu-

lar social circumstances. This means that African Americans were not wholly autonomous; it does not mean that their predicament resulted from pathology. But while providing for a degree of autonomy and minimizing pathology, ghettoized institutions like the churches became places within which the community's social and economic divisions emerged. Very much in evidence today, these divisions are important in determining the direction and extent of African American protests against racial discrimination and injustice.

The second part of this book examines the writings of African Methodist intellectuals, ministers, and members to delineate their theology and ideology. African Methodism, as its name suggests, was based on a marriage of two different traditions. On the one hand, its adherents were "Methodists," believing that they had more in common, theologically at least, with white Methodists than with black Baptists, Episcopalians, or Catholics. On the other hand, they were "African," believing that their African-ness separated them from mainstream Methodist churches. Their African-ness, however, stemmed more from the social experiences of blacks in America than from distinct African forms of worship. African Methodists were distinguished from black Baptists and the more emotive denominations in that they eschewed religious practices that might be seen as African by the larger white community.

The argument that African-ness was subordinated to Methodism during the period of this study has certain implications for the study of African American churches generally. It walks a tightrope between the integrationist framework of E. Franklin Frazier and the black liberationist framework of James Cone. Frazier's *Negro Church in America*, like most of the analyses of black churches before its publication in 1963, employed an integrationist framework (derived largely from the works of Robert E. Park and his associates in Chicago) that presented a particularly unsympathetic view of the established black churches.[31] Frazier clearly wanted black churches to be similar to their white counterparts, particularly in quickening the pace of secularization. Yet he also wanted them to respond to the needs of the community beyond their own congregations.[32] As white churches seldom undertook both projects, Frazier's goals were unrealistic.

Frazier's integrationist view affected his analysis of the churches and the migration. While he was pleased that churches had begun to lose their "other-worldly outlook" and "to focus attention upon the Negro's condition in this world," he nevertheless held them accountable for the development of cults and for the failure of southern migrants to adjust to their new urban environments. In this vein he wrote, "The most important crisis in the life of the Negro migrant was produced by the absence of the church which had been the center of his social life and a refuge from a hostile white world." Yet, in some respects, in order to serve the migrants the churches needed to avoid becoming secularized. Frazier half acknowledged this fact when he wrote, "The inadequacy, from a religious standpoint, of the institutional denominations accounts for the 'storefront' churches which one finds in Negro communities in American cities."[33]

Frazier's confusion resulted in some very unfair criticisms of the older black denominations. For example, he attacked black preachers for having authoritarian personalities and for being anti-intellectual.[34] Yet many preachers were attacked at the time for being too scholarly, while those accused of being authoritarian and anti-intellectual, commonly known as "jacklegs," were often the only ones who could appeal to newcomers and provide them with important services.[35]

James H. Cone's concept, *Black Theology*, which emerged at the same time as the Black Power movement of the 1960s and 1970s, was developed in response to Frazier's integrationist framework. Cone avoided the contradictions inherent in Frazier's work, but while he turned the sociologist on his head to produce a separatist framework for studying black churches, he nevertheless criticized the black churches with equal if not greater vehemence.

Cone defined *Black Theology* by placing liberation theology based on the Exodus story within the context of the 1960s black struggle. For Cone, such a theology applied "the freeing power of the gospel to black power under white oppression."[36] This "ghetto theology" placed Christ on the side of the downtrodden against their oppressors. It employed Biblical texts such as Matthew 20:16, "The last shall be first and the first shall be last," and Luke 7:22, "The blind receive their sight, the lame walk, the lepers are cleansed, the deaf hear, the dead are raised up, the poor have the good news preached to them." Cone concluded that "unless theology can become . . . a theology which speaks to black people, the gospel message has no promise of life for the black man—it is a lifeless message."[37]

Cone argued that prior to the development of the ghetto, black churches accepted the "white lie" that "Christianity is primarily concerned with otherworldly reality." Blacks were taught to believe that they would get their reward for suffering oppression in the afterlife. "Instead of seeking to change the earthly state," he wrote, "they focus their hopes on the next life in heaven."[38] Taking the opposite vantage point from Frazier, criticizing the churches for being too white rather than too black, Cone nevertheless reiterated the sociologist's negative assessment of the churches and their ministers.[39]

Following the work of Peter J. Paris and Delores S. Williams, I attempt to move beyond a merely racial analysis of black churches. As Paris suggests, the intellectual connections between African Methodists and the white denominations were of great importance, even as ghetto-ization occurred.[40] The most important difference between white and black theologians was not one of doctrine but the blacks' belief that white Christians were not practicing what they preached. Another nonracial way of looking at the African Methodists is from the perspective of African American women, who, according to Williams, regard God not as a liberator (as described by Cone) but as a resource and a provider of sustenance and hope.[41] Together the analyses by Paris and Williams provide the key to understanding African American theology generally; both emphasize neither integration nor turning the world upside down but a politics of pragmatism and of overcoming persistent disappointment. More sparks from the anvil of oppression.

The importance of Black Theology for developments in the Great Migration should not be underestimated. In many respects, one of the most neglected features of African American migration is its Protestant-ism. Protestants think a great deal about their role in the world, and it is unusual for them to be totally removed from it (that is, eschatalogical). Even when they are fundamentalist, a very clearly articulated social agenda accompanies their rhetoric of world abandonment. The other side of the coin, however, is that they almost never make good liberation theologists. The closest they have come to such a theology has been the Social Gospel, which was especially popular during the period of the migration and which was founded on "social uplift." This theology explicitly established a hierarchical scale (very similar to that found in Social Darwinism) on which gender, class, and racial (color) differences became crucial in situating a particular Protestant denomination in the larger society. Consequently, even as hands reached out to aid the less fortunate, ideological barriers based on gender, race, and class were placed in the way of a firm embrace. In a phrase, the plethora of Protestant denominations within black communities made unified responses to migration and ghettoization difficult to achieve.

Part III of this book examines the response of African Methodists to the Great Migration.[42] Between 1910 and 1920, 554,000 black Southerners (7 percent of the total black population in the South) moved north, with most of these concentrated in the years between 1916 and 1918.[43] This migration took off for a number of reasons, which have been delineated by many sociologists and historians and which are generally perceived of as "push" and "pull" factors. Migrants could be pushed to leave by the threat of violence or the inability to make a living in the South, or they could be pulled North because of the availability of high-paying jobs, civil rights, and education in northern cities.[44]

In Philadelphia the Great Migration occurred when it did because of economic developments in the North.[45] The cessation of European immigration owing to the outbreak of war in Europe and the increases in northern production, first to supply Britain and her allies and second in preparation for America's own engagement in the hostilities, created a chronic shortage of labor in the North. To counteract this shortage, firms that had never before hired African Americans opened their gates to black laborers. Labor agents were sent south to find workers and northern newspapers, including black ones like the Chicago *Defender*, began a propaganda campaign to persuade blacks to leave the South.[46]

Hostile conditions in the southern states were important in persuading blacks to move, but these alone do not account for the sudden increase in migration north. Owing to the decline of cotton agriculture, African Americans had been moving off the land for many years prior to the war, but they had generally been moving to cities in the "New South," Richmond, Baltimore, Atlanta, Savannah, and Jacksonville, to name but a few. One white commentator wrote as early as 1903: "The negroes are leaving the cotton fields very fast. They are migrating to the cities by the thousand, and it will soon be a serious problem with the planters as to how they will cultivate and gather their crops."[47] During the First World War, these people began to move to northern cities instead of southern cities without a dramatic change occurring in the southern rural economy.

Lynching was one push factor persuading many people to leave their homes, but there was no uniform increase in the number of lynchings just prior to the Great Migration, and earlier lynchings had not resulted in a regionwide migration northward.[48] The importance of lynching may, in fact, be linked to the need for labor in northern cities. The greater the need for labor there, the greater the imperative for northern newspapers to focus on the violent nature of "the South" to persuade blacks to leave their homes. The association of lynching with "the South" had two impacts on the migration: First, fewer lynchings could have greater impact on migration rates as northern newspapers now focused on them more intensely; and second, people feeling threatened by this violence could no longer believe that they would find a haven in a nearby town or in nearby counties where race relations might be better—they now felt they needed to leave "the South" altogether.

The end of the war brought a brief return to pre-1916 migration levels as white soldiers returned to the labor force. In 1922, however, the rate of migration took off again and even exceeded the wartime rate. The labor shortage was still great in northern industries, and the new nativist sentiment coupled with informal immigration controls (formalized in the 1924 Immigration Act) limited the supply of European labor. During the twelve months following September 1922, therefore, over a half-million black men, women, and children made the journey north. As the city with the second-largest black community in the North, "the city of brotherly love" attracted many of these migrants; between 1922 and 1924 about ten thousand migrants moved to Philadelphia each year.[49]

This section of the book focuses in particular on the diversity within the migrant population and looks at how African Methodists responded to the Great Migration. *Diversity* is the operative word here. Attempts have been made recently to delineate the *complexity* of the migration, but the importance of diversity, and how it relates to the organization of churches in ghettoized communities, has not been stressed sufficiently.[50]

Most studies of the Great Migration have tended to describe the African Americans who took part in the exodus from southern states as an undifferentiated mass of people moving from "field to factory."[51] So accepted has this description become that it has been enshrined in the title of the popularly acclaimed Smithsonian exhibit.[52] Occasional references are made to people who do not fit into this model, but no systematic analysis of the migrant population has been undertaken to determine whether the rural-South-to-urban-North model is appropriate. Recently this view has come under attack from Carole Marks, who argues in *Farewell—We're Good and Gone* that a majority of the migrants were "urban, nonagricultural laborers, not the rural peasant usually assumed."[53]

There has also been some disagreement recently about how historians should refer to these travelers. Were they, as Allen Ballard has suggested, "refugees" fleeing "the cumulative impact of a sustained terror" in the South?[54] Were they, as James Grossman describes them, "migrants" acting "to better their condition by seizing control over their own destiny," and "ambitious men and women venturing North" in search of "independence," "mobility," and "the perquisites of American citizenship"?[55] Or were they, as Carole Marks argues, "mudsills" displaced by southern industrial development and brought North by northern industrialists who wished to keep labor costs down?[56] More recently still, Peter Gottlieb has argued that until the Second World War the northbound people were migrants but that thereafter they should be seen as refugees.[57]

The attempt to describe African American migrants in uniform ways weakens all of these descriptions; instead, as becomes apparent in Chapter 8, historians need to see the migrants in terms of a continuum stretching between the two extremes of Marks's "urban migrant" and Ballard's "rural refugee." Far from being a homogeneous group of people, these men and women came from diverse backgrounds and had different levels of preparation for the urban North.

This diversity virtually thwarted attempts to create a unified "black community" in the face of racial oppression. Creating a community out of the many kinds of black people from the South was like trying to make a single community out of Irish and Italian Catholics. For Irish Catholic immigrants to use ethnicity to consolidate their communities was relatively easy, because Irish Catholics were represented by a single church. The same was true, to a great extent, for many other ethnic groups. But when black Americans attempted to do the same thing using the same institution, they heard many discordant voices, not just from a plethora of Protestant denominations but from Catholics, Muslims, and even Jews. For many immigrant groups, emphasis on ethnicity could lead to increased solidarity, for African Americans, who arguably needed solidarity more than those who did not have to deal with the legacy of American slavery and racism, such emphasis on tradition was likely only to lead to increased division along the lines of region, religion, color, class and (as is becoming increasingly apparent in recent years) gender.[58]

Thus, the existence of a migrant continuum points us toward the increasing intraracial tensions found in emerging ghettos, and churches provide the key to understanding these developments. Nearly all migration and ghettoization studies have recognized the centrality of churches in the black community, yet none has organized its analysis around the way these churches operated during the period of migration and ghettoization. As the ghetto developed around migrant communities, churches began to be associated with class groupings more directly than ever before. This is shown most clearly in the fate of the city's African Methodist churches. Until the large influx of rural migrants during the First World War, the A.M.E. Church, with an ideology derived from the close proximity of white and black communities, was able to maintain its dominant position in the community, appealing to and speaking for all sections of black Philadelphia. With the Great Migration and the ghettoization of the black community, African Methodist theology and ideology could no longer unite people who arrived in the city from such different backgrounds and who, once there, were increasingly cut off from the white community. Instead, the Episcopal and Presbyterian churches attracted and spoke for the new professional class, while the Baptist, Holiness, and Spiritualist churches, alongside the so-called cults, began to represent the new "reserve army of unskilled laborers."

At first, northern churchgoers encouraged migration from the South because it brought new members into their congregation who would be assimilated easily and who could contribute, both financially and spiritually, to the churches. Owing to the ongoing nature of migration of urban people from the South, most of Philadelphia's churches had a majority of members who were born in the South. During the period of what is termed the Great Migration, however, these established churchgoers were forced to deal with the influx of rural people, or "greenhorns" as they described them, with whom they had nothing in common. After encouraging black Southerners to come North, they soon began to discourage new arrivals from joining their churches. When these newcomers managed to become members of the established churches, friction ensued. More often, though, constitutional methods were used to make church membership available only to the right sort of migrant, one who had been a member of a church of the same denomination in the South.

On their side, rural migrants rarely found the large urban churches appealing. Migrants who had worshiped in a small building among a few friends and relatives did not care to join a church where they would be merely one of perhaps a thousand members worshiping in a building of Gothic design where they knew no one, and where the style of worship was more restrained than they were accustomed to. The combination of hostility and alienation caused rural migrants to stay away from established churches and instead form their own storefront congregations. But while these new religious bodies could provide the emotional support that a newcomer to the city required, they less often provided the material benefits that were customary at the large churches. Membership at one of the larger established churches represented advantages, but rural refugees were less likely to receive them.

The underlying premise of this work is that examining separately ghettoization, northbound migration, and African American churches distorts all three. Thus, to understand developments within Philadelphia's black churches during this century, I consider them in the context of both the city's emerging ghettos and the northbound migration. The manner in which ghettoization occurred in Philadelphia had an enormous impact on developments within black churches, as did the diversity of migrants arriving in the city. When the three spheres are considered in conjunction, and are given equal significance, new pictures emerge of African American communities. The one described here is of African Methodists struggling to survive in a city that was becoming increasingly inhospitable to their particular ideological mix of protest and accommodation. Their sparks grew dimmer, while those of other groups, religious and secular, grew brighter.

PART I

Churches and Ghettos

Previous Page

On the steps of 1235 Bainbridge Street, April 1914.
Courtesy Temple University Urban Archives

CHAPTER 2

"Drowned by a Torrent of Migration"

Certainly none of us can deny that the migration retarded the steady march of progress of the colored people in Philadelphia.

SADIE TANNER MOSSELL, 1921

Philadelphia's black community of the nineteenth century was not so segregated from the white community as the ghettos of the twentieth century would become. It was not a modern ghetto, defined by racial segregation, intense overcrowding, and minimal economic opportunities.[1] In 1912, according to Richard R. Wright, Jr., the distribution of the African American population was still "very regular." Parts of the city, like the eastern part of the Eighth Ward, were often described as "Negro sections," but black people were still in the minority in these areas (see Map 1). Even the Seventh Ward, which housed the largest number of African Americans, was not truly a "Negro ward."[2]

As W.E.B. Du Bois and R. R. Wright, Jr., showed in their studies of Philadelphia, African Americans at the turn of the century resided in alleys and streets near the places where they could find work. For many this meant being near the larger townhouses, for others it meant living near the warehouses around the docks or near hotels.[3] According to Wright, in *The Negro in Pennsylvania*,

> in Philadelphia to-day, while on Spruce street and Walnut street, many of the wealthiest Philadelphians live, just behind them the Negroes are on Pine, Addison and Lombard streets, in parallel lines. In West Philadelphia, the well-to-do whites live on Walnut and Chestnut streets, the Negroes live on the small streets just behind them.[4]

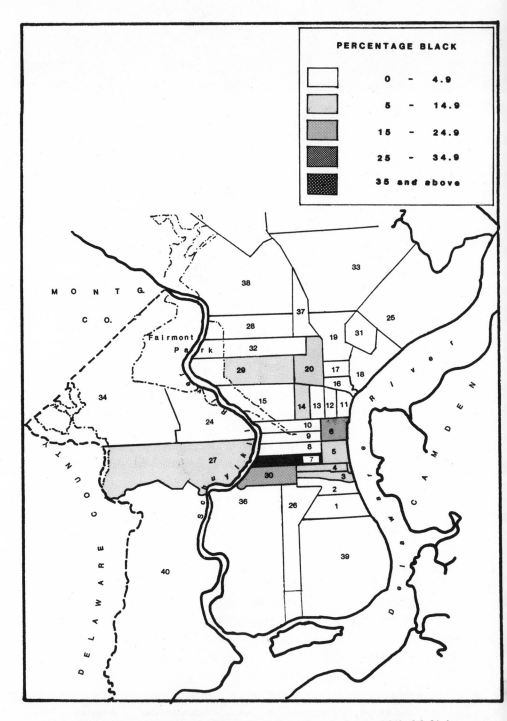

PERCENTAGE BLACK

	0 — 4.9
	5 — 14.9
	15 — 24.9
	25 — 34.9
	35 and above

Map 1. Concentration of African American Population in Philadelphia's Wards, 1900

Consequently, before the Great Migration the black community could only loosely be described as a ghetto. African Americans were seldom totally segregated by alleys or streets, let alone by sections of the city.

While slum areas existed before the Great Migration, the majority of blacks did not live in them, and according to Wright, the worst of these sections were not inhabited by black people. Further, like European immigrants to Philadelphia, African Americans were not trapped in these areas to the same extent that they would become trapped later. "Gradually," Wright asserted, "[Negroes] have moved from the lower eastern side ['the real poverty quarter'] further toward the banks of the Schuylkill River and many hundreds of them to-day occupy houses which a few years back were occupied by well-to-do whites."[5] In Philadelphia, at least, the black community seemed to be fulfilling the American ideal of upward mobility, enabling certain members to move into more prosperous areas of the city. In Wright's words,

> the home-owning and the more prosperous Negroes are, as a rule, moving out of the distinctively Negro neighborhood. In Philadelphia, west of 15th and south of Bainbridge, in Elmwood and Germantown, a large number of the better class of Negroes have settled within the past ten years. The largest number of home-owners is outside of the most densely settled Negro district, but which is chiefly inhabited by foreigners. (pp. 64–65)

In 1912, then, the Philadelphia black community did not appear to be an especially "demographically vulnerable community."[6] As Wright's own work of the period evidenced, black Philadelphians at this time had cause for optimism about developments in their community.

During and after the First World War the outlook for the black community changed dramatically. This change cannot be attributed solely to the influx of migrants. Discussions of the Great Migration often overlook the fact that migrants had been coming north from the southern states for many years, and, like the European American communities, the African American community had been adjusting to this influx reasonably well. Prior to the Great War, the black community was not noted for tensions between established Philadelphians and newcomers, and the gradual nature of the influx did not cause particular alarm in the white community.[7] In 1908, 35 percent of Philadelphia's black business owners had been born in Virginia and a further 25 percent in North Carolina.[8] These business people had arrived in Philadelphia and, because they were believed to be making contributions to the community, had been assimilated very quickly. In some respects, therefore, the black community of 1912 looked more capable of absorbing newcomers than other ethnic communities, some of whose members arrived in Philadelphia with no compatriots waiting to help them adjust to the new life and with no knowledge of English.

Two important changes made the wartime and postwar migrations qualitatively different from those that preceded them. First, the arrival at the gates of the city of roughly forty thousand southern blacks during the war years alone was bound to be a burden on the community.[9] Not only were there difficulties assimilating such a large number into the community at once, but the racism already evident in the city was heightened. White Philadelphians began to separate themselves from their black neighbors in all spheres, segregating not only housing, but accommodations, services, education, and religion. Black people were barred from all center-city restaurants, hotels, lunch counters, dime-store counters, and theaters.[10] At the same time, attempts were made to segregate Philadelphia's schools.[11] Churches were already generally divided between black and white congregations, but those churches that still had interracial congregations now split along racial lines. The black Protestant Episcopal Church of St. John the Divine, for instance, was founded in 1920 after its pastor, Rev. J. Da Costa Harewood, had been ejected from the white St. Michael and All Angels Church.[12]

The second important change was in the origin of the migrants themselves. Prior to the war, most had come from the upper South, in particular from Maryland and Virginia. After 1916, a larger proportion of new arrivals came from the lower South, from the Carolinas, Georgia, and Florida. Before the war, newcomers to Philadelphia generally had lived in such places as Richmond, Baltimore, and Washington, D.C. A large proportion of these people had experienced city life before and were familiar with the same urban culture that black Philadelphians prided themselves on having. Large numbers of the wartime newcomers did not have the same kinds of connections and resources and, more often than had been the case earlier, came straight from rural areas. Consequently, they more often found the experience of moving into the city an alienating one and hence needed greater assistance.

The conjuncture of an increased rate of migration and a change in origin of the migrants led to the problems facing the black community after 1916 and made a community that had not been "demographically

weak" very vulnerable to ghettoization. At the same time that whites
increased their discrimination against blacks as a group, the more established members of the black community found that they had to aid newcomers with whom they felt little or no connection. A few farsighted
people recognized that a larger black community would yield more political power in the long run, but more often the newcomers were resented.

Above all, the optimism that had once characterized the Philadelphia black community seemed to vanish in the period of the Great
Migration. It is ironic that as thousands of black Southerners began to
make their way to their "Promised Land," the people already residing
there felt that the newcomers signified the end of all promise. In Sadie
Mossell's words, the presence of so many "untrained, often illiterate
[people, who were] generally void of culture . . . crushed and stagnated
the progress of Negro life." She continued, "The pessimist groans that
[the black community] will never regain [its former position] and points
to the previous culture level of Philadelphia Negroes as if it had been
permanently drowned by a torrent of migration."[13]

Changing Residential Patterns

Between 1890 and 1930, as Maps 1 and 2 show, the black population of
Philadelphia shifted as new areas in western, southern, and northern sections of the city witnessed the emergence of black settlements. The
dispersion of African Americans into West and North Philadelphia had
already become noticeable during the 1890s. In 1890, 58 percent of the
black population of the city still remained in South Philadelphia, but the
black population of the northern section had started to grow rapidly. In
that year, the 12,538 black people in North Philadelphia constituted 32
percent of the city's African American population. By 1900, 23,272 black
people (36 percent) lived in this area, and twenty years later 53,570 black
people (40 percent) lived there. By then, the proportion of the black
population in the southern section of the city was only marginally larger,
around 43 percent.[14]

A similar growth of black population occurred in West Philadelphia, though African Americans moved into this section at a slower
rate than into the northern area. In 1890, only 10 percent of the city's
black population lived in West Philadelphia, while in 1900 and 1920 the
figures were 12.5 and 17 percent. By 1940, 65,479 black people lived

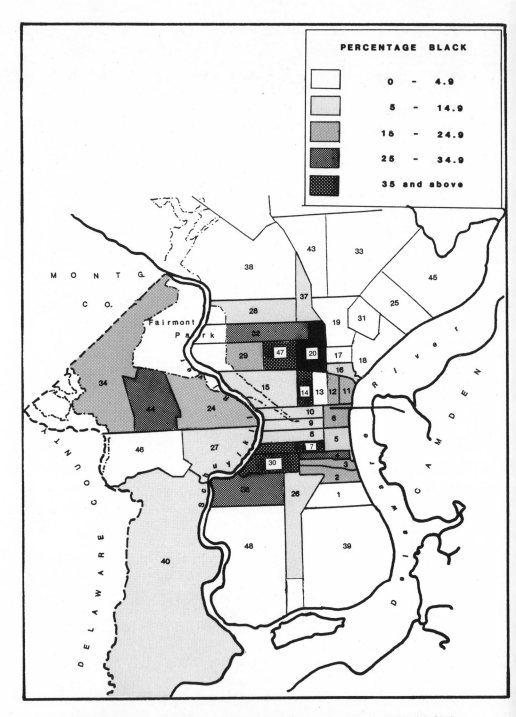

Map 2. Concentration of African American Population in Philadelphia's Wards, 1930

west of the Schuylkill River; they constituted 26 percent of the black population. By this time, the black population of Philadelphia was fairly evenly distributed among three sections of the city: West Philadelphia housed 26 percent, South Philadelphia 27 percent, and North Philadelphia south of Lehigh Avenue, 37 percent.[15]

Southern migrants made up a large number of the black population moving into the northern and western sections of the city. In 1921, Sadie T. Mossell chose to perform a budget study of families in the Twenty-ninth Ward, located in North Philadelphia, primarily because the population in this section was, in her words, "practically limited to migrants."[16] Generally, however, the first people to move into a settlement were wealthier middle-class blacks. After they had broken the residential color bar, less wealthy members of the black community found it possible to follow them. White property owners and real estate agents realized that vast profits could be made from buying up houses owned by whites who wished to flee the area and then selling or renting them at inflated prices to black people. This practice contributed to the resentment of more established African Americans toward the city's new arrivals. They reasoned that it was they, after all, who faced the intense hostility of white neighbors as they sought to live outside the worst areas of the ghetto. A renowned black Baptist minister, Dr. William A. Creditt, met substantial white opposition when he tried to move south of Market Street in West Philadelphia.[17] Similarly, when a black "woman of means" moved into 2396 Ellsworth Street, in a white neighborhood of South Philadelphia, a race riot broke out in which two men were killed and sixty people injured. After managing to settle in such hostile environments, middle-class blacks believed that the same slum conditions they had sought to escape were taking over their new neighborhoods.[18]

The movements of the black population greatly affected black institutions, particularly the churches. First, new churches and missions had to be established to cater to new black settlements. West Philadelphia, therefore, saw the creation of numerous churches and missions in the last decade of the nineteenth century and the first two decades of the twentieth. Ward A.M.E. (founded in 1890), Mt. Olivet Baptist (1896), Pinn Memorial Baptist (1908), Mt. Zion Baptist (1914), and Reeve Memorial Presbyterian Mission (1917) were just a few of many churches created as a result of the dispersion of population. Second, churches situated in areas where the black population was declining needed to relocate. For example, Wesley A.M.E. Zion, which had been

situated almost opposite Bethel A.M.E. on Lombard between 5th and
6th Streets, decided to move west in 1921 to 15th and Lombard, to a
church previously owned by a white Presbyterian congregation. This
move took the church from the Fifth Ward, in which only 816 blacks
lived, to the Seventh Ward, in which there were 12,241 black people.[19]
Indeed, as Richard R. Wright, Jr., noted in his 1912 study, *The Negro in
Pennsylvania*, the only one of the old churches remaining in its original
position was Mother Bethel A.M.E. Church, which was by then "entirely
surrounded by Jews."[20]

After 1916, African Americans also became more concentrated and
more segregated from the white community, in spite of the fact that they
were moving into new areas around the city. In South Philadelphia during the nineteenth century, the black population had been dispersed
among seven wards. Between 1900 and 1920, they became more concentrated predominantly in three wards, the Seventh, Thirtieth and Thirty-
sixth, which saw a dramatic increase in the number of black people and
an equally dramatic withdrawal of whites. In 1900, the Seventh Ward
had been 37 percent black, while the Thirtieth Ward had been 16 percent, and the Thirty-sixth Ward 4 percent black. By 1920, these figures
were 47 percent for the Seventh Ward, 52 percent for the Thirtieth, and
24 percent for the Thirty-sixth. And by 1940, the population in the Thirtieth Ward was 80 percent black.[21]

In North and West Philadelphia similar concentrations emerged. In
the north of the city, the black population increased greatly. By 1920, the
area bounded by 7th Street on the east, 21st Street on the west, Susquehanna Avenue to the north, and Fairmount Avenue to the south had
approximately 19 percent of the total black population (Wards 14, 20, 32,
and 47). This area by 1930 had about 34 percent of the total black population, while the black community had pushed farther north to Lehigh
Avenue.[22] West Philadelphia, however, differed from southern and northern parts of the city in being an expanding area. Both white and black
people were moving west of the Schuylkill, and the residential divisions
between the races were not initially so distinct as in other black districts.
Nevertheless, after 1920, the concentration of black population above
Market Street, which divides West Philadelphia, grew, while the area
below Market remained more exclusively white.[23]

African Americans became increasingly concentrated in segregated
communities. South Philadelphia had been renowned for its slums in the
nineteenth century, but in terms of deprivation, those slums did not

compare with the newly emerging ghettos. The new black communities were situated in areas providing little skilled employment because of early attempts to relocate industry outside urban centers; and when skilled jobs were available, black people were excluded by the unions.[24] The major source of income in these areas was service occupations in the hotels, restaurants, and inns of the adjacent white communities.[25]

The deprivation in these neighborhoods was exacerbated by over-crowding due to the white community's restrictive covenants and the high rents black people were forced to pay. In 1920, the average density for the city was roughly 111 persons per acre, but in principally black wards the densities averaged about 150 persons per acre.[26] Sadie Mossell believed that overcrowding was the direct result of "the determination of white people that the migrant should live in that part of the city in which Negroes had previously lived."[27] Whites failed to halt the dispersion of blacks entirely, but they managed to ensure that black neighborhoods became overcrowded. Often, vacant houses in sections of the city populated by whites were not for rent or for sale to blacks regardless of their means.[28]

Philadelphia's black community expanded at a time when a housing shortage already existed. In *A Century of Negro Migration*, Carter G. Woodson noted that, throughout the country, "owing to the high cost of materials, high wages, increasing taxation and the inclination to invest money in enterprises growing out of the war, fewer houses are now being built, although Negroes are pouring into these centers as a steady stream." Consequently, he added, "the usual Negro quarters in northern centers of this sort have been filled up and the overflow of the black population scattered thoughout the city among white people. Old warehouses, store rooms, churches, railroad cars and tents have been used to meet these demands." Woodson went on to describe a situation in which a large percentage of black people lived in tenements or rooming houses, and many were unable even to find individual rooms. "Sometimes as many as four or five sleep in one bed," he continued, "and that may be placed in the basement, dining-room or kitchen where there is neither adequate light nor air."[29]

Woodson's description of the national situation was shown to be true for Philadelphia also, both by Mossell's study and by the 1924 study of migrants carried out by the Philadelphia Housing Association. According to Mossell, many migrant families had to share apartments in row houses with other families. Sometimes there might even be a family in each room of an apartment. "Press comments," she wrote, "describe the Negroes herded together like cattle."[30] As many as 30 percent of heads of households interviewed for the 1924 migrant study complained about overcrowding in their homes.[31]

In an article entitled "Problems of the Southern Migration Movement," written for the *Evening Public Ledger* and reprinted in the *Tribune*, Clarence Whyte declared that housing was the most important problem facing blacks arriving in Philadelphia. He noted that many migrants not only came north with resources but also quickly found employment in the city. The problem was that they became trapped in overcrowded districts, being "taken into houses already overcrowded." In one part of the city, which he called the "Middle City Area" (the area lying between Girard to the north, Washington to the south, and the Schuylkill and Delaware Rivers), the overcrowding was particularly deplorable: "One house of four rooms was found occupied by four new families," he wrote, "one of these families consisting of a man, his wife and six children. Another house of six rooms was found with five families; and within the next two weeks, the house next to this one, which had been occupied by one family, had increased to a three family tenancy." Even in West Philadelphia, a section of the city to which black people had only recently moved, the overcrowding was excessive. "Above a small garage in West Philadelphia," Whyte reported, "a migrant rented a room for herself, an adopted son, three married children and their families, making a total of sixteen persons. This place had neither yard nor toilet and the filth and waste were thrown into a vacant lot adjoining." It was general for houses converted to multiple occupancy to have substandard sanitary equipment, and many did not comply with city housing requirements.[32]

Woodson's description of the condition of many of the accommodations in which blacks lived in northern cities was also accurate for those surveyed by the Philadelphia Housing Association:

> Some of their houses have no water inside and have toilets on the outside without sewerage connections. The cooking is often done by coal or wood stoves or kerosene lamps. Yet the rent runs high although the houses are generally out of repair and in some cases have been condemned by the municipality. The unsanitary conditions in which many of the blacks are compelled to live are in violation of municipal ordinances.

Added to these structural problems, African Americans also faced problems of vice, crime, and disease in these rundown areas. The overcrowding, the dilapidated dwelling places, the high level of unemployment, and the generally low-paid, low-skill jobs that provided a living for those who were employed, gave rise to these problems. While a crime wave did not occur, according to Woodson, certain criminal activities focused around "the saloons and denizens of vice, which are furnished by the community itself."[33]

Disease in these black ghettos was a further problem. Southern elites had tried to persuade blacks not to move north and in doing so had argued that black people were not meant to live in the harsh northern climate. Their arguments were specious, yet the new overcrowded ghettos were certainly not good for the health of their occupants. Both Emmett J. Scott and Clarence Whyte focused on the health hazard as one of the great dangers arising from overcrowding. Referring to the new arrivals in Philadelphia, Scott wrote: "It was necessary . . . upon their arrival in that city for them to crowd into the district largely restricted to negroes, giving rise to such unhappy conditions as to jeopardize the peace and health of the community." As a result, Scott asserted, "Numbers of these migrants died from exposure during the first winter, and others who died because of their inability to stand the northern climate made the situation unusually alarming."[34] Whyte described the "super-human" efforts of the Division of Medical Inspection of the Bureau of Health to limit the spread of smallpox during summer months among black migrants living in overcrowded and unsanitary houses. During the summer of 1923, "the medical inspectors were obliged to quarantine forty-two districts and to vaccinate every unvaccinated bed resident of those districts. Every [smallpox] case in these localities was found [in] a Negro family recently come from the South. In one house occupied by thirty-eight recent arrivals seven cases were found, and this record was duplicated and even surpassed in one or two other instances." Cases of smallpox were not brought from the South but developed among southern blacks after arrival owing to their contact with the disease in congested housing.[35]

Pneumonia, bronchitis, tuberculosis, and influenza were also a danger for the new arrivals in Philadelphia.[36] Woodson noted that the sudden change from a warm climate to a cold climate made it difficult for many black people to resist these infections.[37] However, writing as he was just before the flu epidemic of 1918, which killed millions of people worldwide and thousands in Philadelphia, even he underestimated the problem. Blacks' living conditions in the city were such that the flu virus could thrive, as the congested sections "vitually present[ed] culture centers for the development of epidemics."[38] The *Tribune*'s reports on the epidemic reveal that many members of the black community were aware of this situation at the time.[39]

Another cause of overcrowding, which Woodson and others alluded to, was the high rents in black neighborhoods. Despite the dilapidated conditions of the ghettos' living units, rents were as high as, or higher than, those in surrounding white communities. Landlords clearly made large profits from the overcrowding in black neighborhoods. With their high unemployment and low wages, African Americans committed a much higher proportion of their earnings to rent than did whites, and newcomers found that any savings they had brought with them from the South or had eked out from their wages were soon used up. As a result, these people were forced to share apartments or take in lodgers. An article in the *Public Ledger* mentioned a room measuring sixteen by twenty feet in which twenty men slept on the floor and for which each was charged $1.50 per week.[40]

Overcrowding remained oppressive throughout the period of this study. By 1940 it was possible to find more than fifteen thousand families, or more than sixty thousand individuals, in a black neighborhood of row houses, seven blocks by fourteen, between 7th and Broad Streets and Fairmount and Susquehanna Avenues (Wards 14 and 20).[41] This area was roughly the same size as the Nineteenth or the Twentieth Ward, which had only forty thousand inhabitants each in 1940 and which between them had a mere twelve hundred black residents.[42] Moreover, housing stock in the black neighborhood was of a far lower standard than that in the two white wards. Many houses had been demolished, leaving vacant lots covered with trash and debris. Of houses standing, 44 percent were substandard, either needing repair or lacking sanitation facilities.[43]

Occurring at the same time as the influx into the city of so many black Southerners during and after the First World War, the rapid deterioration of living standards of the majority of black people gave credence to arguments that the newcomers should be shunned because they brought deterioration with them. These arguments were even more compelling for those whose employment opportunities suffered because of the changing occupational patterns within the modern ghettos.

Employment Opportunities

The increasing separation of black and white neighborhoods caused a decline in wealth and sometimes unemployment for many who depended on white customers or white employers for their livelihoods. The black communities of the nineteenth century had been situated near white middle- and upper-class populations, who wanted caterers, barbers, and domestic servants. Once white people began to move to the suburbs, after improvements in urban transport, many African Americans were left unemployed but living in the same locations. Without the economic patronage of the white elite, black people found that they had to rely increasingly on other African Americans for employment and custom. The effect on the black caterers and barbers was dramatic. In 1908 there were eighty-four black caterers; by 1935, their number was so small that the *Philadelphia Independent* did not even include them in its survey of black occupations. The decline in the number of barbers was almost as precipitous.[44]

The position of African Americans in Philadelphia's labor market improved during and after the First World War, and, for a brief period, this compensated for the community's losses in certain trades. Philadelphia companies, spurred on by the increase in production as America prepared to engage in the war in Europe and fearing the labor shortage that would result from the cessation of European immigration and from white workers joining the armed forces, became more willing to give blacks employment. In 1916, the Armstrong Association, Philadelphia's branch of the Urban League, negotiated an agreement with the Pennsylvania Railroad whereby the company would hire 1,100 black maintenance-of-the-way men in railroad camps near the city. Following this initiative, blacks gained access to higher-paid industrial jobs that had never been open to them in stevedoring, construction, building maintenance, and shipyard, garment factory, and clerical work. Eddystone, Hog Island, Fort Mifflin, Philadelphia Navy Yard, Marine Quartermaster Corps, Cramps and Sun Shipyards, and other employers began to hire African Americans (see Table 2.1).[45] With the postwar boom and the recommencement of the Great Migration in 1922, even more firms began to hire black men and women (see Table 2.2). The jobs that became available to black people, however, were the lowest paid and least skilled and had the highest turnover rates. The apparent benefits of the period were in some ways illusory. They represented the establishment of a "reserve army of labor," which, far from leading to increased opportunities, would in the long run make it more difficult for members of the black community to escape from the ghetto.[46]

African Americans fortunate enough to have had some training when they were young were able to take advantage of new oppor-

Table 2.1. Black Laborers Employed in Industrial Plants in 1917

Plant	Number
Pennsylvania Railroad Camps	
Girard	170
Mantua Junction	300
Frankford Junction	60
Eastern Pennsylvania Camp	150
Baltimore & Ohio Railroad Camps	120
Reading Railroad Camps	300
Midvale Steel Co.	4,000
Atlantic Refining Co.	1,000
Franklin Sugar Co.	700
Keystone Paving & Construction Co.	1,100
Westinghouse-Church-Kerr Electric (Chester)	600
Eddystone Munition Corp. (Essington)	600
Disston Saw Co. (Essington)	400
Total estimated number in plants visited	8,400
Estimated number in plants not visited	7,750
Estimated number of women and children	16,250
Estimated total	33,500

Source: Sadie T. Mossell, "The Standard of Living among One Hundred Negro Migrant Families in Philadelphia," *Annals of the American Academy,* 1921.

tunities. Rev. Matthew H. Jones, for example, came to Philadelphia in 1921 after training as a mechanic at Hampton Institute in Virginia and the New York Electrical School. In 1922, he secured a job at a Buick dealer, earning 55 cents per hour. Because this wage would not support his family, he quit after his superintendent announced that no one at the shop was getting a raise. He then became a stevedore earning 80 cents an hour, though he had needed a large slice of luck to get this job. One day, looking for work, he had walked down to Pier 40 where ships were being unloaded. He arrived just as the driver for Captain Riley and Captain Sullivan was struggling to start their car. Jones walked up and asked, "What are you trying to do, run your battery down?" And, when they suggested that he would be unable to solve the problem, he lifted the hood, took the distributor cap off, separated the points, and got the spark plugs working. Once the car was running, he was given the job of fixing a truck that was needed the following day to take workers to Pier 98 to unload another boat that had just docked. This was easily done. He removed the carburetor, scooped half a cup of mud off it, boiled it in

Table 2.2. Businesses Employing Blacks, ca. 1923

Firm	Skilled	Semi-skilled	Unskilled	Total	% Employees
Henry Disston & Son	2	87	148	237	7.0
Fels & Co.	0	0	74	74	20.0
Westinghouse Electric Co.	0	56	371	427	18.0
Exide Storage Battery Co.	7	0	33	40	1.0
Bethelehem Steel Works	0	0	100	100	0.7
Wilson-Martin Co.	7	10	58	75	50.0
Wm. Cramp & Son	0	0	250	250	—
Lukens Steel Works	142	172	246	560	27.4
Atlantic Refining Co.	42	151	463	619	15.0
Midvale Steel Co.	9	100	400	509	20.0
Philadelphia Rapid Transit	0	59	596	655	5.9
Pennsylvania & Reading Railroad	44	164	827	1035	10.0
Baldwin Locomotive Works	—	—	—	1393	7.7
United Gas Imp.	18	144	278	440	19.0
Pennsylvania Railroad	2	301	1643	1946	7.4
Franklin Sugar Co.	0	47	102	149	20.0
Du Pont Co.	0	68	27	95	—
Barret Co.	0	40	20	60	18.0
American Ice & Coal	—	—	—	95	10.0

Source: Negro Migrant Study, Urban Archives, Temple University, Urb. 31, Box 1, folder 2.

water, and replaced it, and the truck worked perfectly. After doing some work on the piers, Jones was soon placed in charge of Sullivan's and Riley's car.[47]

The termination of hostilities with Germany and the return of the troops in 1918, along with the end of the postwar boom in the early 1920s, ended the honeymoon period for black people. Unemployment increased to levels higher than in the prewar period, and the black community now had to deal with all those who had been encouraged by company agents to leave the South. Having flocked into cities like Philadelphia to end the labor shortage, blacks remained during the 1920s, often without much possibility of holding down a well-paid job.

The hard times of the depression of the 1930s may not have seemed to many black people much different from the "good" times of the 1920s, but employment problems for African Americans were heightened after the Wall Street crash. In its report, entitled *Unemployment Sta-*

tus of Negroes, the National Urban League estimated that of Philadelphia's 247,000 unemployed, between 30,000 and 50,000 were black people. In December 1931, the Bureau of Unemployment Relief provided relief to 34,036 families, of which 15,387 were black. The report stated: "The percentage of colored families for the two months previous remained between 44 per cent and 46 per cent of the total, although Negroes form but 11.3 per cent of the total population of the city." When it came to laying off workers, blacks were always dismissed first, partly because they had less seniority at their jobs than whites, who had not been restricted from employment for years. When the seniority rule did not apply, charges of "inefficiency" or "impudence" were raised against the black employees to achieve the same effect.[48] By the end of the decade, then, most of the advances made in industrial work during the 1920s had been erased, and just prior to the Second World War 60 percent of black men and 90 percent of black women were still working in the most ghettoizing of occupations, service work.[49]

Randy Dixon, reporting for the Philadelphia *Independent*, believed that the depression had had a very negative impact on black employment. "The depression," he wrote, "has forced many an erstwhile laborer, mechanic, porter, elevator operator and whatnot into adopting unthought-of methods to earn a living." Dixon found Andrew Green standing behind a pushcart at 12th and South Streets selling strawberries. Green was proud of his trade and stated that it was "merely the best manner available for him, at present, to earn a living." Jills Dozier, who had also lost a steady job owing to the economic collapse, was seen painting signs to make ends meet.[50] Yet Green and Dozier's attempts to adjust to unemployment represented the happier side of the depression. Robert Tiller's suicide represented the anguish that often resulted from an inability to adapt. Tiller had resided in Philadelphia for thirteen years, having come north from Georgia when he was twenty-seven years old. By September 1935, he had been unemployed for three years, and helping his wife to support their five children had become almost impossible. After trying to stab his wife, he ran into the street, poured kerosene on himself, and burned to death.[51]

For black women the period from 1890 to 1940 brought a similar decline in fortunes on the labor market and the same temporary upswing during the First World War that men experienced.[52] As early as 1896, Mary Church Terrell pointed out that black women were being swept aside by the new white immigrants. "Where there was formerly a constant demand for colored cooks, chambermaids and nurses," she wrote, "there is now a well-defined movement to supply their places with foreign help at advanced wages."[53] Consequently, a serious problem confronted not just black women but the black community as a whole. Black women generally contributed more to family income than did white women. Thus, any threat to women's work had a very negative impact on the welfare of the whole community.

By 1900, this problem had become so noticeable that Terrell once again needed to call attention to "the alarming rapidity with which [black women] are losing ground in the world of labor—a fact patent to all who observe and read the signs of the times. So many families are supported entirely by our women, that if this movement to withhold employment from them continues to grow, we shall soon be confronted by a condition of things serious and disastrous indeed."[54] This problem was exacerbated by the fact that, at the same time that positions for black women were evaporating, thousands of young women were arriving in the city fresh from Maryland and Virginia and hoping to obtain employment. This must be considered, in light of historians' neglect, an "invisible Great Migration," the kind of invisible migration that continues to this day as thousands of young women come into American cities from such places as the West Indies and the Philippines.[55] Because they are young and single and do not make inroads into the more "significant" occupational groupings, these women are not considered part of a migration movement.

In 1905, the Philadelphia Association for the Protection of Colored Women was established to aid the many young women arriving at Philadelphia's docks. Such an organization was essential, the *Tribune* believed, because

> The situation which faces the colored woman in the North, especially the untrained Southern woman, presents more difficulties than in the South. Most industries other than domestic service are closed to her; domestic service in the cities requires training and skill; good temporary lodgings in a decent neighborhood at reasonable cost are hard to find; employment in good families without references is hard to obtain; work in cafes and public restaurants often carries with it great moral risks; the cost of living is double that in her home in the South; good associates are not easily picked up, and when the day's work is done, where can she go for

recreation? The streets are not safe and the dance halls and other amusements open to her are worse.

Moreover, the young woman fresh from the South was "poorly equipped" to deal with this environment.

> She is usually untrained in domestic service, comes from a rural community, has been urged to leave her home by an employment agent who gets a big fee for her, and leaves her home without sufficient clothing or money and no information about her Northern home. Often she has not carfare to get across the city after she arrives. Where she is not the victim of the employment agent she often leaves in the same irresponsible way, hoping to find friends or work. Beyond this reckless journey and blind faith lies many a story of failure, of want, of crime, of poverty, of disease that might be avoided had the girl only been safeguarded.[56]

Mrs. S. W. Layten, founder of the organization, established a home at 1506 Catharine Street, at which training was provided in domestic skills. During the first seven years of its existence, the organization met at the docks and the station over seven thousand women and girls "who have been protected from degenerating and corrupting influences of the city." A temporary home and shelter was furnished for about one-half the number met.[57]

The reason for the loss of ground in the employment of black domestics was clearly racial prejudice, though white employers boycotting black domestics claimed that the latter were "neither skilled in the trades nor reliable as working women." According to Terrell, "in the majority of cases colored women are not employed because of the cruel, unreasonable prejudice which rages so violently against them." Black women were placed in a difficult position. With white employers hiding behind the excuse that they were unreliable and unsuitable workers, black women were forced to make themselves more "reliable" and more "suitable." Even Terrell felt that the way out was to ensure that blacks were so highly trained that whites found it impossible to complain. "To stem the tide of popular disfavor," she wrote, "we must offer efficient, reliable domestics who can demand good wages and establish a reputation because of superior service rendered."[58] Yet however close black domestics came to being superwomen, they continued to find many jobs closed to them. Training them could not overcome the essential fact of white prejudice.

The loss of jobs for black women in domestic service was not matched, as it was for some white women, by a corresponding increase in clerical and sales work. Frances E.W. Harper's novel, *Iola Leroy, or Shadows Uplifted*, revealed as early as 1893 that such advances would not be forthcoming. In a northern city named "P—," fitting the description of Philadelphia, Iola finds work at an unnamed department store bearing a striking resemblance to John Wanamaker's or Lit Brothers. Iola's skin is very light, and her features enable her to pass as a white woman. However, her co-workers become suspicious when she says that she attends a church that they know has a black congregation, and one of them decides to follow her home. When the evidence is brought before the management that Iola is indeed black, she is summarily dismissed.[59] This fictional event clearly reflected numerous women's experiences. Black women were not employed as saleswomen until well into the twentieth century, and by 1935 there were still only five hundred black salespeople in Philadelphia. Considering that 787 stores were owned by blacks, it is likely that only one or two black women worked, like the fictional Iola, in the city's department stores.[60]

In *Labor of Love, Labor of Sorrow*, historian Jacqueline Jones has provided a complete account of the forms of labor open to black women in this period and of how they coped with menial jobs they despised. After the brief period during the war when they were able occasionally to find industrial jobs with higher wages, black women were once again reduced to service work, either as domestics in a declining labor market or as laundresses in the large laundries that had grown up in part to do the work formerly done by servants. One way out of the wage-labor grind was for a woman to open up rooms in her family space for lodgers. This practice became increasingly popular during the migration, when pastors and other leaders asked members of the community to help house newcomers to a city with limited housing units. But it had drawbacks as well as benefits. While it gave some women greater independence from the uncertainties and exploitations of the labor market, it sometimes also trapped them in the home and in household work. It also exacerbated overcrowding, to say nothing of the problems arising when male members of the household faced unemployment.[61]

Based on his *1908 Philadelphia Colored Directory*, Richard R. Wright's 1912 study of blacks in Pennsylvania portrayed a black community that seemed to have fairly good prospects for the future. In almost all of Wright's selected criteria—home ownership, business and institutional development, labor market participation, and so on—African Americans seemed to be improving their position in the state. Their economic situation was comparable to that of other ethnic communities, in spite of racial prejudice.[62] By the end of the 1920s, however, the black community had become far more separated from the rest of Philadelphia society; the vast majority of blacks lived in overcrowded conditions and worked, when they could find work, in unskilled positions. Only a small minority—the urban black professionals—found that development of the ghetto provided new opportunities.

The Rise of Black Professionals

As Kenneth Kusmer has shown in his study of Cleveland, some African Americans prospered from the increased segregation of the black community.[63] While barbers and caterers no longer had customers, the black professional class of lawyers, doctors, and preachers prospered. Prior to the 1890s, few black men could get established in the professions. Given a choice, blacks tended to prefer white lawyers and doctors over blacks because they assumed, often unfairly, that whites were better trained. The increased segregation of the black community eliminated this choice. As a result, black-run and -owned hospitals, like Frederick Douglass and Mercy, began to appear, along with many new black legal practices.

Between 1908 and 1935, while the overall black population increased by 350 percent, most professional groups increased by much higher percentages (Table 2.3). The only exceptions were lawyers, policemen, and clergymen. Lawyers and policemen were part of a single system of law and order. Prospects for black lawyers may have been limited by the fact that black defendants preferred white attorneys because they would be tried by white judges, white prosecutors, and white juries. At the same time, white city administrations clearly desired to keep the number of black policemen to a minimum and restricted opportunities for them. The numbers of black lawyers and policemen kept pace with the overall increase in black population because these professions functioned within the white system; in contrast, the proportion of black ministers in the population was stable because black religious institutions were already well established by 1908.[64]

Other middle-class groups underwent a staggering growth during the process of ghettoization. The prosperous careers of men like Edward Cooper Brown, director of Brown and Stevens Bank; Nathan F. Mossell,

Table 2.3. Black Professionals in 1908 and 1935

Profession	1908	1935	% Increase
Homeowners	802	9,855	1,229
Stores	281	787	280
Doctors	28	200	714
Lawyers	14	32	229
Dentists	11	101	918
Clergymen	73	250	342
Druggists	1	40	4,000
Schoolteachers	54	553	1,024
Nurses	18 (graduates)	250	1,389
Insurance agents	10	102	1,020
Real estate	18 (dealers)	109	6,056
Undertakers	11	89	809
Policemen	70	219	313
Total black population	62,600	235,000	375

Sources: Richard R. Wright, Jr., *The 1908 Philadelphia Colored Directory* (Philadelphia: Philadelphia Colored Directory Co., 1908), pp. 10–17; *Philadelphia Independent*, June 2, 1935, p. 3.

founder of the Frederick Douglass Memorial Hospital; Walter W.H. Casselle, the leading black undertaker; Ed Bolden, president of Hilldale Baseball Club; John T. Gibson, owner of Gibson's Standard Theater; Christopher J. Perry, owner of the *Philadelphia Tribune*; and the lawyers Robert N.C. Nix, Sr., Raymond Pace Alexander, and Sadie T. Mossell Alexander signified the emergence of a black middle class in spite of the general impoverishment of the people they depended on for their livelihoods.

The black middle class was not so secure as its white counterpart, and many of its members fell victim to the depression. Their insecurity was crucial to the way race and class interacted in the ghetto and, in particular, in the churches. The limits to advancement in the larger society meant that members of the black middle class during this period needed to increase their prestige within their own community. They often achieved greater status by gaining entrance into particularly prestigious organizations, such as an Episcopal or Presbyterian church, one of the two South Philadelphia Y's, or the Masons and Odd Fellows.

Because black churches played an important role in conferring status, they could not perform the same unifying function as churches in other ethnic communities. The creation of the ghetto did not enable blacks to unite in the face of racial oppression, as one might expect; instead, it forced one group to gain prestige at the expense of others and thereby undermined the potential for black solidarity. For this reason historians and sociologists alike have to treat the interaction of race and class with care. One cannot discern a decline in the significance of race in the development of class distinctions within the black community.[65] The black middle class developed in the way that it did as a direct result of racial oppression and the emergence of the ghetto.

In *A Ghetto Takes Shape*, historian Kenneth Kusmer introduced the notion that the ghetto is a paradox, meaning that the isolation of the black community from whites helped "unify the black community and provided the basis for the future struggle against racism and all its manifestations."[66] But the true paradox of the ghetto may be that while African Americans uniformly experienced racial prejudice, they seized upon cultural and class differences to differentiate among themselves and thereby created a complex class structure within, or in relation to, the ghetto.

Two patterns emerge from the reactions of established black Philadelphians to black migrants and the development of the city's modern ghettos. First, members of the community who suffered as a result of the deterioration of living standards or of changing occupational patterns resented the new arrivals and made them scapegoats for structural problems. The argument, put forward by some of its members, that the community had been strong and was now being "drowned by a torrent of migration" was persuasive during the 1920s. The emergence of modern ghettos seemed to occur immediately after the commencement of the Great Migration, and it was easy to blame the migrants for the ghettos. While other, equally persuasive arguments were made regarding the benefits to the community from the migration, many black Philadelphians saw in the emergence of the city's black ghettos the termination of prospects for their own and their community's "steady march of progress."[67] Consequently, they often responded negatively to the migration. The second pattern emerged from those who benefitted from ghettoization; cut off from advancement into larger American society and seeking prestige and self-esteem within the black community, these people felt threatened by migrants who came north with resources.

As a result of these negative responses toward the migrants, there was a tendency among established churchgoers to exclude from membership those newcomers who did not fit in with the congregation and a marked increase in strife within church congregations as new members sought to move into the prestigious positions dominated by long-time members. Fortunately for the migrants and for the black community as a whole, however, these tendencies were not so pronounced that work on behalf of the migrants ceased and the less fortunate newcomers were excluded entirely. Relations between old and new Philadelphians frequently transcended such resentment, and other influences, such as the bureaucratic imperatives of the churches themselves and the idealism of ministers and church members, counteracted the tendency toward divisiveness.

CHAPTER 3

Evangelism and Social Service

---

*The Church is dominant in the small town largely because of its
monopoly. In a large city things are different. . . . Instead of
having a monopoly on the Sabbath day, [the city church] must
compete with theatres, skating rinks, baseball games, saloons, pool
rooms, race tracks and amusement gardens, as well as with
Sunday labor and Sunday picnics and society functions.*

RICHARD R. WRIGHT, JR., 1907

During the "Great Migration" all aspects of African American churches[1]
were undergoing change, from their forms of worship to their commitment to charitable programs. Nevertheless, the churches endeavored to
retain their position at the center of community life by increasing their
evangelism and providing social services both to attract new members
and to retain old ones.

Prior to 1890, the black community was located largely around the
southern section of the city.[2] Within this community, churches were the
center for social life and discourse, and they provided valuable services
for their congregations. The churches answered both the spiritual and
the secular needs of members of the community. According to historian
Theodore Hershberg, the "benefits and services" that churches provided
in antebellum Philadelphia made church affiliation "a fundamental pre-
requisite to a decent and, indeed, bearable existence."[3] These benefits
were still evident in 1896, when W.E.B. Du Bois undertook his research
for *The Philadelphia Negro*. Besides playing an important economic role,

churches were also social centers for the black community. According to Du Bois, churches acted as newspapers, intelligence bureaus, and amusement centers; they were indeed "the world in which the Negro moves and acts."[4]

Each church congregation represented a particular section of black society. After visiting many of the city's congregations, Du Bois noted:

> At St. Thomas' one looks for the well-to-do Philadelphians, largely descendents of mulatto house-servants, and consequently well-bred and educated, but rather cold and reserved to strangers and newcomers; at Central Presbyterian one sees the older, simpler set of respectable Philadelphians with distinctively Quaker characteristics—pleasant but conservative; at Bethel may be seen the best of the great laboring class— steady, honest people, well dressed and well fed, with church and family traditions; at Wesley will be found the new arrivals, the sight-seers and the strangers to the city—hearty and easy-going people, who welcome all comers and ask few questions; at Union Baptist one may look for the Virginia servant girls and their young men. (p. 203-4)

Each church prior to 1900 formed its own social circle and, according to Du Bois, few strayed beyond its bounds. "Baptism, wedding and burial, gossip and courtship, friendship and intrigue," all happened within the church walls. Differences among individual churches were not entirely self-conscious, however. The churches had become the center for social intercourse, according to Du Bois, "without wholly conscious effort," and the special characteristics of each church had evolved over a long period of time. Moreover, the churches were not noted for extensive debates concerning what sorts of individuals they wished to attract, and while rifts were later to become endemic there were relatively few during the nineteenth century.[5]

However, Du Bois's analysis did not reveal the full extent of the lack of self-conscious distinctions among black churches. His description of Philadelphia's black churches was misleading owing to the clear association he drew between denominations and particular kinds of churches. In the 1890s, each denomination had churches of all types. With a different selection, Du Bois could have created a different picture. A few examples will illustrate this point. The Protestant Episcopal Church of the Crucifixion had a more impoverished congregation than St. Thomas's "mulatto house-servants"; Berean Presbyterian's relatively poor congregation was very different from Central Presbyterian's "older, simpler set of respectable Philadelphians"; and, lastly, First African Baptist (also noted for its large number of light-skinned blacks) would have been more akin to Du Bois's description of St. Thomas's than his description of Union Baptist.[6]

Within the African Methodist Episcopal denomination churches also varied in type. For example, while "Mother" Bethel was noted for having "the best of the great laboring class," Morris Brown was noted for its more elite congregation. According to Levi J. Coppin, who served both churches, "The Morris Brown people . . . gave [a] certain caste to the Church that still characterizes it."[7] Similarly, Union A.M.E. Church had a more elite congregation than, for instance, Mt. Pisgah, a newer congregation with many fewer members.

Readers of Du Bois's *Philadelphia Negro* forty years after its publication in 1899 would have found black religious institutions transformed in their own time. Although Du Bois foresaw that change was likely and recognized areas of tension in congregations, he could not have predicted the extent of change. While churches were reasonably stable in the last decade of the nineteenth century, they were plagued by both financial instability and internal conflicts by the 1920s. While most churches were housed in large, formal buildings in the earlier period, the average church by 1929 was a small storefront establishment. While most of the congregations studied by Du Bois numbered at least one hundred members, in the 1930s some churches had even larger congregations, but most had fewer than thirty congregants. Lastly, while black churches had been dominated by established Philadelphians, by the end of the 1920s southern migrants had become a majority in many congregations and often constituted entire congregations.

By the 1930s, many African Americans believed that the church had lost its central position in the community. As early as 1915, Robert H. Pierce, pastor of First African Baptist Church of Germantown and editor of the *Tribune*'s "In the Pulpit and the Pew" section, wrote an article entitled, "Cause of Church Losing Its Hold." In it he asserted, "The spirit of the church of today is so much different from the church of former days that the reverence for it is not the same at all."[8] In 1935, Lania D. Davis, a reporter for the *Philadelphia Independent* (the city's second black newspaper), started a series of articles designed to highlight the continuing strength and importance of the churches. In the first she wrote: "There are many who have expressed the belief everywhere to writers of this paper that the church is becoming obsolete, and that the average Negro considers going to church on Sunday an ordeal, that pastors no longer receive the respect of their congregations, and that the average Negro's allegiance has been transformed to 'good-times and numbers.'"[9] Davis disagreed with this position, as did Bishop Wright when his physician–friend questioned the value of giving to churches; but the fact that these opinions were widespread signified a change in the status of churches. In the 1890s, not even an agnostic like W.E.B. Du Bois would have questioned the position of the church in the African American community. By 1940, the black church was no longer "the sine qua non of institutional life" in this community.[10]

Numerous threats to the dominance of the church in the black community existed by this time. The church's social role was being taken over to some degree by new bodies. The church as the locus of social interaction was largely superseded by the new entertainment industry. Black ministers now were forced to ask themselves, "How do we compete with the movie theater, the dance hall, and the gambling den?" Often they found competition impossible. Rev. Pierce criticized ministers for becoming increasingly liberal because they feared alienating sinful people. "Members of the church," he wrote, "are allowed to do and engage in anything that worldly people [do], get drunk, live immoral lives, and in fact do any and everything they please, and it is known by the pastor and officers too—and yet they are not questioned." He believed that even the pastors themselves were patronizing the beer wagons.[11]

Even the church's role as welfare provider was being taken over by other institutions—by national and local governments and by groups like the Armstrong Association (Philadelphia's Urban League affiliate). While the church played an important role in providing relief to the unemployed and poverty stricken during the 1930s, the initiatives of Harry W. Mackey, mayor of Philadelphia, and Franklin Delano Roosevelt were also crucial to the welfare of church members. Even young children seemed attuned to this development and were sometimes heard singing, "Let Jesus lead you; and welfare feed you."[12] At the same time, the church's political role diminished somewhat. It is particularly noticeable that whereas black political power brokers were usually ministers at the turn of the century, by the 1940s they often belonged to a new group of secular professionals, particularly lawyers. In Philadelphia, this movement away from church leadership was symbolized by the work in 1918 of the short-lived Colored Protective Association, which represented one of the last coordinated efforts of the established churches, and by the rise of the National Association for the Advancement of Colored People.

By the 1930s, the dominance of established churches was also threatened by the rapid growth of new forms of communion, known at the time as cults. Many African Americans found the older churches spiritually unrewarding and turned to flourishing groups such as the Holiness and Spiritualist Churches, the Moors, the Black Jews, Bishop Cherry, and the Father Divine Peace Mission Movement.[13] Consequently, the older denominations (Episcopal, Catholic, Presbyterian, Methodist, and Baptist) represented a smaller proportion of Philadelphia's black population in 1930 than at the turn of the century.[14] The position of these black churches in the community was now that of *primus inter pares*, first among equals.

Ironically, while the church, as a collective unit, became less of a power within the community, individual churches and sects were establishing a firmer hold over their members. Evangelism required greater self-consciousness as churches sought to attract new members by emphasizing the qualities that distinguished their church from others. This self-consciousness led to differences among denominations as class distinctions became increasingly important in the modern ghetto and as the black community became divided between a new professional class and a "reserve army" of unskilled laborers. Denominational designations now began to have greater importance than distinctions among particular congregations. With few exceptions, Episcopal and Presbyterian congregations had the wealthiest members, while Baptist and Holiness congregations had the poorest. African Methodist churches meanwhile became known for serving the middling classes of the African American community.

The transformation of black churches can be analyzed in terms of "community"—an "association which flourishes on the basis of 'natural,' 'intrinsic' solidarity"—and "communion"—an association that is consciously created as a result of "an actual experience of common feeling."[15] In the 1890s, churches were fairly stable communities; each congregation catered to a different segment of the black community, but the differences among those segments were less significant than the similarities. Cultural differences among denominations and among congregations were generally divorced from class.

By the 1930s, the term "communions" is more appropriate for describing the churches. People were no longer born into a particular church community. Instead, they gravitated toward one that met certain economic, social, and spiritual needs. While social standing in the nineteenth century had required church membership—the important social division was between church members and nonmembers—it now was related to the particular church one belonged to. In a society that restricted upward social mobility outside the black community, churches became crucial for African Americans who wished to distinguish themselves in the ghetto and increase their prestige. Thus, while culture had been separate from class in the earlier period, class designations in the black community now became closely linked to cultural distinctions.

Although evangelism was undertaken in part to fortify the position of black churches, it in fact only accelerated the transformation from "community" to "communion" and diminished the churches' role as a unifying force in the community. By the 1930s, the unity and cooperation among Baptist, Methodist, Episcopal, and Presbyterian denominations that had prevailed in the 1890s had diminished, and there was greater variance in religious practices among them (the plethora of new sects and denominations that had appeared on the scene only added to the religious diversity in black communities). One of the ironies of ghettoization was that as African Americans became increasingly cut off spatially from the white community, their churches actually came to reflect more closely the association between denominations and class groupings common in white churches.

Black churches, including those of the Methodist denominations, responded to ghettoization in two ways. First, they attempted to ensure their own survival by dealing with any financial crises resulting from either the deteriorating living standards of many of their members or the need to pay off mortgages on new and expensive church edifices. Second, they attempted to reach out economically, socially, and politically to help both established members who were facing hard times and newcomers to the city who might make important contributions to the spiritual and economic well-being of their churches. These two responses were meant to be complementary. By providing services for their members, churches would both appeal to outsiders and keep the support of people already in the congregation; and when membership increased, churches would be in a better financial position to supply essential services.

Financial Insecurities and Evangelism

While undertaking her study of Philadelphia migrants in 1921, Sadie T. Mossell discovered, not surprisingly, a strong correlation between the amount a person was willing to donate to a church and the size of his or

her family income. "Irrespective of the size of either family or the income," she concluded, "83% of the families included in the study financially supported the church and . . . the size of income alone influenced
the contributions by limiting their amount." Consequently, as the standard of living of members declined, the income (both real and potential)
of many churches declined also. Mossell also noted that for churches to
fulfill their social functions properly it was necessary for each member to
donate at least $31.20 per year, and yet as many as 85 percent of the
families she studied failed to contribute this amount.[16]

The worsening of living standards for many members of the black
community was bound to have some impact on the financial security of
many churches. For some churches this problem was exacerbated by the
fact that as class divisions grew more distinct in the community, wealthier members moved to other churches whose congregations had higher
social status. This left a rump of largely impoverished members who
were threatened with foreclosure because they could not pay church
debts.[17]

The payment of the mortgage, the major part of church expenses,
had been a burden even before ghettoization. Almost without exception
churches were in debt, as Levi J. Coppin noted in his autobiography,
Unwritten History.[18] For the many buildings constructed during the 1890s
and 1900s and for others bought from white congregations, the churches
had taken out mortgages, believing that the size and relative wealth of
their congregations would enable them to meet their monthly payments.[19]
But the wealth of many of their members declined, many churches faced
the threat of foreclosure, and during the depression actual foreclosures
among churches reached epidemic proportions.

Even the congregations with affluent members were financially
troubled. Morris Brown A.M.E. Church, which had some of the most
prestigious black families among its members, continually appealed to its
sister churches for assistance. The advertisement placed in the denomination's journal, the *Christian Recorder*, in August 1891 was typical of the
appeals the church made during the period. It read:

> Morris Brown A.M.E. . . . has been struggling for a number of years to
> free itself from debt. Each year they are paying $300 on ground rent, and
> also carrying $1400 in the Building and Loan Association.
>   The membership of this church is about forty so there is little that
> can be accomplished by these and the congregation, without the aid of
> our sister churches.

On Sunday, September 29, the church is striving to raise two thousand dollars of this amount. Quite a number of churches have pledge[d] themselves to assist us by donations.

AMOS WILSON, PASTOR[20]

Perhaps the problem for Morris Brown arose from its exclusiveness. At least until 1916, when Preston Paul Gaines encouraged migrants to join the congregation, the church seemed unwilling to respond to financial hardship in the usual way by endeavoring to increase membership.

As a result of efforts to deal with financial difficulties, the churches turned to strict accounting methods and placed increased emphasis on raising money through church classes. Mother Bethel used both strategies to reduce its financial burden, which arose from the 1890 construction of the building still standing at 6th and Lombard. In 1891, the *Christian Recorder* congratulated Bethel on issuing "the Official Record," which provided "a clear exhibit of all receipts and disbursements of the Trustee Board."[21] By congratulating Bethel, the journal encouraged other churches to follow suit. At the same time, classes became increasingly important in financial endeavors. They had been started in England, in 1742, in response to financial necessity. Originally, a leader was placed in charge of twelve or more members and given the responsibility of contacting them at least once a week to collect at least a penny. Ministers and members soon recognized that while classes promoted community feeling by providing members with a sense of belonging and keeping the pastor informed of individual members' hardships, they were also extremely effective financial agencies.[22] In 1891, Bethel reported in the *Christian Recorder* the results of a class rally at which $2,539 was raised. Listing each class's contribution encouraged a sense of competition and pushed members to contribute more.[23] These techniques became general throughout black churches in the twentieth century.

Increased evangelism was another way to deal with financial insecurities. All ministers seemed to recognize the wisdom of the view summarized so well by Bishop Henry McNeil Turner in 1891: "The more a church is spiritualized the more liberal the people will be. I can take a spiritualized church and raise there three times as much from it as any man can from a dead formal congregation. The more people are taught to respect and reverence God, the more liberal they will be towards anything that God enjoins."[24]

On the whole, ministers were very successful in their attempts to rally congregations to raise money to pay off church debts. Usually the threat to the church was so apparent that members could be appealed to, rifts between members smoothed over, and a unity of purpose created in the war against debt. When Coppin arrived at "Mother" Bethel in 1896, for example, he found an enormous debt remaining from the erection of the new church building in 1890 and a membership that "had begun to go with the city trend, west and southwest." He realized that he would be unable to accomplish anything unless he dealt with the church debt. "My first effort," Coppin wrote, "was to increase the attendance and organize a financial rally that would net a larger sum of money than the average rally produced." He invited his bishop to the rally and also another minister, John W. Beckett, who had had great success at such rallies. Coppin was very proud of the results. "The day was fair," he wrote, "the attendance large; enthusiasm high, and the amount realized was thirty-two hundred dollars. This was before the days of Drs. Carl M. Tanner with his sixteen thousand, and W. Sampson Brooks, with his thirty-three thousand, and was, I think, about the largest amount up to that time, raised in one day by one of our churches."[25] The history of black churches is replete with stories of overcoming debt. Almost every congregation remembers, and many even commemorate, the day the last mortgage was burned with a special ceremony. Each burning was in a real sense an independence day.[26]

Holding rallies and revivals became the common means of dealing with financial problems. Immediately prior to these events, the minister sent out appeals to members, warning them of church indebtedness and telling them of the targets for the coming weeks. J. Campbell Beckett, pastor of Union A.M.E. Church, for example, wrote to his members in September 1924:

> The Fall Rally is called a Mortgage Rally. Our goal is $4,000. The purpose is to meet our obligations, and pay off the mortgage indebtedness. Will you help? I know you love old "Union." Help free "Union" from debt. Subscribe and pay on or before Rally Sunday, October 26, 1924. I know you will do your best to help liquidate our indebtedness.[27]

Likewise, in one of its issues of the *Bulletin* from 1930, St. Matthews A.M.E. Church announced the "Drive to End all Drives." The pastor wrote, "The church has never failed you! Please don't fail your church."[28]

Letters from the Rev. E. K. Nichols, pastor of Union A.M.E. Church, to Walter C. Beckett, a prosperous undertaker and member of this church, highlight some of the methods used to raise money in Philadelphia churches, the problems facing members during the depression years, and the charity work of a member of Philadelphia's black elite.[29] One such letter, dated August 11, 1931, began with Nichols telling the layman that he had been missed at the previous Sunday's services and that the minister wanted him to know that "whenever you are absent you are greatly missed." Such flattery was not surprising, given Beckett's prominence in the community. Nichols then informed Beckett that the church's mortgage interest note would become due in September and that it was imperative that the church raise five hundred dollars almost immediately. He continued:

> Knowing as we do that a large number of our members are [in] really dire need themselves, without work, many of them, and without the means of procuring the bare necessities of life, I am asked that the strong among us follow the Scriptures, "the strong should bear the infirmities of the weak." Therefore I am asking that ten of our members who can do so give $20.00; twenty give $10.00 and the rest give $5.00 and whatever they can. Three thus far have pledged $20.00 and four $10.00. Will you please give me your subscription? I am sure you will not fail the church in this distress.

On July 15, 1932, Nichols congratulated Beckett on being selected commander-in-chief of the forthcoming rally and predicted that he would "lead the forces to a great victory." He enclosed some clippings concerning "rally aids" (cards, small fact sheets called gleaners, and other advertisements), the use of which, he worried, would offend some of his members. Nevertheless, he determined to use these aids because they would "bring us many a penny and dime amounting to considerable sums, which we would not otherwise get."

Often, as at Mother Bethel during Coppin's pastorate, outside ministers were asked to help a pastor in his endeavors. After 1900, churches began to employ special evangelists, who went from congregation to congregation merely to help raise money during revivals. One such evangelist was Arthur Wilbank, who came to Philadelphia from Washington, D.C., in the spring of 1915 and became known in the local press as "Black Billy Sunday" because his antics resembled those of the well-known white evangelist.[30]

Evangelists made important contributions to black churches. As William A. Creditt, pastor of First African Baptist Church, pointed out, most black preachers had been schooled in white seminaries, where they had learned to regard black religious practices as undignified and wrong. "We became apt pupils," Creditt wrote, and he continued,

> a new sort of colored preacher began to appear, he has education, refinement and culture. We have retained much of the deep religious feelings of our fathers, but we seek to control it in order to do what our white teachers taught us. As a result you will find today all over the South and the North colored churches whose services are as quiet and dignified as the most dignified of our white churches and white ministers.

Consequently, many of the ministers were not adept evangelists and were unable to employ the techniques that attracted large audiences or encouraged people to give away their hard-earned dollars and cents.

According to Creditt, the white Billy Sunday had learned his moves on the baseball diamond and had "carried his bodily activity from the baseball field into the pulpit." The new evangelists were similar to their predecessors in slavery, who "had learned their actions in the common plantation dances and while working in the fields and in their frolics."[31] However, these new evangelists also learned from their experiences in the ghettos.[32]

One of the risks of employing these evangelists was that they might outshine the pastors of the host churches. They also tended to reinforce among church members an association between entertainment and donation, thus leaving the educated minister unable to appeal to his flock for funds unless he was willing to imitate the evangelist. As a result, there was a higher proportion of poorly educated ministers in the pulpit in 1930 than at the turn of the century, and clergymen were often unwilling to reveal that they had been well educated.[33] In the case of Arthur Wilbank, Varick Temple A.M.E. Zion found him costly in terms of the damage he did to the church. Wilbank was displeased with his treatment at Varick. "He thinks," a *Tribune* reporter noted, "that the agility he displayed in climbing the organ should have yielded him fairer consideration from the pastor, Dr. Corrothers, and the press agent, Charles Fred White." But Sylvester L. Corrothers was also annoyed because, according to the reporter, the pipe organ would need to "rest for a long while."[34]

Financial conditions in some churches were so bad that almost anything might be tried. When Mt. Zion A.M.E. Church was threatened with foreclosure in 1927 because of a debt exceeding thirty thousand dollars, the pastor invited Herman Rucker, better known as "Black Herman," to use the church for his "voodoo campaign" in return for a fee.[35] Black Herman's voodoo included faith healing, predicting the daily number, and selling charms. His most powerful charm was the "John the Conqueror Root." About this root, Orrin C. Evans, the *Tribune* reporter who undertook a personal campaign against Herman's "nefarious practice," wrote:

> [It was] a few gnarled pieces of root to which has been attributed more wonderful and phenomenal properties than any other root or herb we have heard of. It is believed by certain Voo-Doos and Hindu Priests that persons carrying a piece of this root in their pocket will never be without money and can obtain anything they desire. They will always feel strong and powerful and have much luck. . . . If a man were fearful of losing his job or position all that was necessary was for him to spit in front of his employer [having chewed the root] and he could not be dismissed.

Other healing potions were sold, such as "Sea Spirit," "Queen Elizabeth Root," "Oriental Gum," "Devil's Shoe Strings," and "Dragon's Blood."

The endorsement of Black Herman illustrates the extremes to which a church might go in order to remain financially solvent. Rucker's business was very profitable. He sometimes brought to the church as many as fourteen hundred people at a time and usually more than two hundred, all of whom paid an admission fee. Not surprisingly then, Rev. T. J. Askew defended Herman's practices when pressed on the issue by Evans, saying, "If I did not approve of it I would not permit it in my church. My Presiding Elder, Cooper, was down here one night and sat through an entire performance and he thought that it was entirely creditable and above reproach." Unfortunately for Mt. Zion, however, Herman Rucker did not remain in Philadelphia long. On the basis of one of his guesses a woman took out a warrant for the arrest of another woman on a charge of larceny. When it was discovered that the crime could not have been committed by the accused, Black Herman hastily left town for New York.

Tindley Temple Methodist Episcopal Church (formerly East Calvary) also experienced difficulties with their evangelist. In the last years of Rev. Charles Albert Tindley's tenure as pastor of the church, when he was less compelling and energetic than in his younger days and when building a new edifice left the church in dire financial straits, the trustees decided (against the pastor's wishes) to employ an evangelist. In 1930, G. Wilson Becton was invited to bring his "World's Gospel Feast Party" to Tindley Temple. Becton's antics, which included the consecration of every dime that was donated, were at first very lucrative. The church was full at almost every service, and reporters and photographers exploited his newsworthiness. Eventually the novelty wore off, and Becton was asked to leave Tindley Temple. Unfortunately for the church, the evangelist decided to establish himself and his group at the Olympic Arena, situated at Broad and Christian Streets, a few blocks away from Tindley Temple. Almost three thousand Tindleyites followed him, leaving the Methodist congregation worse off than before Becton had arrived, but its predicament was short-lived. Mysteriously, Becton was assassinated as he left the arena one evening, and his Gospel Feast Party died with him.[36]

The growing presence of evangelists led to many complaints about the "gross mercenary spirit" permeating black churches. A black New York newspaper claimed that these churches drained "the time and small money of their membership" and that their leaders regarded "church building and money raising as the principal business of the preacher."[37] But this commercialism did provide the churches with the sound economic footing essential, as Bishop Wright argued, to providing social, economic, and political assistance to members of their community.[38]

Benevolent Work and Social Service

The churches' customary role of providing services to their members became even more crucial with the emergence of the new Philadelphia ghettos. On the whole, black churches rose to the challenge, though they could not be expected to resolve the problems confronting the black community. Writing in 1912, Richard R. Wright, Jr., noted the large amount of charitable giving and community service done by black church members:

> It is quite difficult for anyone who has not kept in close touch with the Negro church to realize the amount of casual charity done by Negro church members. Many times they give a part of their last dollar to the church and to the poor. "Give till you feel it," is an expression often heard from the Negro pulpit, and not seldom obeyed by the faithful Negro Christian. Nor is it an uncommon thing for the hard worked Negro cook, or washer woman, or housewife, after doing service from ten to fourteen hours a day, to visit the sick and sit up nearly all night with the distressed.[39]

The emphasis of this community work changed according to the needs of the moment. In the early years of the twentieth century, churches placed most emphasis on self-help and vocational training for members. With the Great Migration, they were forced to concentrate on providing housing for newcomers to the city. After the war, providing food and basic necessities to the poor, members and nonmembers alike, was emphasized. Throughout the period churches took it upon themselves to represent the black community politically, a responsibility that they gave up to the National Association for the Advancement of Colored People, once this body became firmly established in the city.

Between 1890 and 1915, black churches concentrated on providing training programs and self-help schemes for their members. The guiding light in these endeavors was Berean Presbyterian Church under the leadership of Matthew Anderson. Berean was established in 1878 as a mission of Central Presbyterian Church, and Anderson turned it into an institutional church. The church's pastoral field was in North Philadelphia, between 12th Street and the Schuylkill River, and between Montgomery and Market Streets, an area of the city where black people were just beginning to live. The six thousand African Americans in this area were generally poor, and there were many slums and a considerable amount of vice.[40] By 1899, according to Du Bois, Berean owned "a fine piece of property bought by donations contributed by whites and Negroes, but chiefly the former." The church conducted a successful Building and Loan Association, a kindergarten, a medical dispensary, a seaside home, and numerous church societies. "Probably no church in the city," Du Bois wrote, "except the Episcopal Church of the Crucifixion, is doing so much for the betterment of the Negro."[41] By 1906, Anderson had created the city's largest black building and loan association, which had purchased more than 169 houses at an average cost of three thousand dollars.[42] He had also started the Berean Institute, a school for industrial education financed by white businessmen such as John Wanamaker and Robert Ogden.

Other churches followed the example of Anderson and Berean. First African Baptist under William A. Creditt, for example, established its Insurance Society in 1903, the Cherry Building and Loan Association in 1904, and the Downingtown Institute (another industrial school) in 1905.[43] Generally, Methodist churches did not establish their own manual training institutes in Philadelphia but supported colleges established by the A.M.E. Connection (the members' term for the denomination) throughout the country. They also supported the Institute for Colored Youth, a black college initially established by the Society of Friends. The principal of the institute during the 1880s was Fanny J. Coppin, a prominent member of the A.M.E. Church and wife of Levi J. Coppin.

Methodists were also involved in banking initiatives. In September 1920, for example, Major Richard R. Wright, Sr., and his son, the editor of the *Christian Recorder*, organized the Citizens and Southern Bank and Trust Company. The board of directors included four African Methodist bishops, Levi J. Coppin, John Hurst, W. S. Brooks and William H. Heard. More than six hundred people, many of them migrants from the South, bought stock in the company. Owing both to skillful management by members of the Wright family and its association with many churches, the company survived through the depression years, while many others went bankrupt.[44] The directors sent letters to prominent church members inviting them to buy shares and attend meetings[45] and often called meetings of church pastors (who afterward presumably advised their members to invest).[46] Association with the churches also influenced the way the Wrights ran Citizens and Southern. They believed their bank had more important functions than just earning profits. "We looked upon our bank not only as a mere business," the younger Wright maintained, "but as a social service. Major and his associates went into the banking business not just to make money, but to try to lay a firm financial foundation for our people."[47]

With the increase in migration during the First World War, churches were forced to turn their focus from self-help and training to housing the newcomers. As will be discussed at length in a later chapter, church members did a great deal to aid the migrants by making their homes available to lodgers; other church members became heavily involved in organizations like the Philadelphia Housing Association, the Armstrong Association, the Commission on Work among Colored People, and the Society for Organizing Charity.[48] Black ministers established the Interdenominational Ministerial Alliance in 1917 to deal with the same problems. This alliance included William A. Harrod of First African Baptist, Wesley F. Graham of Holy Trinity Baptist, Charles Albert Tindley of East Calvary Methodist Episcopal, John W. Lee of First African Presbyterian, and Robert J. Williams of Mother Bethel A.M.E., among others. These pastors used their churches to hold meetings to discuss the migrants' problems and to help find lodgings among churchgoers for the new arrivals in the city.

The churches' response to the migration was formidable. Through no fault of their own, however, churchgoers responded in a way that may have been counterproductive. As Chapter 2 showed, overcrowding was an essential part of the problem of ghettoization. By doing the "Christian" thing, bringing migrants into their homes as lodgers, churchgoers may have added to the overcrowding in the community. There were, of course, few viable alternatives open to ministers and their congregations. They might have pooled their political resources to attempt to end residential segregation, but the relatively small size of the black community and its lack of support in city administrations would have limited their effectiveness.

During the depression years, churches turned from the question of housing to focus more directly on charitable giving to unemployed and indigent blacks in the city. Some churches had been doing this kind of work for many years. The Protestant Episcopal Church of the Crucifixion under its rector, Henry L. Phillips, had established a shelter for the homeless on Lombard Street in the 1890s.[49] "Here," according to the rector,

> a number of old women of the church have always found a resting-place between the time they have become too feeble to support themselves and that of their transition. Here a door for homeless women and children, free of charge, and without regard to race or creed, has been kept open. This is the first institution in the city where meals were regularly prepared for the outside poor and sick who desired to have them.[50]

But, as both Phillips and Du Bois noted, this was one of the few efforts churches in this area made at the time.

By the mid-1920s church intervention on behalf of the poor had become imperative. Unemployment for blacks had grown steadily after the end of the postwar boom, and with the lack of social services and benefits in the society, it was left up to the churches and other voluntary organizations to help the poverty-stricken. As usual, Tindley's church led the way. During the winter of 1918, Tindley's East Calvary was cooking fifty buckets of soup daily and handing out coal to those who needed it.[51] Other churches followed East Calvary's course. Rev. D. D. Mattocks became known as "the community pastor" for doing similar work at St. Mark A.M.E. Zion in West Philadelphia. In 1924, St. Mark built a new church structure so that it could better fulfill its community services. The new building provided rooms for recreation as well as classrooms that allowed for the establishment of kindergarten classes.[52]

Another concern facing churches at this time was the problem of disease in the black community. Ministers and members were well aware that death rates in the overcrowded slum dwellings were higher than in other parts of the city. In October 1922, therefore, all churches and social agencies in the Seventh Ward were invited to attend "The Church and the Community Conference," which convened at Central Presbyterian Church. Twenty-eight people attended; three were social workers, while the rest represented five different black churches. At the meeting, the pastor of Central, Rev. William Lloyd Imes, read the minutes of the previous conference held at Mother Bethel. Miss Jane Turner then spoke of her work with the Philadelphia Anti-Tuberculosis Committee, and the Rev. E.A.E. Palmquist (secretary of the Philadelphia Federation of Churches) discussed the need for social uplift work in the Seventh Ward, suggesting that each church or organization be given specific city blocks in which to do social work.[53]

While black churches very effectively delivered services to those in need, they often were not able to attract those who might benefit from the social life of the church. An employment situation might considerably affect a person's attendance at church. This was particularly the case for some women laborers. Live-in service workers and some household day workers often could not attend church. The former were usually too cut off from the black community—they lived in white households—to get to church. Often, they had to work on Sundays. Day workers, however, while they did not have the same restrictions as live-in workers and usually had Sunday to themselves, might have to give their day of rest to their own family's concerns and thus be equally unable to go to church regularly.[54]

Further, the onset of hard times might result in a family's withdrawal from the church. Members did not necessarily wish to receive aid from other church members. To go to one of the Sunday services, families would dress in their Sunday best. If family income declined, the finery could not be replaced when it wore out, and the family might cease attending church to avoid the humiliation of attending a service in everyday clothes. Ella May Storey, for example, who, since coming north during the war with her parents, had attended Varick Temple A.M.E. Zion Church regularly and had also sung in Union Baptist choir, stopped going to church after she married and began bearing children. She said, "I had children fast and them days you didn't make much money. . . . And I had been raised a certain way; then I begin to not have the things that I would like to have to go to church. So I just stayed away, that's it."[55] The responsibility of raising children, rather than pushing Ella May to go to church more frequently, actually led her almost to stop going. Thus, while black churches provided substantial aid for those who were not their members, people who needed help felt reluctant to join the church if their inability to dress fashionably might advertise their poverty.

The onset of the Great Depression itself brought economic catastrophe to many church members. "When the depression of the early 1930's started," Richard R. Wright later recalled, "I saw my church membership being laid off from their jobs; first temporarily, then permanently. I saw small savings dwindle to nothing and then my people grew desperate. What was true of my church was true of all colored churches over Philadelphia, and over most of America."[56] Wright added that as conditions grew worse black churches banded together to try to help the needy. Many, Mt. Olive A.M.E. and Zoar M.E. in particular, made important contributions toward alleviating the problems of the unemployed. At the former, J. R. Reed undertook "a great fight against the depression," and in so doing provided assistance to many of the five hundred members jamming the church auditorium at each service. Zoar, meanwhile, sponsored its own social work department, which provided assistance to 2,380 children and adults; 139 families received relief, 583 were given free dental service, and 1,997 patients were treated in the baby clinic.[57]

Black church leaders also attempted to put pressure on a committee of white Philadelphia businessmen who had organized for relief purposes to spread their funds among the black poor as well as the white. According to Wright, however, the committee was not forthcoming. The churchmen had more success when they put pressure on the city government to provide relief for black unemployed. Mayor Harry W. Mackey organized a small committee with Wright as chairman, William A. Harrod of First African Baptist as secretary, and Tindley as treasurer. Each of the other major denominations, including the Church of God, was represented on the committee. The mayor placed two thousand dollars at the disposal of this committee every week. Baskets of food were given out, along with coal, and soup kitchens and distribution places were opened. The committee also persuaded the American Stores and A&P Markets to make groceries available at cost. Besides providing food, the committee also attempted to furnish work. As Wright wrote later, "Where the churches would undertake repairs to their property and would furnish the material, the committee would pay for the labor. In that way, many unemployed skilled mechanics' families were helped, along with others."[58] Unfortunately, the churches were limited in the amount of improvements they could make because of their own financial difficulties.

Involvement of the churches in politics was essential in any effort to respond to discrimination. Racial antagonism grew, particularly after the large influx of migrants during the First World War, and black churches were forced to come together to protect members of their community who were victims of prejudice. With the murder of Riley Bullock while he was in police custody and the outbreak of race riots at the end of July 1918, black ministers organized the Colored Protective Association.[59] The purpose of this association was

> to protect the colored people who have been arrested unjustly, and who are sent to prison often because they have no friends to speak for them. The Association will speak for the friendless Negro in the courts. . . . In a year thousands of Negroes are sent to prison, not because they are guilty, but because they have no one to represent them.[60]

The C.P.A. also supported the right of black people to move into any area of the city, and it provided counsel for any African Americans who felt they had been discriminated against while securing a place to live or work, or in the schools and places of amusement. The association was determined "to reach the last Negro in the city of Philadelphia, to bring all colored people into one organization for the purpose of having a permanent organization of protection."

The fact that the large majority of leaders of the association were ministers contributed to the organization's success. Like the Interdenominational Ministerial Alliance, the C.P.A. was able to involve ministers from all denominations. Richard R. Wright, Jr., Robert J. Williams, J. Campbell Beckett, and Bishops Levi J. Coppin and William H. Heard, among others, represented the A.M.E Church; J.W.H. Eason and Bishop J. S. Caldwell represented the A.M.E. Zion Church; Tindley and F. H. Butler represented the United Methodists, and Henry L. Phillips the Episcopalians. All the leading Baptist ministers were involved, including Abraham R. Robinson, Wesley F. Graham, William A. Harrod, and William H. Moses. Hundreds of dollars were raised for the C.P.A. at interdenominational rallies sponsored by numerous churches, such as Graham's Holy Trinity Baptist, Pinn Memorial Baptist, and Mother Bethel A.M.E. Churches.[61]

Once united, the ministers were able to bring together a large section of the black community and create a united front against the city administration of Mayor Thomas Smith. As a result of the C.P.A.'s work, Roy Ramsey (the policeman who had Riley Bullock in custody when he was killed) was prosecuted for murder, and Patrolman John Schneider was prosecuted for another assault on a black man named Preston Lewis. Further, the city government initiated an investigation of the practices of the police in the Seventeenth Ward. The C.P.A. argued that had more black policemen been hired, and had more of them been patrolling the riot areas, most of the violence could have been avoided.

Historian Vincent P. Franklin has argued that one of the reasons for organizing the C.P.A. in Philadelphia was the failure of the NAACP to involve itself in Philadelphia cases in which blacks were the victims of racial discrimination and police brutality.[62] Perhaps another way of looking at this is to suggest that the political strength of the churches in Philadelphia allowed the NAACP to channel its resources elsewhere, to places where blacks were not represented by so formidable a force. The establishment of the Philadelphia branch of the NAACP during the 1920s may symbolize the decline in power of the established churches and their increasing inability to unite to protect the rights of black people in the city.

The Colored Protective Association represents the swan song of unity among black churches in Philadelphia. With increased ghettoization and the migration of thousands of blacks from the South into the city, the different denominations tended to move further apart from each other as they came to represent different sections of the community. Where, in 1918, an organization like the C.P.A. could be led by African Methodists working closely with Baptists, Presbyterians, and Episcopalians, after the 1920s the Baptists (along with the new Holiness and Spiritualist sects) would tend to lead lower-class blacks, while the Methodists would more often represent a middle-class grouping and the Episcopalians and Presbyterians would represent the black elite.

Such divisions were heightened by the decline of the Republican Party in Philadelphia. Individual African Methodists had been linked to the Republican Party machine through their membership in the Citizens Republican Club and in ward organizations, and as a group they received leadership from the *Tribune*, which sustained a strong Republican editorial bias.[63] This commitment gave them influence over the city's mayors from which community benefits could be reaped. In 1934, for example, black Republicans were able to persuade Mayor S. Davis Wilson to commit himself to ending jim crow hiring policies in the police force.[64] But the rise of a black democratic organ, the *Philadelphia Independent*, bolstered by the popularity of President Roosevelt's New Deal policies, led many African Americans to sever ties with the Republicans. The onset of the Great Depression undermined old loyalties to "the Party of Lincoln," which gave way to support for the party of Franklin and Eleanor Roosevelt. This process further diminished African Methodist influence in the city.

The desire among many churchgoers to blame newly arrived Southerners for the deterioration in Philadelphia's black community ought to have been counterbalanced by both evangelism (the desire and need to increase the size of congregations) and a strong tradition among churchgoers of service and commitment to uplifting "the race." African Methodists had learned from the Baptists' experience during the first decade of the century that the quickest way to expand a congregation was to welcome new arrivals to the city. In 1912, Richard Wright, Jr., had pointed to the prodigious rise of Baptists in Pennsylvania. "For three quarters of a century," he wrote,

> the Baptists as a rule had the less influential and intelligent class of Negroes in its membership and held rather an insignificant place among churches of the state. During the present generation, however, the Baptist denomination has taken a front rank among Pennsylvania's Negro churches, both as to number of churches and influence. The increase of the influence of the Baptist church has been due chiefly to the influx of Negroes from Virginia, where the Baptist denomination was probably the first established and where it is to-day stronger than any other denomination. Many of the ministers of this church are Virginians.[65]

This lesson was not lost on Wright's fellow African Methodists. Migrants represented an attractive resource for ministers in search of members, particularly because a much larger proportion of them than of the more sceptical Northerners were churchgoers.

In the process of becoming evangelical, however, churches accentuated what was unique about their theological and ideological identities. Consequently, while they solidified the commitment of people who already shared their outlooks and appealed to others who were persuaded by the fresh presentation of these ideas, they repelled larger numbers who had not shared the same heritage. In other words, evangelism brought to the fore particular religious, class, and gender attitudes that would be attractive to people for whom those ideas had some relevance. Meanwhile, other people were likely to be alienated.

Evangelism, then, signified two things: weakness in the face of a threat from outside social forces and the realization that the church or denomination was no longer a "community"; and reliance on religious uniqueness rather than on shared spiritual values in attracting new members to what was now a "communion." African Methodists, like other Christians, had developed a theology that reflected their position in society. As this position changed with the development of ghettos, African Methodists were unable to make significant adjustments to reflect the new social reality. For African Methodists, who, perhaps better than anyone, had managed to speak for the whole African American community, evangelism would mean the end of their leadership role. Thousands of newcomers swarmed into the city, but African Methodists were often unable to appeal to them and other denominations profited. Part II deals with the distinctive class and gender aspects of African Methodist theology and practices that compromised the denomination's ability to take advantage of the Great Migration.

PART II

"In the Pulpit
and the Pew"

Previous Page

Mother Bethel, 1916. Courtesy Atwater Kent Museum, Philadelphia

CHAPTER 4

Uplifting "Backward Peoples"

*What [the mission of Methodism] is may be expressed in one brief
but pregnant sentence: Patient, loving, Christlike leadership
towards all that make for the salvation and uplifting to complete
manhood of the backward peoples.*

BISHOP GEORGE W. CLINTON,
A.M.E. ZION CHURCH, 1912

From its foundation at the end of the eighteenth century, African Methodist theology had evidenced two apparently contradictory strands: conservative Methodist forms of worship and a liberal, sometimes radical, political philosophy. The former strand, which grew out of Richard Allen's commitment to Methodism in the face of Absalom Jones's defection to the Protestant Episcopal denomination, was solidified after the Civil War in the writings and leadership of Bishop Daniel Payne, who in many respects followed the direction of white Methodist theologians.[1] The latter strand also developed early in the denomination's history; it began with support for abolitionism and Radical Reconstruction, which were followed by opposition to segregation and disenfranchisement in the South. African Methodists often formulated political positions that were more radical than those of white Wesleyans, particularly concerning race relations. The political and social oppression that characterized the period provided conditions in which African Methodists could couple conservatism in forms of worship with a political progressivism without feeling any sense of contradiction.

This linkage of liturgical conservatism and political radicalism was also typical of the Social Gospel movement, supported by most religious reformers of the Progressive Era.[2] The Social Gospel movement, was distinct from liberation theology in that its adherents were not intent on reshaping theology to reflect the aspirations of impoverished and oppressed peoples; rather, they concentrated on "uplifting" oppressed people so that they could share in the advances and advantages of "civilization." Liturgical reform was not deemed desirable.[3]

The need of the Catholic church to secularize the operations of the clergy was absent from African Methodism, largely, of course, because the language of worship was already English as opposed to Latin. However, other theological reforms could have been demanded. Traditional Wesleyan hymns could have been replaced by Gospel songs, Gothic church edifices could have been replaced by more open and inviting architectural forms, and both certification and appointment of ministers could have better reflected the needs of individual congregations than the exigencies of a bureaucratic, episcopal structure.

Although one of the earliest composers of gospel hymns, Charles A. Tindley, was a Methodist, African Methodists tended to eschew the singing of gospel hymns in their services. Tindley himself only employed his music during "songfests" that developed out of his sermons and at prayer meetings; he did not make his hymns official parts of the church service performed by the choir and congregation.[4] In marked contrast, black Baptists decided in the early 1930s to recognize officially the gospel hymns of Thomas A. Dorsey and thereby endorsed what was already happening within their congregations. Likewise, while some denominations found the storefront an appropriate place of worship for a ghettoized people, African Methodists tended to view storefronts only as temporary establishments until a congregation could afford a "proper" Gothic church building.

The Social Gospel had important consequences for the development of African Methodism in the twentieth century. First, as black ghettos developed, African Methodists did not feel the need to reform their political positions dramatically to speak to the problems facing their congregants and black people generally. Social Gospel thinking made uplifting "backward peoples" seem relevant both for people in rural areas and for those in ghettos. However, like other Progressives who believed that they could cross class boundaries and represent people on both sides, African Methodists failed to see that emerging social divisions in the black community would deprive them of both rich and poor. Their complacency would lead to a shrinking constituency.

Second, the liturgical conservatism of African Methodist theology never gave way to a more liberation-oriented theology. There was no need for it to do so because it had coexisted with political progressivism for a long time before the development of the ghetto. The sectarianism of African Methodists (matched by that of black Christians in other denominations), which arose out of conformity to separate conservative liturgies, inhibited the development of a "Black Theology" and made an interdenominational response to oppression difficult to achieve.

Third, the Social Gospel movement influenced the reaction of Philadelphia's African Methodists to the influx of new migrants from the South during and after the First World War. African Methodists tried to help the newcomers adjust to their new environment, but at the same time they welcomed more readily into their congregations those who had been members of the denomination in the South, since these people were familiar with the liturgy and would feel more comfortable in their pews. This does not mean that they were deliberately exclusionary. Rather, their Methodist religious practices were not appealing to non-Methodists who had made the trip north and who perhaps wished for familiarity in their worship to compensate for the lack of familiarity in their new urban surroundings.

These impressions are based on a close study of articles published between 1888 and 1925 in the African Methodist Episcopal Church *Review*. This quarterly was founded by Bishop Benjamin Tucker Tanner in 1884 to fulfill a different role from the *Christian Recorder*, the denomination's weekly newspaper covering general events in the churches and the denomination. Through the *Review*, Tanner hoped to provide an outlet for black intellectuals and to increase debate on matters relating to both the race and Methodism.[5] He invited anyone who wished to contribute to do so, but most contributors were members of the A.M.E. Church.[6] Financial constraints forced the journal to rely on three sources for its writers: friends of the editor, ministerial and lay members of the A.M.E. Church, and young men and women aspiring to be writers.[7]

The dependence upon members of the denomination was sometimes a hindrance to an editor trying to produce a quality journal, as Levi J. Coppin later noted in *The Unwritten History*:

> The selecting of articles for the Review was no easy task. Our main
> support—financial support—was not from the most scholarly class, and it

> often happened that one who had not gained a reputation as a writer
> would send in an article, and feel that on account of the material support
> given by himself and his friends, it should appear. This was especially
> true of ministers connected with our conferences. They began to say:
> "We support the Review, and we want to be given a place in its
> columns."[8]

But because of this reliance, the journal provides a window on the theology and political philosophy of the African Methodist elite during the period.

Whether these views were shared by churchgoing members is less easy to discern. It is unclear just how widespread the readership of the *Review* was. Certainly, though, ministers were encouraged to subscribe to the journal by the editor, who promoted his wares at a local conference, and sometimes by a bishop. Coppin remembered having difficulty at a local conference persuading a minister to subscribe to the *Review*. Bishop T.M.D. Ward, then the bishop of that conference, overheard the conversation and came over to help the editor:

> "What is the trouble there?" asked the Bishop, his mouth twitching with
> a characteristically humorous smile. "He was asking me to take the
> review," responded the minister. "It is one dollar and a half," said the
> Bishop. "But I do not care to take it," replied the minister. "One dollar
> and a half," said the Bishop again. "But suppose I haven't got the
> money," said the minister. The Bishop leaning forward, said again, "One
> dollar and a half." Upon this, the contending party took the amount from
> his pocket and entered the list of subscribers. (pp. 256–57)

This passage reveals that the journal had some official support in the A.M.E. denomination. It begs the question, though, whether other bishops supported it as much as T.M.D. Ward did. It also suggests that some ministers may have been reluctant to subscribe. Nevertheless, it is likely that the *Review* made a significant impression on church members, either through its readership or through the dissemination of its ideas by pastors in the pulpit.

African Methodist Liturgy

Articles in the *Review* between 1890 and 1915 reveal that African Methodist religious beliefs conformed fairly rigidly at the turn of the century to those found in white Methodist churches. African Methodists did not object to white Methodists on theological grounds; they objected to whites discriminating against them. The initial break with the white denomination was viewed as a necessity rather than an ideal, and this belief was still accepted in 1900, as can be seen in the many debates about rejoining the Methodist Episcopal Church.[9] African Methodists did not feel that it was necessary to reform the practices of white Methodists, and they often looked to the white denomination for direction in theological matters. Bishop Tanner understood the nature of this relationship with the white church. At a service commemorating Mother Bethel A.M.E. Church's one-hundred-and-nineteenth anniversary, in 1908, the bishop considered what was original about the African Methodist Episcopal Church. "It is not doctrine," he argued, "for as Methodists we hold these in common with the Methodists of the world." Instead, he concluded that the church's originality lay in its ecclesiastical independence, which allowed blacks to administer their own affairs.[10]

Many of the theological articles in the A.M.E. Church *Review* could quite well have appeared in a journal of white Methodist churches. Furthermore, white Methodists frequently contributed articles on theological matters to the *Review*. The journal would publish an article from a white religious paper or a speech given at a white Methodist conference. Partly as a result of such contributions black writers often modeled themselves on white theologians. Many blacks believed that equality in all realms would be realized when whites saw what blacks could achieve. In their theological writings, this meant demonstrating their ability to write articles that white theologians would accept as sound theology.

Consequently, African Methodism could not easily be distinguished from Methodism generally. Because the church had not arisen out of a theological controversy, there was no need for African Methodists to depart from "the theological heritage of Methodism."[11] Articles by John T. Jenifer, a regular contributor to the *Review* from Richmond, Indiana, clearly show that A.M.E. theology stayed within the bounds of the Wesleyan tradition. African Methodism, according to Jenifer, was "a Method of holy living with all the enlightening and reforming agencies of Methodism, formed into a separate, distinct and free church organization, which is controlled by men of African descent, being peculiarly fitted by blood, temperament, experience and sympathy to so use these agencies as to reach all classes of their race, and to enlighten and rescue them from degradation and death."[12] No separate theology, derived from African American history, underlay this definition. Jenifer did not feel that white theological practices and theories were insufficient for black people, and he willingly accepted the practices of Methodism.[13]

Ironically, the fact that A.M.E. churches were racially separate institutions allowed them to deemphasize race as a theological issue. Black theologians did not have to dispute issues with white theologians, nor did they need continually to justify themselves to white churchgoers. In black churches they had the freedom to neglect the issue.[14] Consequently, the separation from white churches led to a tendency toward conservatism. African Methodists were free to establish churches that were essentially similar to those of white denominations because one of the central internal tensions in white Methodist churches, that revolving around the issue of race, had been dealt with.

African Methodist theologians avoided concentrating on the unique religious experience of blacks and instead emphasized the hypocrisy that they felt was apparent in the white practice of Christianity.[15] In general, *Review* authors stressed the similarities between the religious expressiveness and inclinations of members of black and white races. A. C. Garner, in an article discussing revival methods used in black churches, made this point clear. "I regard nothing psychical as peculiar to the Negro," he wrote. "The elements of the human race are essentially the same in all races. History, heredity, environment may modify but cannot destroy this truth."[16] While William H. Ferris suggested that blacks had a richer "emotional endowment than any other race," he nevertheless downplayed the differences between whites and blacks, writing, "I know you will say that the Negro is prone to emotional excitement, but the only difference between the Negro camp meetings and the camp meetings of poor whites is that you can hear the whites singing and shouting two miles away, while you can hear the Negroes singing and shouting three miles away." Moreover, Ferris maintained that black religious history was not a phenomenon separate from the historical development of the rest of the human race, by which he meant adherents of Christianity. "In [the Negro's] religion, as in the white man's religion," Ferris argued, "we see but stages in the evolution of human thought. The colored man is gradually shuffling off his old superstitions and absorbing from his environment materials for further growth."[17] The argument advanced by most *Review* authors concurred with this assessment. Blacks were deemed similar in most aspects to whites; they merely needed to be "uplifted" through the continued experience of freedom to share the religious sensibilities of members of the white "race."[18]

The debate over unification of Methodist denominations illustrated the manner in which African Methodist intellectuals ignored race as a theological issue. The major arguments against unification were that it was too difficult to accomplish and that it was unwise because whites would not treat blacks as equals.[19] Even so, some African Methodists still adhered to Bishop Payne's view that unification was inevitable and that the denomination, along with all others, would eventually be absorbed into a universal Christian Church.[20] "Sure and certain it is," James Porter pronounced, "that all the Methodists of America are going to cluster and unite. First, the AMEZ [A.M.E. Zion]; then the other colored Methodists; then the ME South; then the ME North; and the great central power of attraction, unification and amity will be our grand old mother the AME Church."[21] No contributors to the *Review* argued that union was impossible because of the divergent religious experiences of blacks and whites.[22]

African Methodists focused on white discrimination and hypocrisy in their discussion of organic union partly because they did not wish to endorse, let alone celebrate religious practices that might be described as "African." Indeed, *Review* authors emphasized the need to stamp out any practices that were unique and to conform to those of white congregations. Articles on forms of worship and music had no particular racial emphasis, which is surprising given the historical importance of spirituals in slave and freed black communities.[23]

Many members of the African Methodist elite wished for reforms so that there could be no doubt that their practices conformed to those they believed were practiced in white churches. In the long term, this was to be achieved by educating ministers, and *Review* authors were unwavering in their demands for an educated ministry.[24] R. R. Downs, for example, wrote, "It is to be deeply regretted that from many African Methodist pulpits we can hear only words of reproach and condemnation for the educated minister."[25] Considerable support was also given to the denomination's theological seminaries throughout the pages of the *Review*.[26]

In the short term, these reformers tried to change the behavior of both ministers and members. In an article on "Sunday manners," for example, Dr. Edward A. Clark provided a list of "dos" and "don'ts" for ministers and congregations. The ten prohibitions for ministers in the pulpit were: "don't spit, lean on the pulpit, cross your legs, pose, rant, be funny, apologize, use profane language, hold conversation, and spat." The requirements were: "begin on time, stop when you are through, have something to say, say it distinctly, talk English, get behind the message, regard the occasion, be reverent, be well-brushed, and be in love with your job." This advice might well have been provided in any theological seminary at the time. Members in their pews, meanwhile, were given a similar regimen to follow, which included coming early, keeping children under control, not overlooking the collection plate, not sitting when the congregation stands, and not rising to go out when sinners are called forward.[27]

Reformers wished to change revivals in particular. Numerous authors discussed the proper way to carry out these services in African Methodist churches. In general, they complained about the ejaculatory aspects of revivals and the limited nature of conversions achieved by these methods. James Porter, for instance, complained of "filling the churches to overflowing with sinners of every grade and class."[28] Abraham Lincoln Gaines believed this practice resulted from the short-sighted approach of ministers. "Frequently herculean efforts are put forth to induce hearers to advance to the 'anxious seat,'" he wrote, "with the idea that, then, the work of the minister is complete."[29] These writers remained within the tradition of Bishop Payne, who had earlier carried out his own campaign to root out "heathenish" practices.[30]

Scott B. Jones had developed the same theme as Gaines in an article of 1891. "It is my candid opinion," he wrote, "that many of the revivals in our churches would be productive of better and more lasting results, if much of the trickery used to catch souls were banished from them. Christ called preachers to be 'fishers of men,' and not tricksters of them." Jones went further in his attack on ministerial practices: "In my humble opinion some evangelists commit almost as many sins in their efforts to save as have been committed by those whom they desire so much to have saved. A revival is the last place for sin, yet, I am sorry to say, it abounds in the shape of falsehood."[31] Such a criticism of revival practices was common at the time and was not exclusive to African Methodists.

An even more revealing criticism of African Methodist practices came from A. C. Garner. Like other authors, he complained about the concentration on number rather than quality of conversions and about the encouragement given the man who is more able to entertain than to teach. More than this, however, Garner criticized aspects of revivals peculiar to African Americans. He recognized that blacks' revival singing was "unique" and that "it stirs to action," but he continued:

> Born of suffering, these melodies ring with true emotion. Made in the childhood of the race, they lack the depth of maturity. One is moved more by the singing of them than by what is sung. When the passionate Augustine was aroused more by the singing than the thoughts of the song, he confessed to having sinned. Our revival songs need more of the sacredness of good sense, more dignity, more of the worshipful. A meaningless ditty may arouse but it does not help onto nobler conceptions of God.

At the same time that "shouts" were becoming increasingly popular in black congregations, Garner attacked what he called animalism. "Noise cannot save us," he claimed, "and the jargon of tongues in our day has no justification in Pentecost."[32]

The main purpose of discussions about revival methods, then, was to keep black churches in line with white ones. The authors either did not focus on the uniqueness of black revival methods or dismissed them as inferior. This was characteristic of the whole emphasis of African Methodist theology during the period of this study. Rather than relying on black experience in slavery and freedom to provide the vision for a new theology, African Methodists attempted to do corrective surgery on established theology. This is understandable given the integrationist sentiment of the times, but it did not bode well for the future of these black denominations in the age of the Great Migration. At a time when many black Southerners were entering northern cities, northern African Methodists were attempting to eradicate those religious practices most common among the newcomers.

African Methodist Women's Theology

The writings of African Methodist women outlined a theology that was in many ways different from, but nevertheless complementary to, that of the leading intellectuals within the denomination. Women did not write directly about theological issues in the A.M.E. Church *Review*. Perhaps they assumed that this was the province of men with theological training, but more likely the editors of the *Review* discouraged women from encroaching on the province of professionals. Nevertheless, female churchgoers based their beliefs and practices on theological propositions, even though they did not debate those propositions with the likes of Levi J. Coppin. They developed these ideas in novels, poems, and other texts.

One woman who developed a clear theology using the novel form was Frances E.W. Harper. In *Iola Leroy*, one of her leading characters, Robert, reveals the nature of his Aunt Kizzy's religious beliefs:

> Many a time . . . have I heard her humming to herself in the kitchen and saying, "I has my trials, ups and downs, but it won't allers be so. I specs one day to wing and wing wid de angels, Hallelujah! Den I specs to hear a voice sayin', 'Poor ole Kizzy, she's done de bes' she kin. Go down, Gabriel, an' tote her in.'" Den I specs to put on my golden slippers, my long white robe, an' my starry crown, an' walk dem golden streets, Hallelujah!"

If Kizzy's words are anything to go by, African Methodist women put great emphasis on service, survival, and nurturing and on doing the best they could in the face of oppressive circumstances; they appropriated passages from the Bible that highlighted these things. One of Harper's characters, for instance, was likened to Hagar because she "went out into the world to seek a living for herself and child."[33]

Josephine D. Heard, whose husband was a pastor of "Mother" Bethel and later a bishop, revealed aspects of her own theological beliefs in poetry. In one poem she echoed Kizzy, writing:

> *When I am gone above me raise,*
> *   No lofty stone perfect in human handicraft*
> *Say this of me and I shall be content,*
> *   That in the Master's work my life was spent*
> *Say not that I was either great or good,*
> *But Mary-like she has done what she could.*

Like Harper, Heard emphasized service and the need to do God's work without the hope of "rich reward" until the afterlife, citing the example of Mary Magdalene, who anointed the feet of Jesus and dried them with her hair.

Katherine D. Tillman, another prominent African Methodist woman, also incorporated the Hagar-like theological position in one of her poems.

> *On through the long night of oppression and wrong,*
> *   On with a smile and on with a song,*
> *Where darkness is deepest then follows the dawn;*
> *   The soul of my soul go upward and on.*
> *So rich so pure her jeweled womanhood*
> *So consecrated to her fellow's good*
> *   That on and on,*
> *Shall shine her life in other happier spheres,*

> *Undimmed for'er by mortal ills and tears*
> *Through years unborn.*

Tillman used other genres to put across her theological views. For example, she quoted authors with whom she agreed. Josie Heard was one of
these; another was Nannie H. Burroughs, a prominent black Baptist.
Burroughs had written, "You will never come into your own until you
put at the service of the Almighty all of your powers—mind, body and
soul," showing that these beliefs about service were interdenominational.[34] Tillman also wrote several plays and pageants including characters like Aunt Betsy, who proclaimed, "De lawd hab pervided. . . . I was
an unfaithful servant to doubt Him for a moment. Didn't he feed 'Lijah
when he was in the wilderness, an' aint He promised to feed His children."[35]

Given their emphasis on service, African Methodist women may
have believed that their time should be spent doing things that might
help "conquer the world for Christ" rather than discussing theological
propositions. Harper perhaps represented the opinions of other women
when she revealed, in *Iola*, her sympathy for Uncle Daniel, an unedu-
cated southern preacher who had no time for theology. Harper wrote:

> "Uncle Daniel," asked Robert, "are you still preaching?"
> "Yes, chile, I'se still firing off de Gospel gun."
> "I hear some of the Northern folks are down here teaching theology,
> that is, teaching young men how to preach. Why don't you study
> theology?"
> "Look a yere, boy, I'se been a preachin' dese thirty years, an' you
> come yere tellin' me 'bout studying yore ologies. I larn'd my 'ology at de
> foot ob de cross. You bin dar?"[36]

While women members may have been sceptical about the importance
of theological learning, their notion of "service" complemented the belief in "uplift" adhered to by African Methodist theologians.

African Methodist Political and Social Criticism

The political and social beliefs of African Methodists prior to the Great
Migration were greatly influenced by the Social Gospel movement,
which was at its height at this time. The Methodist Episcopal Church, to
which the A.M.E. Church often looked for liturgical and political direction, issued its Social Creed in 1908. This creed in some respects represented the climax of the movement for social reform. It pushed for such

things as industrial conciliation, elimination of factory hazards, abolition of child labor, protection for women in industry, abolition of the sweatshop, reduction of the hours of labor, and the increase in leisure time. In December of the same year, the Federal Council of the Churches of Christ in America, in which the A.M.E. Church was represented, asserted that it was "a Christian duty to make the influence of Christ effective in all human relations,"[37] alluding to the fact that industrial and social relationships clearly were not being run on these principles.[38]

Articles in the *Review* focusing on political and sociological concerns show that the Social Gospel influence was of great importance for African Methodist intellectuals as they developed their responses to both racial and class oppression. The authors revealed their ambivalence toward American society. While they were extremely critical of a society that discriminated against them, the men and women of the A.M.E. Church shared notions of progress and civilization with other Americans.[39] Their political philosophy easily fits the description, "Progressive."

African Methodists at the turn of the century were understandably preoccupied, given the deterioration of race relations that was occurring at that time, with political and sociological issues. They felt that it was the duty of ministers, therefore, to involve themselves in the key issues of the day. C.O.H. Thomas, for example, believed that ministers needed to understand the circumstances facing their members and to address the problems arising out of them. "If Sunday preaching is to be of any importance," he wrote, "it ought and must be adapted to the conditions of existing circumstances—in the present—NOW; and not only in the pulpit but in all the broad and varied realms of moral, industrial, commercial, material and political society."

In his article, "Politics, Ministers and Religion," Thomas represented the majority of *Review* authors, by writing:

> It must be accepted by all, that all great reforms which are by nature to be brought about by political action have necessarily the closest connection with morals; and morals are the rock-bottom foundations of "pure and undefiled religion." The clergy, therefore, cannot, without being recreant to their high calling, be indifferent to these great reforms. Their attitude should be a most positive one and their action aggressive.

Justification for political action among clergy, according to Thomas, came from the fight against slavery. If the church was justified in fighting slavery, opium trade, and rum traffic, then it ought to be involved generally in moving people politically along a path of righteousness.

The church, then, failed in its mission when principles of righteousness were neglected and when it failed to "impress upon its members the obligations of citizenship." It was not merely that clergy were justified in becoming involved in political matters; they had a moral imperative to do so. Furthermore, according to Thomas, churches "commit suicide" by ignoring politics:

> Say nothing against "vested rights," political treachery, . . . legal proscription and class legislation. In short, give everything over to the control of the dreaded Socialist or fiendish Anarchist, give to them all the vital questions of the day, and confine the pulpit to "Children's Day," "Missionary Day," "Educational Day" and other meetings. . . . At this rate, it will not take the common people very long to discover that "the salt has lost its savor." . . . It is thenceforth good for nothing, but to be cast out, and to be trodden under foot of man.[40]

Motivation for reform came as much from fear of the "dreaded Socialist" as from fear of those with "vested rights." This was a common position among Christian reformers at the turn of the century. Nevertheless, the sentiment for reform was strong, as was the belief that ministers ought to be involved in the process of change. This belief was founded on the principle that in order to survive the church must respond to the political and social concerns of its members.

The state of American race relations roused the invective of many African Methodists. Ironically, though, their anger revealed their commitment to the United States. African Methodists tended to protest against their exclusion from American society, not against the society itself. Rev. John William Norris, for example, condemned the "unchristian" behavior of white America and, in the harshest possible terms, lynch law. His continued support for the Constitution, however, was clear. He expressed his opposition to "all violators of the law, let them be white or black," and argued that provided "colored" people were "condemned for their willful wrongs and commended for their manly acts," then "the Negro will be a better citizen." Norris wanted "[the Negro] to take his place more proportionately among the best and most useful of our countrymen."[41] Written in 1892, this was an early formulation of Du Bois's notion of the "Talented Tenth."

Sometimes the tone of the criticism was extremely militant. G. Herbert Renfro attacked the Afro-American League for not being aggressive enough in its condemnation of white racism. Renfro's solution was clearcut:

Let the Negro have both his Bible and his rifle—aye, powder and shot and dynamite for his own protection. Where the one fails let the other apply. . . . Tell me, in Heaven's name, while we fast and pray, must we live like sheep and die like dogs? Shall it be said that the Negro would pray less fervently when he has weapons of defense near at hand? Our inaction, our servility and our failure to unite and adopt reasonable means of protection are our sin, our folly and our bane. Let us have the wisdom to unite for our own defense.[42]

More often, however, African Methodists were conciliatory, focusing on the identity of interests between whites and blacks rather than on racial conflict. "Interests of black and white are identical," J. B. Stansberry argued in "The State of the Country." "Bitterly as the thought would be resented by many, the Americans, whether white or black, are in fact already one people—one nationality, one in religion, and very largely one also in blood."[43]

Throughout the 1890s and 1900s, African Americans discussed among themselves and with a few white educators the kind of education that would be most appropriate for members of "the colored race." Even before Booker T. Washington rose to prominence, the debate between proponents of liberal or "complete" education and those of industrial education raged. S. F. Williams, a Louisiana educator, for example, argued in 1890 that industrial education should not be considered a mere "craze," for it was a necessity that blacks could not afford to ignore. A liberal education was unnecessary for them given the kinds of jobs that they were likely to secure. "We have the pitiable sight of college graduates as Pullman porters, dining-room servants, bootblacks and loafers," Williams wrote. "All labor is honorable: but college-training, algebra and Greek are not necessary concomitants of boot-blacking and servitude. If such was to be their occupation, some years were lost at school that could have been more profitably used in furthering their material interests." Williams believed that industrial education was the cure to most of the problems blacks faced, which resulted from one central cause: idleness. "Idleness is a plant of quick growth," Williams wrote. "Vice is its companion and the prison its ultimate home. All this could and would be avoided if industrial education was a part of the curriculum of every school. The cunning of the head needs the cunning of the hand to equalize the balance."[44]

The other side of the argument was advanced by James A. Handy in an article (originally an address at Allen University) published in the same issue of the *Review* as Williams's piece. Handy's main complaint against industrial education, echoed later in W.E.B. Du Bois's attacks on Washington, was that it did not allow for the possibility that African Americans would rise above the menial jobs they were being trained for. "You ought by no means to think of relinquishing the study of arts and sciences," he wrote, "merely because you have passed through the usual collegiate course, or because your labors are chiefly to be employed in one profession. What you have already obtained is merely to enable you to pursue further and to greater advantage." And he added, "It is no small recommendation to the ancient languages, that those who have been most thoroughly acquainted with them have generally been most eminent in other branches of learning."[45]

With the rise to prominence of Booker T. Washington in 1895, debate about the value of different types of education died down (at least until Du Bois began voicing his complaints against the Washington regime); the issue had been decided in favor of industrial education. Attention turned, instead, to questions concerning the importance of black business initiatives. Not surprisingly, articles focusing on this issue almost unanimously favored such initiatives, indicating that, as Du Bois noted in 1903, some blacks had imbibed one part of "the spirit of the time," namely, the pursuit of profit.[46] Blacks and whites alike shared the conviction that business success would improve social status and conditions.

One man who was moved by a different spirit, however, was Reverdy C. Ransom. This spirit was of a more radical nature, similar to that found in the works of people like Henry George, Edward Bellamy, and Henry Demarest Lloyd. Indeed, in 1896 Ransom even advocated socialism. In "The Negro and Socialism," he proclaimed: "The present social order with its poverty and vast army of unemployed, cannot be accepted as final, as the ultimate goal for which the ages have been in travail. If man is the child of God, the present social order is not divine." In Ransom's opinion, socialism allowed for a social system that was more Christian than capitalism permitted, for

> socialism like the Carpenter of Nazareth, places more value upon man than it does upon riches. It believes that the rights of man are more sacred than the rights of property, believes indeed, that the only sacred thing on earth is a human being. Socialism would bring all the people

who participate in the rivalry of life upon a footing of equality, allowing
each individual the widest possible range for the development of his
powers and personality, with freedom to follow wherever his abilities may
lead him.

Because black people belonged almost entirely to the proletarian or industrial class, Ransom maintained, it was inevitable that the program of
socialism would in time "powerfully appeal to the American Negro." At
the same time, he felt that the involvement of those who had been most
oppressed was crucial to the success of socialism. Thus he wrote, "The
battles of socialism are not to be fought by white men, for the benefit of
white men. It is not, as we have said, a question of race, it is the question of man. So far as America is concerned, this question cannot be
settled without the Negro's aid."[47] Ransom's view was not a popular one.
In fact, the article stands out as an island of radicalsim in a sea of gradu-
alism. Almost twenty years later, many African Methodists still remembered the article, and when he was appointed editor of the *Review*, Ransom's "socialism" once again came under attack.[48] By that time, however,
he would no longer have considered himself a Socialist.

More acceptable for most African Methodists was the liberal position put forward by H.C.C. Astwood three years after Ransom's essay
was printed, in an article entitled "Social Economy." Astwood attempted
to mediate between the forces of capital and those of labor. He criticized
capital by writing, "Accumulated wealth gotten out of the unnatural
profits of self-sacrificing labor, is the great problem that seems to be
undermining our social fabric." But he was unwilling to follow Ransom
down the road to socialism. Instead, he proposed that capital and labor
"find a common adjustment of the unequal conditions which confront us
as a people, . . . [for] in consequence of the advanced civilization attained by us, these two elements in our social economy seem to be indispensable." He argued, therefore, "The principle requirement for full
fruition of social economy must be complete harmony between capital
and labor."

Astwood, however, like many other Progressives, kept his harshest
criticism for labor unions, which "have made themselves greater masters
and oppressors than the capitalists themselves."[49] Astwood's position was
similar to that of white upper- and middle-class reformers who, during
the first decade of the twentieth century, attempted to tamper with
some of the excesses of capitalism but at the same time feared organized
labor. On the one hand, Astwood's antiunion stance was perhaps influ-

enced by the racially prejudiced practices of unions affiliated with the American Federation of Labor. On the other hand, his attitude toward capitalists may have been affected by the knowledge that some business leaders were known to support churches and church undertakings among blacks.[50]

Theology and the Migration

African Methodist theology had an important bearing on the way the denomination's members responded to the incoming migrants. The development of the Social Gospel among African Methodists at the turn of the century made this response seem contradictory: they appeared to stretch out a helping hand to the newcomers arriving in the city, while holding back from fully embracing them.

African Methodists were indeed genuinely concerned about the newcomers, not least because of the emphasis they placed on the hypocrisy of white Christians. They realized that they were open to the same charge if they shunned other African Americans. And this charge was made with regard to the migration. In 1917, for instance, the *Tribune* editor wrote: "If we are unwilling to hail [the migrant] as a brother and lend him a helping hand then we must cease to blame the white man for his prejudiced refusal to recognize the colored man as a brother."[51] African Methodists' fervent belief that they had been discriminated against by white Methodists counterbalanced their tendency toward exclusionary behavior.

But liturgical conservatism dampened any welcoming spirit among them. Reverdy C. Ransom, editor of the *Review* during the Great Migration, was one person who recognized the problem facing A.M.E. churches as they endeavored to proselytize among the former Southerners. Referring to the migrants, he wrote later: "There has crept into many of our churches so much ritualism and formalism, a spiritually hungry people could not find sustaining spiritual food in the cold and formal programs and services conducted in so many A.M.E. churches."[52]

It would be wrong to suggest that African Methodist liturgy remained unchanged during the period of the Great Migration. Certainly, as residential segregation became more widespread and blacks became ghettoized in depressed urban sections, African Methodists less often viewed white churches as the standard by which they should be judged.

Further, the possibility of a cross-fertilization of ideas between white and black Methodist denominations (either in seminaries or through a shared literature) diminished, along with the desire of black theologians and ministers to emulate white Methodists. This should not be overstated, however. Rev. Matthew Jones of the A.M.E. Church remarked that some of the strongest influences on the development of his religious ideas during the 1920s were white radio preachers. Their programs, which were popular in Philadelphia, seem to have crossed the race barrier.[53]

Nevertheless, even if African Methodists' direct emulation of white Methodists diminished, conservative worship and liturgical practices remained fairly well entrenched as the foundation for African Methodist theology. This was one of the things that some southern migrants found frustrating about northern A.M.E. Churches. These churches were reluctant to adapt rituals and practices to fit the needs and desires of their newest communicants. African Methodists were particularly slow to incorporate Gospel songs into their services despite, or perhaps because of, the fact that these songs were clearly unique to black people.

CHAPTER 5

"Pulpit Extension"

*Being yet a child race, perhaps also the backward race, our powers
and possibilities are not yet known. As in the other arts and
sciences, we are yet to shine in noonday brilliancy. Let the soul still
be kept in tune. The soul, the God-like function of the body: the
soul, without which the body would be as an earth without a sun.*

LEVI J. COPPIN, 1912

African Methodist minister–editors, men like Levi J. Coppin, Hightower
T. Kealing, Reverdy C. Ransom, and Richard R. Wright, Jr., all adhered
to the philosophy of "uplift" that was central to Social Gospel thought.
Consequently, their efforts to reach out from their pulpits to the uncon-
verted were not always as fruitful as they hoped. Their theological and
sociological assumptions often led, unwittingly, toward exclusion rather
than inclusion. Many southern migrants could believe that they were
unwelcome in the African Methodist fold, even while the minister–editor was proselytizing them. The problem, of course, was partly that established congregants did not share the editor's fervor for expansion, but
it was also the minister–editor's conceptualization of the "Negro question" in terms of uplifting the race to the level of white American society. Whether or not the editor felt that he personally had reached that
level, he made it clear that those outside the church had not. Focusing
on the minister–editor's Social Gospel thus adds to our understanding of
the plight of African Methodism during the period of the Great Migration.

Levi J. Coppin

The work of Levi J. Coppin, editor of the A.M.E. Church *Review* between 1888 and 1896 and an influential bishop between 1900 and 1920, was typical of the African Methodist Social Gospel developing at the turn of the century. Born in Maryland in 1848, Coppin was, according to George A. Singleton, a historian of the A.M.E. Church, "tall, robust, and full-bodied. He was a preacher of exegetical ability. . . . He had a peculiar mannerism while preaching. He would clap his hands, slap his left thigh, again put his left hand to the right side of his mouth with open palm to the right, and whisper for emphasis. There was much unction in his words."[1] He was well educated, though like many black ministers born in slavery he was largely self-taught. He received a rudimentary education before the Civil War from his mother, who read to him from the Bible. With the end of slavery he was able to enroll at a Maryland public school. Then, after leaving Maryland and moving north at the age of twenty-one, he began to teach at a high school in Wilmington, Delaware, and attend the Protestant Episcopal Theological Seminary in Philadelphia. This training at a white theological seminary influenced his writings, just as being trained at white-controlled colleges influenced other black churchmen. Coppin recognized his debt to his teachers by dedicating his first book to one of them.[2]

Coppin endeavored to use his position as editor for "pulpit extension"; he tried to make the journal a "messenger of grace, freighted with that which is loftiest in thought and purpose." Through the ministers who read his work he hoped to reach the lay people of the A.M.E. Church.[3] He believed that the work of the religious press was twofold: to represent the formulated doctrinal positions of the denomination it represented and to deal with the broader questions of the day.

On the one hand, therefore, Coppin felt that an editor of a religious journal should not "swap his opinions upon the most vital religious subject for the sake of conformity to a popular sentiment." He continued, "It is true that religion is broad enough to afford standing room for all sects and denominations, but every man of mature religious convictions should represent more than a reed shaken by the wind." This was a doctrinal conservatism that would not brook such things as interdenominational positions (which would have been a feature of "Black Theology").

On the other hand, Coppin felt that the minister–editor should consider "questions that are for the weal or woe of society." These included:

> questions of government in its various forms; of capital and labor, of sociology and the right of the ballot; upon prison reforms and reformatories for youthful offenders; of temperance and child labor; of trusts and the cost of living; of peonage and involuntary servitude; popular education, school curriculums and the length of school terms in the rural districts; the various forms of so-called race problems, and the Golden Rule in modern life.[4]

Such concerns were obligating for anyone professing liberal ideas during the period known as the Progressive Era. Hence, in dealing with the two spheres, religious and political, the minister–editor could be both theologically conservative and politically progressive.

During his tenure as editor of the *Review*, Coppin wrote two theological works complementing his journal writings. These fall within the mainstream of Methodist theology, deviating only occasionally from the standard interpretations of white theologians. Where they are original, it is not because of any racial analysis. His first theological work, entitled *The Relation of Baptized Children to the Church* (1890), was fairly controversial with regard only to Coppin's interpretation of Original Sin, which caused a stir among several theologians. Besides this one area, however, the work conformed to the standard canon of Methodism. Coppin concentrated on the importance of baptism and the crucial role of education in keeping children committed to the path of Christ. He wished to save children for the church not merely by bringing them into the church, but "by not allowing them to leave." The child had to be trained, not just taught. This training was to occur in the Sunday school, where the child would learn to worship Christ and to be committed to the church. The boy or girl would be put "into action and actually drilled."[5] There was no special racial emphasis in his analysis. Some black churchgoers might derive some educational benefit from Sunday school, of course, but Coppin did not consider this possibility.

The Key to Scriptural Interpretation (1895) was more revealing than Coppin's earlier work. It was intended as a guide for Methodist ministers wishing to interpret biblical texts. Coppin clearly delineated a method of analysis for them that was essentially a direct, methodical interaction with the text without commentaries. He felt confident that if his method was followed dutifully all readers of the King James Bible would reach similar conclusions. The problem was that too many people believed that the scriptures were "veiled in mystery." Consequently, he feared, "every individual may claim the right to use his own judgment in the work of interpretation."[6] Coppin felt that his own analysis of the Bible was the correct one, coinciding as it did with those of white Methodists.

One such mainstream interpretation was Coppin's analysis of Mark 10:31—"But many that are first shall be last; and the last first." Following closely on the heels of Jesus' statement about the difficulty for the rich to enter heaven, this passage would seem to have a natural appeal to those at the bottom end of society.[7] One imagines a slaveowner keeping this good news from his slaves (not least because these words appeared in Nat Turner's "Confessions"),[8] or a sharecropper responding favorably to this promise of reward in the afterlife for having had to experience suffering. Even if the reward was to be delayed, poor people could still feel that God was on their side and that the essential message of Christianity was one of liberation.[9] But Coppin contested such a reading of this text, fearing that analyzing it in terms of race might be detrimental to black people. "Some have concluded," he noted, "that [the passage] refers to the different races or nations; that those who at one time were first among the civilized nations, have suffered a reversion, and become last." Instead, Coppin felt that the word "many" should be emphasized and he argued that "the language is not intended to establish a rule, but to declare a possibility." In his mind, there was no promise that the world would be turned upside down. He believed that the context of the passage suggested that the comment, directed at Jesus' disciples, was a "mild rebuke . . . to all, whose work, like that of the disciples, is to save souls."[10] In short, the passage was supposed to ensure that a pastor would not become complacent and believe he had saved enough souls; it was not intended to have an inspirational social message for the downtrodden.

Given this doctrinal conservatism, it should not be surprising that Coppin wanted his journal to be respected in white Methodist circles. While editor of the *Review*, he consciously endeavored to impress white readers with the erudition and quality of its articles. As he indicated in his autobiography, he often turned to white reviews and literary journals to see how his own review was being judged. He was pleased to note that the judgment was often favorable, "even flatteringly so." "Of course," he commented, "we came in also for our share of criticism." On one occasion, he remembered, Rev. George Brent submitted an article on "The Origin of the White Man" that "proved to his own satisfaction, that Gehazi, the servant of Elisha, who deceived his master, and ran after Naaman and took gifts for his healing by the prophet, was the true progenitor of the white race." Coppin, who might have been pressured to print this article, was upset that Brent's conclusion "was ridiculed by one of the leading Reviews" and that he personally "was severely censured for permitting such to be published."[11]

While Coppin might give a radical passage from the Bible a fairly tame reading, he was less likely to paint so mild a view of American racism and racial oppression. A case in point is an editorial entitled "The Russian and the Negro," in which he shows both determination to protect political rights for blacks and willingness to attack a system that oppressed people. Comparing the situations of African Americans and Russian peasants, he wrote, "the fact that the system is a barbarous one remains the same, and Christianity rises up against it as it does against all other forms of oppression."

While he might at times sound like a black nationalist, Coppin usually evinced an acceptance of the larger society's Progressive ideology. In particular, he felt it was necessary to "uplift" both Russian serfs and black sharecroppers. While the main question was one of justice and rights for all people, Coppin was still "willing to wait for developments along the lines of capability," and he would "grant that the fittest should and will survive." Like other African Methodists, therefore, he hoped for support from white paternalists in this endeavor. "When a man is down," he wrote, "he needs a stronger hand than his own to lift him up; he needs one who occupies a position above him to lend him aid; someone with influence and power 'at the court.'"

This dual emphasis, both critical and accepting of American society, came through clearly in Coppin's discussions of residential segregation and crime in northern cities. Writing critically about the former, he observed, "It is next to impossible for a family, however refined and respectable, to hire or buy a house in a portion of our great Northern cities." And he continued, "The landlords and the real estate agents have resolved themselves, by common consent, into a committee of the whole to force 'colored people' to live in back streets, tenement houses, and immoral districts."[12] Similarly, in an editorial on crime, Coppin discussed reasons for the disproportionate number of offenses committed by blacks. He pointed to the fact that a large majority of "the race" lived in slums. "We knew full well," he argued, "that we [blacks] could not, any more than others, breathe constantly an immoral atmosphere without contracting an immoral disease." Like the typical Progressive or adherent of the Social Gospel, Coppin moved away from a focus on individual sin toward an emphasis on social and environmental causes for individual failings. And like other reformers of the time, he accepted the notion that the lower classes had contracted an "immoral disease."

But these critical statements were balanced by Coppin's appeal for help to some of the people often considered guilty of discrimination and of creating the "immoral atmosphere" he described. He hoped that white people would begin to provide blacks with the resources they needed to uplift themselves, and he noted with approval that "one by one such persons are coming forward and instituting ways and means with a view of changing the present condition of things as it relates to the oppressed of the people."[13] By considering issues such as residential segregation and crime, Coppin revealed his concern for the souls of all black folk. His emphasis on "uplift" and his appeal for white patronage, however, implicitly denigrated the same people he was trying to help and distanced him from their predicament.

Coppin, like many other African Methodist ministers, was also greatly interested in composing both words and music for hymns. In a 1912 article entitled "Soul Culture in Song," Coppin, by then a bishop, focused on the importance of song for African Americans. He commented that while it was generally conceded that black people were able to sing, this was often the only thing they were considered capable of doing, and "singing does not stand very high in the scale of human excellences." He then showed the significance of music to theology, arguing that "the flow of inspiration seems more easily and gracefully, and inspiringly expressed in poetry than in prose: in figure than in plain speech."

Alongside Charles Wesley's hymns in terms of their importance for African Methodists, Coppin wished to place plantation melodies, which he considered "the only really American music." These "soul echoes, born of sorrow, but messengers of hope, are yet to have their day," Coppin proclaimed. And for him, a memorable musical experience occurred when these sorrow songs were performed within a Methodist forum. A bishop from the white Methodist Episcopal Church, South, had visited an A.M.E. conference at which Coppin was present and asked to hear those assembled sing some spirituals. Coppin suspected that many in the convention hall protested the request, but when the choir gave its rendition of "Just Keep Smiling," the "vast congregations were variously moved, and many came forward seeking pardon and peace."

In this article, Coppin also focused on the power of music to bring slaves into the Christian fold. "During the darker days," he wrote, "the power of song was the most efficient means of reaching the unlettered slaves and bringing them to repentance." And he continued: "I fancy, the servants-obey-your-master style of sermons that were preached to them when they heard preaching, never brought about many pentecostal revivals." Instead, the slaves would meditate over a story from the Bible that was read to them and make from it a song with a chorus. "These were the weapons used in their revival meetings," Coppin argued, "and the means by which the truth sent its arrows of conviction to the simple hearted."[14]

Rather than feel ashamed of their musical ability, Coppin concluded, black people should feel fortunate to have this gift, and they should not "shrink from the exercise of this best gift of heaven and earth." Coppin himself lived by this creed, composing many hymns, some of which were included in the A.M.E. hymnal of 1902.[15] But none of his hymns could bring forth the emotions summoned by a Charles Wesley verse; neither did they often speak to the condition of black people. Indeed, white congregations could have sung most of them comfortably. The two exceptions were "Our Father's Church," which mentioned uplifting the race, and "The A.M.E. Church Rallying Song," which made specific reference to all the major A.M.E. bishops.

Coppin's commitment to hymnology was a trait shared by all Methodists. Charles Wesley's hymns had perhaps been even more important in spreading Methodism than the sermons of his brother, John— a point that Coppin made in his article.[16] As one *Review* author put it, the hymns "groan under the mortal anguish of repentance; they throb and quiver with the throes of the new birth; they swell with the triumphs of faith—the full glories of a present salvation." He continued, "They are not versified moralities, not didactic disquisitions, not languidly virtuous sentimentalisms, but they are most intensely alive, and in their spiritual scope, thoroughly practical." Owing to this "peculiarity," they had a resonance for people who were oppressed even though they offered no promise of an immediate end to oppression. They offered "redress for the Negro's woes, and utter[ed] a resurrection from the solitude of his many tombs."

The hymns encouraged people to express themselves through their religion, and in this respect they demanded the inclusion of all people and cultures within the church. The *Review* author noticed this aspect of the hymns in particular. "The whole vitality," he wrote, "not only of the poet, but of the people of the Lord everywhere is in them. The life-blood of the time flows through them. They are big with the great awakening which 'turned the world upside down.'" Indeed, the hymns were almost un-Methodist, for in them, "The clamor of persecution is heard, the shouts of the godless mob; now we see the eager faces of a listening multitude, as the words of life drop into their hearts, and the work goes on."[17] In some ways, these hymns counteracted the exclusiveness of Methodist theology; while members had to conform to Wesleyan doctrines in other spheres, they could allow their own spiritual and cultural backgrounds to influence the way they sang and what they sang about.

A tension has existed in Methodism between sermon and hymn, perhaps even between the aspirations and intentions of the Wesley brothers, and this tension found its way into African Methodist churches. In some respects, it resembled the tension between service and prestige and between men and women, which are discussed in later chapters. How was it possible both to bring people with many different cultural orientations into the church and to have them conform to one creed? How could a church both serve all people and safeguard the prestige of a minority who benefited from the institutionalization and bureaucratization of that creed? And, when providing prestige for oppressed men, how could the church avoid in some way oppressing women? Because such questions cannot be resolved easily, they are sometimes judged better left unasked. And this is what Methodists did. They encouraged all people to come into their house, sometimes using sirenlike hymns to attract them, but they required them, once inside, to conform to the "method." Understanding this tension surrounding Methodist hymnology thus provides a trope for understanding the work of African Methodists during the Great Migration. Their desire was for inclusion, but their practice, ultimately, was one of exclusion.

Coppin did not live to see the full impact of the Great Migration on Philadelphia's African Methodist congregations. From his writings it is clear, however, that he would have responded to the migration in the way that many African Methodists did at the time, treating the new arrivals as people in need of "uplift." During his years as A.M.E. bishop for South Africa, Coppin had to deal with the migration of Africans into the cities of Cape Colony. His response to this problem suggests how he would have responded to southern migrants during and after World War I. Coppin wrote:

> The Native people who leave their homes and come into the cities, especially the large seaport cities, seeking work, should really be somehow placed in the care of Christian guardians. Not that they should be forced by any law to become the wards of the Church, and not treated as free moral agents, but the Church should stand ready to meet them at "the gate of the city" and offer them protection and guidance that an unsuspecting plain man from the country needs, when suddenly ushered into modern city life.[18]

He never considered that the newcomers might not want protection and guidance, and that they might not be as "unsuspecting" and "plain" as he assumed. This was one of the fallacies of the concept of "uplift." To see the migration in terms of a project of uplift was to be already too removed from the beneficiaries of that project to understand what it was that they wanted. Certainly, the vantage point from which the minister–editor of the A.M.E. Church looked down on the world made it difficult to put aside the denomination's methods and to observe the world anew.

Hightower T. Kealing and Reverdy C. Ransom

The end of Coppin's tenure at the *Review* brought an end, briefly, to the journal's influence both within the denomination and among Methodists and African Methodists in general. Coppin had managed to keep the journal above the political fray for many years, or if, as seems likely, he himself was embroiled in denominational politics, he was able to make the *Review* appear impartial. This was possible, of course, because the faction he represented, the denomination's northern intellectuals and professional elite, was dominant at the time.[19] The interregnum between Coppin's tenure and that of Reverdy C. Ransom, a man of similar background to Coppin, thus took on the appearance (at least to their followers) of a slide into the political mire. As such, the ideas propagated in the *Review*, however much they resembled those propagated before 1896, the year Coppin returned to pastoring, could not be endorsed unequivocally by the northern elite.

David Wood Wills, author of an intellectual history of the African Methodist Episcopal Church in the years 1884 to 1915, has suggested that the *Review* underwent a major transition during this interregnum. The election of Professor Hightower T. Kealing represented a watershed in which control of the journal passed from the hands of the deceased Bishop Daniel T. Payne's protégés to a more southern-based group loosely coalesced around Bishop Henry McNeil Turner. However, the impact of this watershed was greater on church politics than on the denomination's theology. While new departments were established in the *Review* (such as one for women), the actual theological and political writings of those who contributed to the journal under Kealing's direction were not markedly different from those produced under Coppin. Indeed, Coppin still contributed to the *Review* occasionally. The change was more in style than in substance. The trend was toward shorter articles and toward reprints from other religious journals. Nevertheless, the essential message remained the same. Kealing was not more radical than Coppin, he merely had less theological inclination so that his message was sometimes less distinct.

The political dimension of the change in leadership was perhaps more important. People who ceased contributing to the journal tended to consider themselves northern African Methodists, even if they had, like Coppin himself, been born in the South. Kealing, meanwhile, along with Bishop Turner, clearly associated with the South. Northern Methodists feared that they were losing control of the church. Turner had begun pushing for his candidates to be elected to the episcopate, and the rapid growth of the church in states like South Carolina, where, in 1890, one-fifth of all African Methodists lived, meant that Southerners began to dominate conventions.[20] The leaders of the First Episcopal District, which included both Philadelphia and New York, clearly felt that their power was on the wane.

This largely unspoken conflict came to a head at the *Review* after Kealing's sudden death in 1911, when the newly appointed temporary editor, Dr. C. V. Roman, attempted to remove the journal's headquarters to Texas. Northern African Methodists mustered their forces and elected their own candidate, Reverdy C. Ransom, to the editorship.[21] The northerners bolstered their position in the church, but at the time it may have seemed like the last gasp of the old order before the new order finally gained ascendancy. Had not the "Great Migration" started, sending many African Methodists northward, Philadelphia in particular, and the North in general, might have lost their central positions in the denomination.

This conflict should not be overemphasized, especially in terms of the denomination's theological and political teachings. While Coppin no longer provided a sense of coherence to the writings in the *Review*, he was elected bishop in 1900 and used this position to influence the spiritual and political leadership of the church. Further, while the denomination's journal no longer favored northern African Methodist ministers and intellectuals, local forums were still available. The Philadelphia Preachers' Association, which met under the intellectual leadership of Coppin, is a case in point.

This association sometimes included as many as thirty pastors and bishops from the Philadelphia area. For a number of years around the turn of the century, it met every week at Allen Hall. The association's importance was more political than theological or ideological. It provided a forum for ministers and intellectuals, once the *Review* had been taken away from them. However, as the minutes of the meetings show, the ideas discussed were not markedly different from those found in the denomination's quarterly and most of the papers presented dealt with topics similar to those in the journal. A typical meeting began with the president directing a pastor to give the devotions. The pastor read a lesson from the Bible and said a prayer. He was then joined in a hymn, such as "O for a Heart—to Praise my God," or "Jesus the Name High Overall." Then a member of the group or a guest lecturer presented a paper, and the ministers present discussed it at length. On November 8, 1897, for example, Coppin talked about Christian Science, while a week later Professor G. L. Newton presented a paper entitled "On the Wonders of the Heavens." According to the secretary, A. M. Buckley, the audience at Newton's presentation was moved to the realization with David that "the Heavens declare the Glory of God, and the firmament showeth his handy work." Other speakers included Frances E.W. Harper, N. D. Temple, William H. Yeocum, the evangelist Miss Mary Jones, and other writers who had contributed to the *Review* under Coppin and continued to do so under Kealing.[22]

With the election of Reverdy C. Ransom, who at the time was pastor of Bethel A.M.E. Church in New York City, the *Review* ceased to be oriented around the Philadelphia African Methodist community. Nevertheless, Ransom's tenure is important because, through his guidance, the journal once again began to have the influence within the denomination it had attained under Coppin and because Philadelphia's African Methodist ministers and lay people continued to read it.

Under Ransom, the *Review* did not veer toward a liberation theology, as might be expected given Ransom's 1896 article proclaiming the similarities between socialism and Christianity. He developed no alternative, or "black", conceptions of Methodism, because he was by now well within the mainstream of the Social Gospel movement. Indeed, later in

life Ransom felt disappointed that he had not enabled the denomination
to separate itself more distinctly from white Methodism. "Our A.M.E.
denomination has not contributed anything original or creative in the
realm of Theology or Church Polity," he wrote. "When Richard Allen
and his group withdrew from St. George's Methodist Episcopal Church,
and organized an independent church, a part of them chose to remain
Methodist and adopted bodily both its doctrine and its polity. To neither
of these have they contributed anything creative or original within the
past 164 years."[23] Ransom certainly made no great claims about his own
theological writings. His concerns were always more political and social.[24]

   With the *Review* back in the hands of northern intellectuals, we
may turn our attention elsewhere. Part of the story of the *Review* no
longer concerned Philadelphia because Ransom lived and worked in
New York. Moreover, while the *Review* remained an important source of
ideas for Philadelphia's African Methodist ministers and lay people, at
this point it began to be overshadowed by the *Christian Recorder*, the
denomination's weekly newspaper. Reverdy C. Ransom and Richard R.
Wright, Jr., editor of the *Recorder*, had worked together and shared many
opinions about theological and sociological concerns. They also agreed
about the need to support southern migration. The *Recorder*'s larger readership and its more frequent publication, however, made it the more
influential of the two denominational organs during the Great Migration,
and it is therefore important to turn our focus to Wright.

Richard R. Wright, Jr.

As editor of the *Christian Recorder*, Richard R. Wright, Jr., needed to be a
different kind of minister–editor from his counterparts at the *Review*.
First and foremost, he was responsible for furnishing "to the church the
news of the church." "It is the editor's place," he wrote, "to serve as a
clearing house for church correspondence, keeping the whole church informed of the most important incidents in each part." But Wright saw his
role in the denomination as encompassing more than maintaining the
connection among the different parts. "Not only should the editor give
through his paper information of current church life," he wrote, "he
should constantly keep before his people such information as will explain the history and doctrine and organization of the church. Hence he
should secure from the most reliable sources such articles as would ex-

hibit these facts in the most authoritative and best expressed manner."[25] Thus, Wright included within his role as editor of the *Recorder* everything that Coppin and Ransom were doing at the *Review*. Doing so enabled him to use his position to influence the denomination's response to the Great Migration. Under Wright's leadership, the *Recorder* became an outspoken advocate of the migration; in many ways, Wright would deserve the title, "the Robert S. Abbott of the Philadelphia migration." However, while the editor of the *Chicago Defender* managed to speak to all Southerners, Wright's influence remained largely limited to his denomination. This limitation reflects the difference between the Chicago and Philadelphia migrations. The latter was shaped by the more highly developed divisions within Philadelphia's black community.[26]

Richard Robert Wright, Jr., was born in 1878, the son of Maj. R. R. Wright and Lydia Elizabeth (Howard) Wright. Richard learned a keen sense of the importance of education from his parents. Major Wright had entered a missionary school on being freed from slavery in Georgia in 1863, had graduated from Atlanta University with an A.M. degree, and had gone on to be president of Georgia State Industrial College in Savannah. As the son later remembered, during his early years both parents stressed education as the means to advancement and employed strong discipline to ensure that he would not stray from its path. The parents' commitment to learning partly accounts for the son's educational accomplishments. After receiving a Georgia public school education and passing through Haines Institute and Georgia State College, he earned B.D. and A.M. degrees at the University of Chicago and a Ph.D. in sociology at the University of Pennsylvania.[27] Like W.E.B. Du Bois, Wright studied in Germany at the universities of Berlin and Leipzig during 1903 and 1904. Clearly, he belonged to the "Talented Tenth" whose achievements Du Bois believed would convince whites that their assessment of the darker race was wrong.

While studying at Chicago, Wright became increasingly involved with the African Methodists. In 1891 he had joined Bethel A.M.E. Church in Augusta, Georgia, but it was in Chicago that he became a Sunday school teacher, superintendent, class leader, steward, and finally assistant pastor. The church at which he assumed this last position was none other than the Institutional Church established in 1900 by Reverdy C. Ransom.[28] These formative years were crucial in the development of Wright's career. Ransom's social concerns clearly inspired the young preacher and were absorbed by him. Wright later commented, "In 1905 there was little awareness of the obligations of Negro-American churches in an organized way, except in the fields of education, missions and personal charity. To be sure, a few pioneers, notably the Rev. R. C. Ransom in the Institutional Church, Chicago, had started something." In 1900, Ransom was still espousing the validity of the socialist message and its congruence with Christianity. Wright never lost his respect for some Socialists, even though he attacked their atheism, and retained a strong commitment to individualism and the pursuit of profit. Further, the Institutional Church was concerned (as were all churches, which attempted to fulfill their spiritual mission by institutionalizing their charity, educational, and social endeavors), with providing services for both the congregation and the surrounding neighborhood. This meant that Wright, more than most young ministers, came into contact with the plight of the urban poor.

Another important influence on Wright at this time was his university experience. His years at Chicago coincided with the rise to prominence of John Dewey and other liberal sociologists. At the divinity school, in particular, where Wright was enrolled, the Social Gospel was beginning to gain converts. That Wright was one such convert is clear:

> My studies threw me in the midst of the social gospel. . . . Brought up as
> I had been, with a theology which took but little account of social
> conditions and concerned itself with "getting to heaven," I found in the
> social gospel a more satisfying meaning and purpose for Christianity than
> ever before. The more I studied the Bible, and indeed the history of my
> own church, the more enthusiastic I became about the social gospel, not,
> however, as the old "gospel of works," but as the necessary outflow of
> the spirit of Jesus. For me there was little else for the church to do than
> to make practical its belief in God and brotherhood, and to help build a
> Christian society on earth.[29]

As a consequence of this adherence to Social Gospel ideas, Wright managed to combine the two major forces shaping his life, his education and his religion. While continuing to seek pastoral positions at churches where he could apply institutional methods, he studied sociology, and in 1905 moved on to the University of Pennsylvania, where he wrote his dissertation, "The Negro in Pennsylvania."

In Philadelphia, Wright resided at the Eighth Ward Social Settlement for two years. During this time he participated in many of the social organizations concerned about the condition of the city's African American population, including the Association for the Protection of Col-

ored Women, the Spring Street Social Settlement, the Armstrong Association, and Mercy Hospital. He then served as pastor of a church in
Conshohocken, which, owing to its small membership, allowed him time
to complete his dissertation. In 1909 he left Conshohocken for Philadelphia again and was appointed editor of the *Christian Recorder*. By this
time, though only thirty-one years old, Wright was already known
throughout the church as a leading African Methodist intellectual. He
had written a number of articles that had brought his name to the attention of church members nationally, including "Social Work and the Influence of the Negro Church" and "Self-Help in Negro Education."
While undertaking his dissertation research, he compiled *The Philadelphia
Colored Directory* of 1908.[30]

In terms of theology, Wright was very much in the tradition of
Levi J. Coppin. When it came to liturgy, he proposed that black ministers follow the lead of the Methodist tradition. This is most clear in his
1911 volume, *The Outline of the Teaching of Jesus: Or, The Fundamentals of
Christian Doctrine*. The work commences with a misleading statement:
"The purpose of this little book is to bring together from the Gospels
the words of Jesus upon the vital points of religion; to interpret them in
the light of their times, and to show their bearing and application to the
life of to-day." The needs of the present and the transformation of styles
of worship to meet the desires of all members would fit within such a
description. However, Wright had conservative intentions, as is shown by
his assertion that "the book may be used as a guide for study by the
inductive method." Limitation upon the individual's capacity to interpret both the world and God are the consequence of this method. Like
Coppin, Wright believed there was a right and a wrong way to interpret
the Bible. In a passage that echoes Coppin's analysis of Mark 10:31,
Wright provides an example of his method:

> Concerning prayer, Jesus says, "Ask and it shall be given you," which
> upon the face of it might be taken to mean that if a man asks for
> anything, even that which he does not need, or which might do him and
> others harm, he will receive it. . . . But read further and this conclusion is
> manifest by these words: "If ye abide in me and my words abide in you,
> ye may ask what ye will, and it shall be done unto you." Here it is clear
> that one must abide in Christ, and Christ in him, before he is entitled to
> ask what he wishes.

The reader could perhaps come to these conclusions alone, but for
Wright guidance was required from the Methodist minister who should

know the inductive method, or from a guidebook such as his own. To "abide in Christ" meant to be within the Methodist fold.

At points in the text Wright shows some liberality with regard to the condition of those suffering in this world, as when he uses numerous biblical texts to aver that "the wickedness of the world shall not always stand." But his sympathies are for the righteous, not necessarily the downtrodden. Further, he makes no reference to racial oppression and incorporates no liberationist notions, even when writing about hypocrisy, that "form of sin which receives especially severe condemnation from Jesus." Wright's moderation comes through when he suggests that "ownership of wealth is not contrary to the spirit of Christ's teachings." It is only when men "make money their god" and "live only that they might accumulate" that they depart from the Christian way. The Progressive compromise between capital and labor was clear:

> The washerwoman who cares more for her wages than for the honesty of her work and the service of her God, is serving mammon just as much as the millionaires who crush out their fellow men or water their stock in order simply to increase their incomes. The wage earner who causes his wife and children to suffer unnecessarily in order to gratify his selfish love of money, is just as much at fault as the factory owner who causes his employees to suffer that his profits may be larger.[31]

Such a compromise encompassed the relations between whites and blacks and allowed African Americans the possibility of allying themselves with capitalists against the demands of their laborers.

Richard Wright's background, with his family's emphasis on education as the route to self-improvement and, by extension, racial uplift, counteracted any tendency he may have had to use less restrained forms of worship and to take radical theological positions. His sermons, by his own declaration and that of a former member of Jones Tabernacle A.M.E. Church, where he was a pastor, were so dry and didactic that they almost never inspired worshipers to any form of exclamation.[32] His influence in the denomination in general was readily apparent, both through his pronouncements in the *Recorder* and in his compilation of the denomination's encyclopaedias, whose biographical sketches heavily emphasized educational attainment. It is possible that Wright excluded biographies of individuals who lacked educational distinction.[33] In many respects, Wright's ascendancy to the bishopric in 1936, while logical given his service over the years, symbolized the unwillingness of the A.M.E. Church to reorient its religious practices to appeal to those outside the Methodist fold, in particular, to people emigrating from the South.

And yet Richard R. Wright, Jr., was one of the most vociferous supporters of the migration. While he had moved north early in life, the rest of his family remained in Georgia until his father brought them up early in 1920.[34] His statements in support of the exodus were some of his most radical. In his editorials in the *Christian Recorder*, Wright described the migration as a reaffirmation of the power of the laborer in opposition to white capital. "Every Negro who leaves [the South]," Wright wrote, "means less money in the white man's pocket. For labor is the very foundation of capital and of all wealth." Beyond this challenge to southern white capitalism, Wright saw the possibilities that migration to the North represented for both southern and northern blacks:

> The movement North is unorganized. 100,000 Negroes have moved without any leader, without any organization, and with nothing but an individual motive and longing. Yet they have set the whole nation to thinking. Now IF ONE HUNDRED THOUSAND UNORGANIZED NEGROES CAN DO THIS WHAT COULD ONE MILLION ORGANIZED NEGROES DO?

The withdrawal of black labor from the South and the anger it caused among white Southerners, provided lessons for all blacks, who, in Wright's view, needed to learn how to organize their consumption to make a considerable impact on American capitalism as a whole.[35]

For Wright, migration would benefit both northern and southern blacks. "Migration through all time has been a great solver of problems," he wrote later in his autobiography, "and for the Negro-Americans, in the North, things were not half as bad as painted." Southern blacks coming to the North, he argued, would get better education and higher wages, and they would be able to organize more easily. Northern blacks would also benefit because the coming of the migrants "would make it possible for their children to become doctors, lawyers, and school teachers, insurance agents, business men, build large churches, and be elected to legislatures and Congress, and build a real foundation for a better American life."[36] Wright would have agreed with the writer for the *New York Age* who noted the political benefits of the migration and pointed out that "a million Negro votes in the free States would make the political power of the race a thing to be reckoned with."[37]

Wright's unequivocal support for the migration represented the culmination of intellectual discourse within the denomination about the position of African Americans in the United States. Here was a chance to advance the race by establishing a political voting bloc in northern cities. But framed as it was in terms of uplift, this support for the migration also fit within the denomination's view of the nature and mission of African Methodism. Therefore, while a powerful voting bloc might develop in the cities from time to time, it would always elude those who, like the minister–editors, wanted to control it. Some members of the community would turn to the new university-trained professional elite, while others would remain committed to ministers who, through storefront churches, serviced local neighborhoods. The Great Migration, though promoted by the minister–editor, in many ways contributed to his demise.

CHAPTER 6

Service and Prestige

When the Almighty God said: "It is not good that the man should be alone; I will make a helpmate for him," He thereby clearly defined the status of man and woman.

JAMES H.A. JOHNSON, 1892

To serve and to gain prestige were the two dominant impulses in African Methodist congregations on the eve of the Great Migration. In theory they seem contradictory, representing two different visions of Christianity—the one ascetic, the other associated with individual achievement and racial advancement. In practice, however, the line between them was not always clear; serving the cause of racial "uplift", for example, could result in increased prestige both inside and outside African American communities. Nevertheless, the distinction should be drawn because of its particular gender and class implications. One of the characteristics that embedded African Methodist churches firmly within the middling classes of the black community was their separation of service and prestige along gender lines, seeing the former as the province of women and the latter as the prerogative of men.[1]

The separation of these two impulses reinforced the belief common among African Methodists that the sexes were divided in their churches. Although women sometimes used the church for their own (or their husbands') purposes, and men sometimes became heavily involved in the service aspects of the church, it was nevertheless true that service was associated with women and prestige (or power) with men. Women, in particular, felt that men used the church to secure avenues for their advancement, while they themselves were more likely to see the church as an extension of the home, another place in which their service was required.[2]

The separation of service and prestige along gender lines did not cause tension because men and women believed that women should perform the functions of service, while men strove to uplift the race through economic and social avenues. In fact, open conflict between the sexes was rare. Women did not try to force men to increase their contributions to service initiatives undertaken by their churches, nor did they try to usurp the power of men in the various bodies in which positions of responsibility carried prestige. Instead, the hierarchical, episcopal structure of the denomination was built around an understanding of the sexual division within the congregations. In other words, men, whether they were class leaders, stewards, members of the boards of trustees, ministers, or even bishops, were to be supported by their "helpmeets" (usually their wives if they had them, but otherwise women in general). Gender roles in the churches reflected those in the larger society. The church was a "home" writ large, with women as the "homemakers" and men as the leaders.

Katherine D. Tillman adhered to this arrangement in her article, "Women as Helpers of the Ministers in the Spiritual and Social Activities of the Church." "The biggest church in the world ought to be just a spiritual home for God's people," she wrote, "where they meet to learn more of Him and how to do His will more perfectly so that His kingdom may come here upon earth and in making this church home spiritually and socially what it should be, who is better suited to help the Minister if she be earnest, intelligent and tactful than the home-maker of the centuries, Woman?"[3] Over time, problems arose out of this formulation as women became increasingly active in church work and as men became (in the eyes of women) increasingly indolent, especially when women began to push for political, economic, and social rights in the larger society. This was the radical side of separate-spheres ideology: political and social reforms advantageous to middle-class women could be promoted by defining society as the home writ large and by attributing to women moral superiority, derived from their role as mothers or from their exclusion from avenues to prestige and advancement. Few men or women questioned this idea of women's superiority or examined whether it could survive the political involvement that many women were demanding. But such questions were only problems on a distant horizon in 1913, when Tillman wrote the aforementioned article.

Gender Roles in the A.M.E. Church

The roles of men and women in society and the church received a great deal of attention in the pages of the A.M.E Church *Review*. The journal was very hospitable to the views of black middle-class women. The editors appeared to be comfortable allowing women to air their concerns and articulate their ideas. Levi J. Coppin did not share conventional male beliefs about women's limitations. His wife, Fanny Jackson Coppin, one-time principal of the Philadelphia Colored Institute, was a leading figure in the A.M.E. Church, and Coppin supported her in all her endeavors. His editorial policy of publishing numerous articles by women indicates that he was supportive of other women as well. Coppin's successor as editor, Hightower T. Kealing, also showed some sympathy for the concerns of women. On one occasion, he wrote of "the hand of women [being] seen in society, improving, uplifting, purifying and healing."[4] It was during his tenure as editor that the journal established a woman's section. This section, it is true, tended to focus less on political concerns than on how to bring up the sons and daughters of "the race," how to help a husband, and how to conform to etiquette. Nevertheless, the establishment of such a page reflected the increased importance of women in the church (though it perhaps also represented a church strategy for containing the broadening ambitions of black women).

As in white America, differences between how black men and women analyzed woman's role in society grew throughout the period. In the early 1890s, male and female writers seemed to hold similar opinions about woman's role. As one woman author succinctly put it: "We are called on to help man to conquer the world for Christ." Woman, then, was seen as man's "helpmeet."[5] In "Woman's Exalted Position," in 1891, James H.A. Johnson put forward the generally accepted view of woman's role in church and society: "When the Almighty God said: 'It is not good that the man should be alone; I will make a helpmate for him,' He thereby clearly defined the status of man and woman." Johnson continued:

> Being made a "helpmate" for man, she was endowed with peculiar qualities—made softer, sweeter and milder than he; being made "mother of all living," she was made clearly understood and respected. Suitable to this calling, she was given a tender heart and a plastic hand, that she

might "rock the cradle and rule the world." She was constituted to
manage the intricate affairs of the family circle, and bring them into a
condition that could not be produced by the unskilful hand of man.

While man is "the outdoor agent . . . made to breast the storms, hue
the oaks, grub the fields and subdue wild beasts," woman has features
that make her suited for "illuminating home-life, . . . extending the influence of the Church, . . . intensifying the excellency of character, . . .
[and] improving the condition of the world." Thus, Johnson concluded:
"Woman is the weaker vessel; but by all reasonable consideration, it is
clearly seen that her weakness is her strength, and that she is as important, in her position, to the human family as the head, the eye or the ear
is to the whole body."

   Johnson not only repeated accepted notions about woman's role;
he also showed his fear that women might no longer deign to act in the
prescribed manner. He reminded his audience that "woman was never
intended to be as a man; she never was intended to talk like him, nor
walk like him. . . . She never looks so well upon a bicycle as she does
upon a throne." He warned that "the woman who claims admission to
every position occupied by man, and is willing to shoulder her musket
and fight for it, is a monstrous outgrowth of the coarser elements of
female nature." The role that woman played in society was "prescribed
both before and after the fall"; to try to alter this arrangement would in
effect be an attempt to change the divine arrangement of society—and
no true Christian could condone such an act.[6]

   On the surface, many women also shared Johnson's view. Mary E.
Lee, poet and wife of the editor of the *Christian Recorder*, for example,
maintained that "if [a woman] should go to the polls, she would become
coarse and rough, and would necessarily neglect her home and children.
No greater calamity could happen to a people than the failure to perform
such an important duty." Lee encouraged women to think of the home
before they became embroiled in politics, for this was "the highest, di-
vinest sphere which is occupied by women; for all the affairs concerning
the civilization of the human family, that of home-making and keeping is
the most important." Nevertheless, she concluded that, hazards notwith-
standing, women should have a larger political role and that woman's
suffrage was "a good thing."[7]

   Under the surface, then, African Methodist women were unwilling
to accept their role as it was defined by men like Johnson. African Methodist women, however, seldom if ever confronted the notion of separate
spheres directly. Even when they argued for an expansion of woman's

public role, they did so from the vantage point of woman's special abilities or virtues. For example, in response to a doctor who had argued that
God never intended women to become physicians and that they should
not be encouraged to do so, Hannah Jones wrote: "Such blind, blind
prejudice! What could be more in accordance with the will of the great
Physician of the universe, than that woman, with her ready sympathy,
natural skill, and her gentle patience, should thus help to repair the work
of His hands?"[8]

Out of the concerns for homemaking, then, could arise an alternative, reform-minded politics. Sometimes the focus of women's efforts
was temperance; at other times it was corruption or the ill effects of
industrial capitalism. Mary Church Terrell, a leader of the National Association of Colored Women founded in 1896, became one of the most
vocal exponents of this alternative politics. Terrell wished to "bring
mothers together" through the association; she believed that "the influence of intelligent, Christian, progressive women must be more directly
felt, before the race can attain to its full stature, either mentally or mor-
ally."[9] In order for women to exert this influence they needed to concentrate their efforts not on national politics but on the home. "If I were
called upon to state in a word where I thought the Association should do
its most effective work," she wrote, "I should say unhesitatingly, 'in the
home.' The purification of the home must be our first concentration and
care. It is in the home where the woman is really queen, that she wields
her influence with the most telling effect."[10]

Terrell's "home," different from that described by male authors,
was intertwined with national politics and the "social question"; it was
not a realm in which women merely served men. It was an arena in
which morality could rise to the surface uncorrupted, a morality that
could then be used to combat the corruption rampant in national and
local politics. The argument was summarized succinctly by Selena C.
Gaines Dickerson, who defined the new responsibilities and duties of
women: "The character of our home life determines the character of our
community life; the character of our community life determines the character of our civic and national life. The character of our civic and national
life determines the character of our civic and national institutions."[11]

Katherine Davis Tillman showed how the special experiences of
women in the home could spur them to political action. "Let us as Afro-
American women pledge ourselves to the elevation of our home," she
wrote. "Let us war against intemperance, against gambling in saloons or
parlors, against bad literature and immorality of all kind, for these are the

demons that destroy our homes. Let us enlist under the banner of Christ and help subdue these evils."[12] Nowhere was the division between men and women clearer than over the question of temperance. Many laymen and even some ministers wished to ease up on the denomination's strictures against imbibing alcohol. Women contributors to the *Review*, however, consistently linked the issue of women's rights to the cause of prohibition, believing that until society was cured of this evil their homes would be threatened. Thus, while many male authors writing about women believed that emphasizing the home would confine women to this sphere, female authors usually emphasized the home because they felt certain that it would radicalize their sisters through an "alternative politics."[13]

Fannie Barrier Williams heralded the organization of the National Association of Colored Women as the "awakening of women." In spite of male chauvinism and the desire to keep women in subordinate positions, she argued, women were breaking through to new levels of independence. "It has been . . . our misfortune," she wrote, "to be regarded and estimated as suited to no other purpose in life than to make the world gay with our vivacity, laughter and social attributes. But when intelligence and that large love referred to begins to lift women out of a social dependency into the larger world of social independence, duties, and responsibilities the very foundations of civilization begin to shake and move forward toward better ideals of life and living."[14] African Methodist women, then, saw themselves leading a movement that would "regenerate" society.[15] They felt that by advancing their own social positions they would be uplifting "the race" as a whole. The emphasis on the home required a concern not for self alone but for family and, by extension, race. As Terrell argued, "It is useless to talk about elevating the race if we do not come into closer touch with the masses of our women, through whom we may correct many of the evils which militate so seriously against us, and inaugurate the reforms without which, as a race, we cannot hope to succeed."[16] African Methodist women were unwilling to consider home as separate from community and society. By ruling the home they believed they could affect all social realms.

These female contributors, not surprisingly, came from an elite segment of the African American community. Usually, they were the wives or daughters of professionals, such as ministers, doctors, and lawyers. It is therefore questionable how relevant this political program of rejuvenating society through the home was to the lives of lower-class black women in service occupations.[17] This was a middle-class political program similar to that found among white middle-class women, and it was only appropriate for working-class women once they had absorbed the values of Victorian womanhood and had risen above the level of domestic employment into the realm of domesticity.[18] African Methodist women were committing themselves to an ideology that increasingly would seem unrealistic as migrants came to the city who had no choice but domestic work and as ghettoization made it increasingly difficult for some men within the denomination to support a family on their incomes alone.

Consequently, organizations like the Philadelphia Association for the Protection of Colored Women, to which these women contributed, were primarily intended to "uplift" working women rather than empower them and embrace them as sisters. This association set out "to give colored women a fair chance to obtain honest employment and . . . a further chance to obtain decent living conditions." Members' assessment of the women to whom they were reaching out, however, was so negative that it created a great distance between benefactors and beneficiaries. "The Southern colored woman is very poorly equipped to deal with [the urban] environment," an article in the *Tribune* describing the intentions of the organization proclaimed. She was therefore susceptible to the corrupting dangers of the streets, the dance halls, and other "worse" amusements, and the migration from the South resulted in "many a story of failure, of want, of crime, of poverty, of disease that might have been avoided had the girl only been safeguarded."[19] Thus, while the association provided many tangible benefits for working women (particularly training in skills like sewing, which were important to the domestic), it nevertheless alienated many of the people it was trying to help. This was symbolic of the Progressive predicament: how to give people benefits without elevating the status of the providers and thereby reinforcing class distinctions. This conundrum was one that Philadelphia's African Methodists had to deal with if they wanted to appeal to the newcomers in their midst.

Men: The Benefits of Church Membership

In a 1913 *Review* article, C. H. Johnson, general secretary of the Laymen's Missionary and Forward Movement of the A.M.E. Church, argued that the church was in crisis because of the failures of men in the area of service. What was needed, he claimed, was widespread commitment of African Methodist men to a laymen's movement such as his own. He wrote:

> The men of the church ought to know each other. There should be special times when they would come together in a social way, and talk over their lives as they relate to the church and the community. The church life ought to be so closely looked into as to bring out the reasons that hinders spiritual life, and plan to meet them. There ought to be a careful notice taken of the masculine attendance to religious service.[20]

In other words, men ought to start acting in the church more like women; out of such actions a stronger commitment to service would develop.

Johnson's disenchantment with men in the realm of service had been shared by Frances E.W. Harper. In her novel, *Iola Leroy*, the protagonist presented a paper on the "Education of Mothers" to a group similar in composition to the Philadelphia Preachers' Association. One of the ministers present acknowledged that, indeed, the need of "the race" was for "enlightened mothers." However, Miss Delany, one of Iola's more radical women friends, quickly interjected that enlightened fathers were also essential. She continued:

> "If there is anything I chafe to see it is a strong, hearty man shirking his burdens, putting them on the shoulders of his wife, and taking life easy for himself."
>
> "I always pity such mothers," interposed Iola, tenderly.
>
> "I think," said Miss Delany, with a flash in her eye and a ring of decision in her voice, "that such men ought to be drummed out of town!" As she spoke, there was an expression which seemed to say, "And I would like to help do it!"[21]

In a more moderate manner, Katherine Tillman feared that "so well have women performed their part of the work that in many instances it has made the men of the church sluggish and inactive in certain lines, notably so in raising missionary funds."[22]

However, Alice M. Dunbar, wife of the author Paul Laurence Dunbar and a staff member of the *Review*, had a quite different perspective regarding the problem of men and the church. She noted, in 1913, that "even if the women do go to Church, they are unable to pull the men with them. In other words, the present-day man has no desire for the Church." There was an alarming decline in attendance at church services, which, she felt, was largely confined to the male sex. Dunbar felt that the Men and Religion Forward Movement proposed by Johnson was doomed to failure because the idea of service would not appeal to men.

Dunbar believed that the church faced a crisis because it had become no more than "a social organization of women, who like to give entertainments." The problem was that the church had ceased to cater to the needs of its men. Members had tried to avoid "sensationalism" and had demanded "a spiritual atmosphere above the sordid and meritricious display of the street." Further, members had tried to make their churches a haven, "a relief from the hubbub of daily life. . . . We drop into the Church pretty much as we do the theatre, as a rest and recreation, when we do attend." Dunbar argued that they had gone too far in this direction. "Now the question is," she wrote, "does the 'spiritual uplift' which comes from a well-ordered service appeal alike to strong men, business men, professional men, and to men of temperament and women? Have we feminized the Church too much, and in decrying virile methods of attack, hung tidies, as it were, over it?"[23] Men needed more from the church than spiritual uplift. They needed to feel that they could make business and professional connections with other men and that they were using their time productively by attending church services. Dunbar believed that the church had a responsibility to men to cater to some of these needs, to provide the "virile methods of attack" previously decried.

These two criticisms of the church, coming as they did from opposite directions—one blaming men for not following women, the other blaming the church for being too "feminized"—reveal the nature of the prime motivation behind male church membership. The church provided black men with good avenues for advancement and for securing prestige in a society that not only rewarded the realization of "manhood" but also blocked avenues to its realization for African Americans.

Membership in a church opened up many opportunities to black men. Often, as mentioned in Chapter 3, ministers were closely associated with black building and loan associations and banks. To secure loans or mortgages, therefore, a recommendation from a minister was often helpful. Further, business success and position in the church hierarchy were closely associated. It was sensible for a church endeavoring to deal with financial vicissitudes to turn to people who had demonstrated in business that they could handle such affairs. Consequently, a system of patronage was available to those who were willing or able to build networks with those in prestigious positions, like president of the corporation, member of the board of trustees, steward, usher, and so on. Some church positions might not be as appealing as others—they might involve more work and fewer benefits, for example—yet even these provided visibility for the person who wanted prestige in the community.

The records of Walter C. Beckett show a symbiotic relationship between churches and black businesses. Churches paid for the printing of their programs and other pamphlets by advertising procured by businesses like Beckett's funeral home. The business establishments no doubt gained from the careful perusal given to church pamphlets during those parts of the Sunday services that seemed to drag on longer than desired. Newly arrived migrants, who came with sufficient funds to establish their own businesses, realized that one of the most effective ways to attract customers was to advertise in church papers. Thus D. A. Hart, a Southerner who joined "Mother" Bethel in 1916 and later followed the Rev. Williams to Mt. Zion Church, advertised his printing firm in the St. Matthews A.M.E. Church bulletin and other church pamphlets.[24]

The church was also a forum in which individuals could learn skills for public speaking and organizational politics. While ministers may have lost a degree of their power within the black community as a whole, those who rose to replace them at the head of the community, particularly the new breed of lawyers, often learned some of their skills in the church class or in helping to organize a church campaign. African Methodists could reap one of the benefits of segregation, that of addressing each other without being continually subordinated to white leaders.

The churches were also closely linked with the fraternal orders, which provided many avenues for advancement. To become a member of a lodge in the Free and Accepted Masons, Odd Fellows, Knights of Pythias, or any of a myriad of other orders, it was imperative first to belong to a church. Not only did a lot of recruiting take place within congregations, but most orders stipulated that members should be churchgoing Christians.[25] Not being a church member would have led to "blackballing" during the stringent examinations of individuals considered for membership.

Most of the larger churches had some connection with the orders. Either they allowed the secret societies to meet in their building or a society developed within their congregation. Masonry was considered "a handmaid of religion," and the other orders were likewise supposed to complement the work of churches.[26] Once a year, in fact, after the brothers had paraded in their uniforms, each lodge heard a sermon from a minister.[27] The orders often provided an important component of the system that gave prestige to men who became members of churches.[28]

As in the church itself, intention and reality in the orders were often very different. "Masonry is a moral institution established by virtuous men," W. F. Teister wrote, "and [it is] intended to recall to our minds the most sublime tenets of Brotherly Love, Relief and Truth." It is easy to see how the orders appealed to church leaders because their precepts were often the same as those taught in church. According to Teister, "Masonry teaches that there is one God, and He [is] the maker of the Universe and all contained thereon. It teaches that God is our father and that all men are brothers. It teaches a high state of moral rectitude. No drunkard, gambler, atheist, or irreligious libertine can be initiated therein."[29]

Similarly, Masonry's appeal among African Americans is easy to understand. "Pure Masonry," Teister argued, "is the equalizer of all peoples of every clime or condition." Two verses from a poem familiar to all Masons, would have an obvious appeal for many black men:

> *We meet upon the Level, and we part upon the Square;*
> *What words of precious meaning those words Masonic are.*
> *Come, let us contemplate them, they are worthy of a thought,*
> *With the highest, and the lowest, and the rarest they are fought.*
>
> *We meet upon the Level, though from every station come;*
> *The rich man from his Mansion, the poor man from his home,*
> *For one must leave his wealth and state without the Mason's door,*
> *And the other finds his true respect upon the checked floor.*

But the orders did not always live up to the levelers' creed. The Masons usually had three classes with distinct privileges and different rules and rituals established to secure these privileges. According to Teister, honor and probity were the recommendations of the first or lowest class, diligence and appreciation qualifications of the second, while the third class was restricted to a few known for their truth and fidelity. Each level had its own signs, passwords, and grips.[30]

Stratification within the orders was so evident and attention paid by members to attaining positions of prestige was such that corruption was frequent. "That the principles of Masonry, like those of Christianity, have too often been perverted, none will deny," S. H. Coleman wrote. He continued:

> Our most wholesome lessons have often been disregarded. Our laws and constitution have been openly violated; and our landmarks purposely forgotten. Many unite themselves with the fraternity with no higher motive than that of satisfying an idle curiosity, or with the design of gratifying some low ambition. There are others who expect to be invested with some wonderful secrets and to witness the most mysterious evolutions.

Masonry was more than just a "half-way house between earth and heaven, [offering] shelter and protection to the weary travelers struggling up from beneath and perishing in the storm."[31] It was part of the struggle itself; the "shelter and protection" it provided was that of increased prestige and, often, increased political power.[32]

The testimony of Matthew H. Jones highlights many features of the orders. Jones joined the Masons fairly soon after arriving in Philadelphia. His chance to join a lodge came about through his work at St. Matthew's Church. As part of his duties as a class leader, he visited a sick man who, unbeknownst to Jones, was a Mason. At the end of his visit, the sick man said to him, "Mr. Jones, you've done for me what my Mason brothers haven't done yet." In response, Jones mentioned that he was interested in becoming a member of the order. Several weeks later, three lodge members "came round" by surprise to interview him. "They wanted to see how you lived," Jones remembered, "how you treated your wife and your kids, so they came by surprise."

Matthew Jones later found out that his visitors reported back to the lodge and the Masons voted on whether to accept him into the secret society. "They used to have a ballot box in which the members would put balls," Jones remembered. "If you received a black ball then you wouldn't be accepted and you would have to go back and try again. If you received too many blackballs, then it wasn't worth coming back." Jones was successful, however. He was elected an apprentice mason and during the next few years worked his way up through craft mason to become a Third Degree Mason, master of a lodge for a year, and a past master.[33] At each stage new rituals had to be learned, new tests (some taken blindfolded) had to be passed, and more surprise visits from his lodge brothers had to be endured.

Jones explained why he did not try to climb further up the lodge hierarchy. He remembered that he "didn't have the funds, nor the energy to go further." By the standards of many in the black community, he was well off and had more money than most, yet he did not have enough. To rise through the thirty-three degrees of the Masonic society, therefore, required both a great deal of political energy and ample financial resources. Jones had "some nice days in the Lodge," but besides gaining pleasure from his association with the Masons, he knew that he could also receive certain benefits. "Being a member was very useful," he said, "though I never used it myself. . . . It provided connections. If you wanted to get something started, you could do it through your lodge brothers." He added, "A Mason would always lend you money, because if you were a Mason and you promised to repay someone, you always would."

Owing to the organization's secrecy, the extent of membership in the Masons is difficult to determine. Once he became a member, Matthew Jones found out that many others in his congregation also belonged to the lodge, and certainly, black membership of the lodges in Philadelphia was large enough to warrant a special section in the *Tribune* covering the secret societies. Jones summed up the impulse behind such membership, as well as some of the impulse behind male membership in churches. He said: "It was good to be recognized as one of them [i.e., a Mason]. We were all poor, obscure people, so anything that helped gain standing or prestige was desired."[34]

A 1917 editorial in the *Tribune*, published during the peak of the wartime migration, confirms the connection between the churches and the orders. It also shows the strength of the fraternities and the concern their members had for their own positions rather than for helping migrants adjust. "Now is the season of sermons and parades of our many fraternal orders," the editor wrote.

> As we view the long ranks of marching men bedecked in beautiful uniforms and immaculate regalia we become reflective. What means this blare of music, this martial tread of hosts of men in serried ranks wending their way along the thoroughfares of our cities?
>
> Is this beautiful display of uniforms and men, this outpouring of fraters to listen to a sermon, at so many dollars per sermon, all it means?
>
> Do we as fraters recall the memory of the sacred obligations taken at the altar, without mental reservation, or is it but a fleeting show?
>
> How often we have thought as we viewed these fine parades, Oh, if we could only impress upon the minds of these men, this great host of brethren bound by solemn vow, the solemnity of these obligations.

If we could only, in truth, as well as in theory, see them united in one grand phalanx for the moral and social uplift of the race.

Their number is legion, their power is unlimited, if only they but realized it.

The *Tribune* editor recognized the differences between theory and reality in the orders and noted that they had become no more than vehicles for individual advancement. He continued,

True they have done much to relieve the suffering, to bury the dead and help one another, but what would their power be if instead of backbiting and fighting each other they would unite in one grand band for the uplift of the race, for the carrying forward of the grand ideals of the brotherhood of man and the fatherhood of God.[35]

It can hardly be a coincidence that this article was placed directly next to one discussing the treatment of migrants and the need to help them adjust to life in Philadelphia. The implication was that the men belonging to churches and fraternities were often too concerned with their own affairs to do their "duty to the incoming brother" from the South.[36]

Women: Conquering the World for Christ

They made the foaming washtub
With honest labor ring,
And in its soapy contents,
Saw many a precious thing.[37]

Just as men in the African Methodist Episcopal Church acted very much in accordance with the spirit of the time in striving for upward mobility and the uplift of the race through their own political and economic efforts, women in the church acted in accordance with that spirit in ways that complemented their partners. In other words, African Methodist women treated the church as the home writ large and endeavored to ensure that their family, the congregation, was "led joyfully in song."[38]

Ever since the establishment of the A.M.E. Church, African Methodist women have been noteworthy for their efforts on behalf of their churches. One of the major themes of the first century of the denomination's history was how and in what capacities women would be incorporated into the power structure of the denomination. By the 1880s, the general conferences had largely decided that women could fulfill many of the same functions as men without being given comparable power or prestige. Women could be licensed as evangelists but not as ministers; they could be made stewardesses, but as Bishop Turner was quick to point out, they were "merely assistants" to "the stewards, class leaders and pastor. . . . They have no legislative or judicial discretion."[39]

However, while women in some ways remained within the confines of the prescribed positions of evangelist, stewardess, and deaconness (a position introduced in 1900), by fulfilling their duties, according to historian Jualynne Dodson, they implicitly challenged "church policies excluding women from formal authority." To be a successful evangelist involved having power over individuals and inspiring them, perhaps even compelling them to come forward to the altar to be saved at a revival. The denomination needed evangelists for expansion, but women's success in evangelism could bring with it the recognition that women were perfectly qualified for the ministry. Likewise, the denomination needed stewardesses to carry out the work of stewards who, in the eyes of many, were more interested in gaining prestige from the position than carrying out their duties. But, again, the success of stewardesses could bring with it recognition of women's qualifications.

By the 1890s several women were prominent in the denomination on both national and local levels. Jualynne Dodson writes of preachers like Amanda Berry Smith, Margaret Wilson, Emily Calkin Stevens, and Harriet A. Baker, who gained national and sometimes even international renown.[40] In Philadelphia, women evangelists were not so common, there being enough male preachers who wanted to minister to the prestigious pastures of the city. But female evangelists occasionally attended the Philadelphia Preachers' Association meetings, and evangelist Mary Jones gave a talk on "Africa's Redemption" to its audience of ministers in 1897.[41]

People commenting on the work of the church nearly always placed special emphasis on the contribution of the women. One of T. G. Steward's impressions of Philadelphia, gained from his trip to the city in 1891, was the work of Annie M. Hall, a member of Union A.M.E. Church. Steward wrote of the "extensive work" of the Industrial Missionary Association, which was presided over by Mrs. Hall, "a very earnest and devout Christian lady." The association had a membership of ninety adults and ninety-six children and held two meetings each week at which sewing was undertaken. During the previous winter the association had been able to help sixty-two families. "The credit of the organization belongs largely to Sister Hall," Steward wrote, "encouraged and assisted as she was by the former pastor, Rev. J. W. Beckett, D.D."[42]

Another woman, Martha Morris, was given special mention by Bishop William Henry Heard in his autobiography for contributing greatly to the success of his revivals at Allen A.M.E. Church. Due to the work of Martha Morris, Allen took one hundred and thirty potential members into a probationers' class during the revival of 1889 and lost no more than eight to ten of them before they became full members.[43]

Lastly, Fanny J. Coppin was the inspiration for many of the women in the church. Born Fanny M. Jackson, she became principal of the Institute of Colored Youth after the Civil War. Under her direction this Philadelphia institute founded by Quakers grew substantially and provided further education for many young men and women who would go on to be leaders of the black community during the early decades of the twentieth century. Jackson married into the A.M.E. Church in 1881, when she and Levi J. Coppin were betrothed (she was already writing a woman's column for the *Christian Recorder*), and for the remainder of her life she maintained an active role in the church both in missionary organizations and in her husband's congregations.[44] So active was her role in the church that H. T. Kealing claimed that "when her husband was elected Bishop in 1900, we heard a man say that since we could not make Mrs. Coppin a Bishop, he had voted for her husband, feeling that in elevating him he was honoring her; and doubtless he was not alone in this."[45]

Women did so much of the work in the congregations, from raising money, to teaching in the Sunday schools and visiting the sick, that it soon became an embarrassment to many church leaders that they could not vote in corporation meetings and were not represented on any of the important governing bodies. Richard R. Wright, Jr., wrote in the *Centennial Encyclopaedia* of 1916, for example, "Where possible women should have voting power in all church corporations, as they support them largely, and 'taxation without representation is tyranny' both in Church and State" (p. 304). During the next twenty years many churches gave women voting power.

Slowly women began to receive some political recognition for the work they undertook. In 1913, Katherine Tillman foresaw a changing status for women in the church. "Women having proven so helpful in the past," she wrote, "it is not surprising that the present trend is to entrust them with larger responsibilities. In the Methodist, Presbyterian and several other large denominational bodies there are immense areas of the church's missionary activities under the supervision of the women of the church."[46] In 1928, at Allen A.M.E. Church, Susie A. Thomas, who had been president of the Senior Stewardess Board under Rev. W. Spencer Carpenter, between 1911 and 1916, was elected trustee under Rev. Charles W. Stewart. Also in the 1920s, Dickey B.W. Prowell, owner of Prowell's Lunch Box and one of the founding members of Mt. Zion A.M.E. Church after its congregation broke away from Bethel, became one of the first women elected trustee and treasurer of a congregation in the A.M.E. Church.[47] During the 1930s, Gertrude B. Lee, an outstanding member of Mother Bethel who had worked as a Sunday school teacher from a very young age, was elected to the board of stewards and became its treasurer.[48] Progress in this direction was slow, however, and even today positions of authority within the churches remain largely the province of men.[49]

In some respects, men are at fault for the sluggish rate at which women have gained political power in the church; men skilfully handled women's discontent and channeled their desire for prestige into safe organizations. For example, they established the Board of Stewardesses and the Order of the Eastern Star (OES), the sister arm of the Masons.

The Pennsylvania chapter of the OES was founded in 1909 by Col. Philip H. Edwards of Mother Bethel. Edwards served as Grand Worthy Patron of the organization from 1909 to 1923. The constitution of the group is interesting. Membership was (and still is) restricted to women related, either by marriage or birth, to a Master Mason. Two things are readily apparent here: first, by belonging to the OES a woman did not bring prestige so much to herself as to her husband—she was not being rewarded for her own deeds but for those of a male relative; second, the organization was likely to divide women in the congregations, since it clearly benefited some women to support their men rather than their sisters. Men could not lose from the establishment of the OES. Indeed, they even retained control of the organization. Masons were (and still are) officially allowed to attend the meetings of their sister groups, and the highest position in the women's order is, in fact, held by the Masons' grand master.[50]

In other respects, however, women moved only slowly into positions of control because many of them were more concerned with fulfilling the role prescribed for them than seeking political power.[51] Mrs. R. L. Chappelle, wife of the bishop from South Carolina, believed in the nobility of aiding a husband in his calling. While she believed that "woman is the world's Motor-power," and "an indispensable factor in the onward march of men things," in her mind women were clearly also subordinate to men. "She is that essence which quickens the pulsations of men and gives soul to his actions." As such, the pastor should assign her "certain territory in his parish to look after," amounting to a separate sphere "of prayer meeting clubs." This territory should have been central to church work, yet Chappelle implied that the territory controlled by men was more important.

Women were to undertake the social work of the church, looking after "that class of our membership who are not in such circumstances as the more favored members assuring them that they are with Christians who care for them and will make them feel it by treating them as their social equals, in the church work, at least." Above all, the women had to counteract "the selfishness of our membership," by which Chappelle referred implicitly to the men, who "feel and act too, in the church, as if they care nothing for anybody but themselves, and then, too would like to have everybody feel that the church belongs to them and their families. This does not only chill the church-work, but drives members from the church." Writing in 1913, on the eve of the acceleration of migration, Chappelle recognized the danger of allowing such behavior to continue unabated in the churches. It was necessary, she felt, for this committee of women to "look after strangers, those who come into our cities and some of these people are our own members coming from other cities and towns, and sometimes from the country, and are naturally timid and fearful among the city people."[52]

To deal with "the current crisis," great emphasis was placed on an alliance between women members and their pastors. This was a natural alliance, Katherine D. Tillman believed: "Woman's quick intuition, sympathy and tact make her an invaluable ally of the Minister, and fortunate is the pastor who is able to marshal the female forces of his church." There was also biblical justification for this alliance. "In the Old Testament times," Tillman wrote,

> we find Miriam mentioned first as a helper of Moses, thrilling the hearts
> of his Israelitish followers with her exultant improvised song of praise;
> Esther is chosen to carry Mordecai's hope of deliverance for his
> oppressed people, the tactful Abigail succors David and his famished
> men, the poor widow at Zarephath divides her last bit of oil and meal
> with Elijah and the generous-hearted Shunamite woman, not satisfied

with her occasional entertainment of the prophet Elisha, persuades her husband to build a room for the prophet, so that he may partake of their hospitality whenever he chanced to come their way.

Women "occupied an important place in their relation to the Minister," Tillman felt. Building on the Ladies' Aid Society, Sewing Circle, and Missionary Band, created specifically "to help the Minister in the various problems of church life," the "thoroughly organized modernized feminine forces of the Church today" could help the minister conquer the church itself for Christ.

Making an alliance with women made economic sense for the pastor also. As Tillman pointed out, "Simply because of the activity of their wives in the church thousands of men who have no hearty interest in the welfare of the Church contribute liberally to its support."[53] Besides inducing men to reach into their pockets, women did most of the fundraising and missionary work. This fact led Tillman to ask, "What would be the condition of the churches of all races and denominations, if the women were to withdraw their moral and financial support?" The answer was, not very healthy, for

> it is the women in our churches who assist the perplexed pastor in
> devising plans for the annihilation of state and church debts, and who
> assume the charge of clothing the pastor and his needy family in a little
> purple and fine linen occasionally; who prepare at home, little feasts and
> invite this everyday hero, that he may fare sumptuously at least one day
> out of seven, and who often seem to their pastor angels in disguise.

The columns of "our race journals," Tillman noted, were full of accounts of the work of African Methodist women raising immense sums for "the erection or renovating of churches or for some Christian purpose."[54]

The most prominent missionary work done by women was channeled through two national organizations, both of which had local affiliates in Philadelphia. Both groups were started at the instigation of men whose own missionary work had been failing miserably. The Women's Home and Foreign Missionary (WHFM) Society was formed in South Bend, Indiana, in 1893, by Bishop Turner and Dr. W. B. Derrick, in large part to help them in their efforts to spread the work of the A.M.E. Church into southern Africa. While this group managed to raise respectable sums of money throughout the country, it did not have the institutional strength of the other missionary organization, the Women's Parent Mite Missionary (WPMM) Society.[55]

The roots of this organization lay in an 1874 editorial in the *Chris-*

tian Recorder, written by Benjamin T. Tanner, stressing the need for women to organize a women's missionary society. "At this moment," Tanner proclaimed, "our missionary [work] in Hayti lies upon its oars, and why? The Church with all its acknowledged riches cannot afford to assist him. Will you not, my dear sisters, lead off in the organization of a missionary society of the AME Church which shall supply the means by which Hayti shall live?"[56] In response to this letter the Mite Missionary Society was quickly established in Washington, D.C., and it spread rapidly around the country. The society was largely responsible for the support of work in Haiti, Sierre Leone, and South Africa.

In 1895 at the connectional convention of the society held at Bethel Church, Fanny J. Coppin proposed the formation of conference branches under one parent organization. The outcome, in 1896, was the formation of the Women's Parent Mite Missionary Society and ten branches, one in Philadelphia. The parent organization was largely headed by wives of the bishops of the connection, while the local groups were headed by wives of prominent ministers in the area: Fanny J. Coppin and Josie D. Heard were prominent in the local organization during the 1890s; in 1916, S. E. Hoxter, Jennie M. Palmer, Clara V. Davis, Laura C. Waters, and Mary F. Parker (all wives of ministers) were among the leaders of the Philadelphia Conference Branch.[57]

More important perhaps even than the minister himself, the minister's wife was arguably the central figure in most African Methodist Episcopal churches prior to the Great Migration. In order to forge an alliance with the women of the church, the minister needed to use his wife as an emissary. As "is pillar of strength," she was expected to "lead off," not merely participate, in the church. According to Mary F. Handy, president of the Women's Parent Mite Missionary Society, she should be "especially interested" in the work of Christian missions and other church work. The women and children in the congregation should consider her the "Big Sister" and in her find "a general advisor and consoler for their woes." In a word, Handy suggested, the minister's wife should act as an assistant pastor: "Always alert to the pastor's interest, keeping abreast with the church, thus educating herself along lines of helpfulness while standing as a support to her husband. Not given to gossip, not an idler; a busy woman in a quiet way fighting the battles of the Lord." While the minister could not always be approached, his wife had to make herself both available and approachable, so that the members might feel "such a nearness that they will not hesitate to discuss their joys and sorrows [with her]." On the basis of what she learned from her members and from her experiences in the parish, she then had to make suggestions to the pastor that might aid, and sometimes even save, his ministry. So important was her position, Handy felt, that "in my opinion many failures in the Ministry may be traced to [the minister's] indiscretion in choosing a companion."[58]

Given the importance of their position, ministers' wives needed instruction in fulfilling their role. In "The Ideal Minister's Wife," Mrs. M. E. Guile told her readers that in order to succeed as ministers' wives they needed both to have their heads, hands, and hearts committed to their husbands' work and to ensure that their characters were as "spotless as the snow on the summit of the loftiest mountain top." In many respects, the job was hardly an appealing one; it required immense effort and provided very little recognition besides the occasional note of gratification from the husband. The qualifications needed were lengthy and often difficult to meet:

> You must be a self-sacrificing, consecrated woman, one who can rise above the little annoyances of surrounding circumstances over which you have no control. You must know how to bridle your tongue when people find fault and ridicule your husband and persecute him. To be an ideal minister's wife, you must be able to brush away the tears that come with an overburdened heart, and answer the doorbell with a pleasant smile. Be pleasant to all callers, always keeping an extra bed and an extra chair at the table. You must visit the aged, the sick and the poor of your community. Do not stay at home, as some society belle would do, waiting for company or the people of the community to call on you, but you, in a business-like way, must go out to meet them and become acquainted with them.[59]

Some of the qualifications, moreover, could not be acquired but were intuitive. "When you are with the aged," Guile wrote, "be so pleasant they will forget age, and when you are with the poor, be so kind and humble with them that poverty and obscurity are forgotten. When you are with the sick, be so generous in your words and smiles and pennies that sickness will not be thought of." And beyond these feats, "Do all you can to bring them to Christ." Even though her work was perhaps as difficult as her husband's was, the minister's wife had to remember at all times that her needs were secondary to his and that her main objective was "stimulating those qualities in her husband that make for the point of development in the ministry."[60]

The role of women in the churches should not be unduly romanticized; women were not inherently good, nor men inherently bad. Women merely did not have access to the political positions that might be corrupting. Moreover, some women did not confine themselves to service-oriented tasks but endeavored to play a political role in the church. Often, a woman could gain a sense of power and prestige from her family's position in the congregation and so contribute to her husband's efforts to rise in the male church hierarchy. Nevertheless, the writings of contemporaries make it clear that the gender division was widely acknowledged at the beginning of the century: the men had the power, and the women provided the services.

The separation of the impulses to serve and to earn prestige undermined a unified response to the Great Migration by the denomination as a whole. Individual congregations could respond in several ways to the influx of migrants. One response—discouraging newcomers from entering the congregation—was exclusionary but considered necessary by churchgoers who, in the face of an influx of their social "inferiors," were anxious to maintain the social prestige of their church and its members. Such a response had serious repercussions for the denomination, because the actions of a single congregation negatively affected the reputation of all African Methodist churches. Another response, promoted by ministers and favored by many churchgoers, was inclusionary: opening the church doors to all migrants and providing services for those in need.

Either of these responses was likely to lead to tensions within a congregation. On the one hand, exclusion could be seen as hypocritical, and since black Christians often criticized white Christians for hypocrisy, black churchgoers were very sensitive to this charge. On the other hand, inclusion might lead to conflict among churchgoers as new members sought to gain the same advantages from church membership that former members had achieved but found access to positions of prestige blocked by entrenched elites.

A third response, a compromise, blended service and advancement into a delicate mix similar to that which had existed prior to the Great Migration. In this response church members remained largely exclusionary, being fairly selective about the people they allowed to become members of their congregation, while at the same time providing services for members and nonmembers alike. In other words, church members looked for people who might make a positive contribution to their church. This was achieved by the requirement of a period of probation for a new arrival unless he or she brought a letter of transmittal from a southern A.M.E. church. At the same time, to counteract the possibility that these "suitable" arrivals would seek to take over positions held by an entrenched oligarchy, certain restrictions were sometimes enacted by trustees to ensure that new members could not vote or stand for election to church offices for as long as three years.[61]

Even while they followed exclusionary practices, however, church members undertook considerable amounts of work to aid incoming migrants. As is discussed at length later, churchgoers undertook their own initiatives, or contributed to collective ones, that endeavored to alleviate many of the burdens facing newcomers to the city. In the short term, the commitment to service usually associated with the work of women in African Methodist churches could be tapped liberally without threatening the prestige of male churchgoers. In the long term, however, the gendered divisions within the African Methodist congregations would make the church seem foreign and unwelcoming to outsiders and would limit both the growth and the influence of the denomination in the city.

Indeed, the Great Migration presented a problem for churches that separated service and prestige. As previously noted, this separation required a particular class, or economic, basis. Given that during the war the migration began to bring into the city many people who did not have a secure economic position, and that the continuing process of ghettoization undermined the economic position of many longtime residents of the city, the adherence to separate spheres ideology only distanced African Methodists from the growing majority of the African American community after World War I.

CHAPTER 7

"Flaming Torches"

If the Preacher in his sermon,
Stands up to tell the truth,
They'll go about and murmur,
With slander and abuse.
They want the whole arrangement
To suit their selfish style;
But God will sit in judgment,
After a while.

CHARLES ALBERT TINDLEY,
from the hymn "After a While"

During the first two decades of the twentieth century the pastor's position in the church began to change. In the 1890s, the pastor had been a successful mediator between opposing groups within the church, depending largely on the commitment of women in his congregation to service and allowing men to control financial and political affairs. His apolitical position within the congregation was maintained partly by itinerancy (the pastor was seldom at one church long enough to build up a political following), partly by the denomination's emphasis on education, and partly also by the pastor's wife, who (as discussed in the previous chapter) was usually able to rally the women of the congregation to the side of the pastor.[1]

By the second decade of the new century, the pastor's position had become more politicized. This change can be attributed to several factors. First, the system of itinerancy had begun to break down, and the pastor was spending more time at each church—long enough to build up support that might challenge groups resistant to his position on numerous issues. Second, a decrease in the number of men involved in church affairs made it easier for a pastor to develop a sufficient following among discontented people within the congregation to contest the power of an established elite. This was made easier still by the fact that two new groups—migrants and women—were beginning to play important political roles in northern churches. Women continued to push for political rights in the churches to match those they sought in the national political system, while the arrival of migrants (some of whom had held prominent positions in their former churches) meant that there was often a disaffected group within the congregation that could be persuaded to follow the pastor's leadership.

Third, the increasing politicization of the episcopacy within the denomination affected ministers. Divisive and often vicious political campaigns undertaken to secure election to the highest office in the church made it clear to ministers that to rise in the church hierarchy they had to act in a political fashion. It was no longer enough to preach well and to be the most erudite minister in the conference; it was more important to be connected to a particular bishop, to enjoy the patronage of one who had already climbed the totem pole.[2]

Lastly, pastors found that they were competing with new forms of entertainment and that the style of preaching they had been practicing no longer attracted audiences as effectively as it once had. And since filling the pews was now more important, the pastor could no longer rely on his training at the theological seminary but in many ways had to begin performing. The new style of preaching tended to reorient the church to a new concentration on the centrality of the pastor, replacing the old emphasis on "service." An uneasy balance between service and advancement, or prestige enhancement, now became subordination of service to advancement, which in turn became the advancement of the pastor.

African Methodist ministers commented increasingly on the political character of African Methodist churches and the difficulty of mediating among contending groups. In 1914, for example, W. Spencer Carpenter, who was then pastor of Allen A.M.E. Church and a leading minister in the city, wrote of the problems he and many of his colleagues faced in their churches. His *Review* article, entitled "The Minister as Big Brother," provides a clear sense of the pastor's position within the denomination, delineating the problems for those ministers who tried to fulfill their ordained purpose in these political churches, and revealing the language in which the pastors' dilemmas were discussed at the time. His description of the almost endless litany of complaints made against pastors is worth quoting at length. It shows the difficulties facing ministers on the eve of the Great Migration:

> If a minister uses manuscript he is blamed for "digging into his barrel"; if he doesn't use manuscript, "he hasn't prepared." If he raises his voice when praying, he is "an old-timer;" if he keeps his voice down, he "lacks fire." If he clenches his fist while preaching he is "a fighter;" if he keeps his hands at his sides he is "so awkward." If, while preaching, his eyes fill with tears, he is called "a baby;" if he never betrays emotion, he is called "a brute." If he parts his hair in the middle, he is a "fop;" if he doesn't part his hair, he is "untidy." If he laughs at a joke, he is "very worldly;" if he cannot see the point of a joke he is a "goody-goody."

Even though he was considered a very successful minister, Carpenter must have been on the point of despair, not knowing how to act:

> If [the minister] begs the people to give money to the church, he is "mercenary;" if he doesn't beg the people's heads off, he is a "poor pastor." If allows a member to insult his manhood he is a "coward;" if he defends himself, he is "marked" at conference. If he keeps his temper under control he is "a weakling;" if he ever loses his temper, "he isn't fit to preach." If, in preaching, he takes an occasional flight in oratory, he is "showing off;" if he doesn't "fly high" when preaching "he just can't hold the people." If he questions the members about themselves, "he is too inquisitive;" if he doesn't, "he is indifferent." If he makes numerous pastoral calls it is "well, what else has our pastor to do?" if he doesn't make pastoral calls it is "the pastor feels he is above us." If he doesn't take a vacation he is accused of "being jealous of an assistant;" if he asks for a vacation, wonder is expresed that "he really needs one." If he doesn't hold out his hand for private donations, he is "too proud;" if he does so, he is a "grafter." If he does not invite other ministers to preach for him "he is afraid of his job;" if he does ask a brother to help him, "he is too lazy to preach himself." If he joins the secret societies he is "looking for the annual sermons;" if he doesn't join the societies, he is "too good to associate with the people who support him." If he preaches against hypocricy and vice he is told to preach "the unadulterated gospel;" when he preaches "thou shalt not commit adultery" he is blamed for "stirring up a mess." If he holds a moment's private conversation with an attractive woman, "there's something between them;" if he doesn't cater to the attractive women in his church "he is afraid of his wife."[3]

It is easy to see that the African Methodist pastor who was trying to cope with the problems of day-to-day survival in the church might not have been in a position to lead his congregation in a unified direction in response to the arrival of large groups of newcomers. "Unified" is the key word here. For, as we will see in the events at "Mother" Bethel, some pastors felt that the influx of migrants provided a solution to their problems, giving them the power base to challenge those who believed that they could do nothing right.

Social Profile

Before the changing role of pastors within African Methodist churches is discussed any further, the reader should know more about these pastors.[4] It is particularly noteworthy in light of the migration that Philadelphia's ministers came from many parts of the country. A much smaller proportion of ministers were born in Philadelphia (only 22 percent) than might be imagined, and more ministers were born in the southeastern United States than in the Northeast (see Table 7.1). This is likely to have been important during the years of heaviest migration. The ministers were probably open and helpful to the migrants if for no other reason than that they often shared a background with some of the new arrivals. J. G. Robinson, in particular, could empathize with many of the new arrivals because he had been "driven out of the South by the Ku Klux Klan."[5]

Prior to the 1920s, the city's A.M.E. pastors were as likely to come from the South as from the North (see Table 7.2). As the most prestigious district in the denomination, Philadelphia attracted the leading ministers from around the country. A change seems to have occurred by 1930; thereafter, very few ministers in the city had not come from the South. Perhaps bishops of the district, like William H. Heard and John Gregg, who both were born in the South, favored southern ministers: certainly during the 1930s and 1940s it appears to have been an advantage to have been born in the South.

Ministers in the A.M.E. Church often came from large families. Of the 19 ministers for whom there is such information, the average number of siblings was 9. However, this average is skewed toward the high side because several ministers came from extremely large families. Robert J. Williams, for instance, was the eldest of a family of 18 children, while W. H. Hoxter was one of 14 and Hodson Waters one of 19 children. It is also likely that large families tended to be mentioned because they were peculiar.

Table 7.1. Place of Birth of Philadelphia's A.M.E. Ministers, 1880–1940

State	Number	% of Total
Delaware	3	4.8
Pennsylvania	14	22.2
New Jersey	2	3.2
Ohio	4	6.3
Illinois	1	1.6
Iowa	1	1.6
District of Columbia	1	1.6
Maryland	8	12.7
Arkansas	3	4.8
Tennessee	1	1.6
West Virginia	1	1.6
Virginia	5	6.3
North Carolina	4	6.3
South Carolina	4	6.3
Georgia	9	14.3
Mississippi	1	1.6
Outside U.S.	2	3.2
Northeast	19	30.2
Southeast	31	47.6
Total	64	

Table 7.2. Origins of Pastors by Region for Each Decade, 1880–1950

	South	North	Elsewhere
1880s	4	2	0
1890s	5	4	0
1900s	8	7	1
1910s	7	10	1
1920s	8	7	0
1930s	11	3	0
1940s	10	2	0

Note: This table reflects the origins of pastors at Philadelphia's churches during each decade listed. One pastor may be counted several times if his pastorates in Philadelphia spanned several decades.

Throughout the period, one of the keys to a pastor's rise in the denomination was early establishment in a Philadelphia church. Generally, it was difficult to achieve this before the age of about thirty-five, unless, like Jabez Campbell Beckett, Henry Harrison Cooper, Jr., and William Richard Gullins, Jr., one's father was a practicing minister in Philadelphia. These three ministers had all grown up in the area and had gone to Philadelphia churches during their childhood years; they had a distinct advantage over ministers not known in the district. Levi J. Coppin's appointment to Mother Bethel in 1879 at the age of thirty-one was a truly exceptional case, especially since Coppin had moved north from Maryland as recently as 1869 and had spent most of the intervening years in Wilmington, Delaware. His courtship of Fanny Jackson, which began at about the time of his Bethel appointment, might help explain his meteoric rise in the church. Usually, though, a pastor reached his late thirties or early forties before becoming established in Philadelphia. Even then he was most often appointed to one of the newer, smaller churches in the district. When, in 1916, Robert J. Williams jumped from the small A.M.E. churches in Chester County, Pennsylvania, to Mother Bethel, he was justified in believing he was heading toward the bishopric, even though he was already forty-five years old.

Between 1890 and 1940, Philadelphia's African Methodist pastors were generally very well educated. Of the 61 pastors for whom there is information regarding educational background, 54 (or 89 percent) had been to college—Wilberforce University being the college most commonly attended.[6] Further, the seven pastors who had not been to college had all graduated from high school, and all except 3 supplemented high school with some form of night school or Bible college. For example, Robert Williams attended the Institute of Colored Youth, while Spencer Carpenter worked with tutors at Harvard and Boston University. Not surprisingly, the pastors for whom information about educational attainment is available tend to have been the more educated ones. Even so, the message must have been clear to young ministers in the denomination: to succeed in a Philadelphia ministry in the A.M.E. Church it was essential to be educated.

The ministers' connections with colleges did not cease after graduation. At least half the sample were recorded as having received an honorary degree such as a doctorate of divinity or an LL.D, many of them from their alma maters. An honorary degree was clearly a mark of success within the denomination; the letters denoting it usually accompanied the names of ministers so honored. Conferring such honors on ministers was probably an important money-raising technique for colleges that were hard pressed for funds.

Two important events in the making of a minister were often associated with his college years. The average age for the conversion to African Methodism, which in some cases meant confirmation of religious affilation, was eighteen, roughly coinciding with a student's first year in college. Licensing on the average occurred when the individual was almost twenty-four years old, often soon after graduation from a college. Harry P. Anderson, who converted while at Wilberforce University in 1893 and was licensed after finishing his theological courses, was typical of many. The age at conversion and the age of licensing reaffirm the importance of college in the minister's training and in shaping the liturgy that the churches would conform to.[7]

The emphasis on learning is not surprising given the importance attributed to education by members of African American communities throughout the United States in the years following the Civil War. This emphasis seemed to decline between 1920 and 1940. Owing to the small sample size, however, a trend cannot be determined with certitude from the information gathered.[8] Nevertheless, other sources suggest that during the 1930s and 1940s emphasis on a minister's education declined markedly. In his autobiography, Bishop Richard R. Wright, Jr., mentioned that several people complained that his style of preaching was too "educated."[9] Further, writing in the 1930s, Mays and Nicholson noted that ministers of all denominations sometimes endeavored to conceal their education, which was considered undesirable in a minister.[10]

From the educational backgrounds of the ministers, we can perhaps infer that the socioeconomic standing of their parents was generally good. Several individuals followed paths like that of Booker T. Washington, who worked his way through Hampton Institute. When he was young, Harry P. Anderson supported his mother and sister on their farm in Pennsylvania by working at a brickyard, and then supported himself through Wilberforce with dining-car service during his vacations. William H.H. Butler left home at the age of twelve, after his father died, and did "chores" to provide income for board and lodging. He then joined the army at the age of fifteen and fought in the Civil War. Similarly, Carpenter helped support his family in Cambridge, Massachusetts, by becoming an apprentice at Harvard University Press. On the whole, though, most men preparing for the ministry must have received some help from their parents for their education, and one suspects that they were not the most impoverished members of the black community. As already noted, several ministers were sons of clergymen.

Before being licensed, 16 (or 25 percent) of the ministers worked. Often employment helped to pay for their education. Frequently, they were teachers at either elementary or secondary schools, showing once again a relationship between the church and education. Very few ministers held down another job while serving in the ministry. In Philadelphia, for most of the period, this would have been unnecessary. The churches were sufficiently well established financially to pay a salary that would enable the minister to commit himself full-time to his work. Matthew H. Jones, who worked at the docks briefly and then owned a garage out of which Yellow Cabs operated, was an exception to this rule. However, his pastorates were at smaller congregations in the Philadelphia suburbs and his ministerial income was never sufficient to provide for his family. Also, his education at Hampton Institute in Virginia and at a mechanical trade school in New York gave him an appreciation of cars that he did not want to surrender.[11]

Two other kinds of information are worth particular attention. Marriage was encouraged by the denomination, and ministers were instructed that they "should marry wherever possible and present an example of pure family life to the community."[12] In both of the denomination's encyclopedias ministers' wives' names are usually mentioned, probably because the character and abilities of the minister's wife were thought crucial to the success of his ministry. Matthew H. Jones, who married twice, noted that his first wife, Marjorie Sougher, whom he had met while at Hampton Institute, had helped him "greatly." Her excellent singing ability was particularly helpful to Jones because she improved the musical content of his services and made them more appealing to his congregations.[13] Of the 64 ministers, 49 (77 percent) recorded that they were married. Twelve were married twice. On the death of the first wife, a minister often felt the need of a second "helpmeet," if only to act as his liaison with the women in his congregation.[14]

Finally, many of the ministers belonged to at least one fraternal order and some belonged to several. Some resistance to the fraternal orders had characterized A.M.E. churches during the nineteenth century, partly because it was believed that the orders might divert male members from church. According to the *Centennial Encyclopaedia*, the General Conference of 1836 had passed a resolution declaring "that no preacher should be permitted to graduate with ministerial functions who is and continues to be a member of any Free Masons' Lodge." In 1844 and 1848 petitions opposing Masonry were presented to the general conferences, but they were ignored; the Conference of 1848 resolved to take "no further action on the subject." "Since that time," the *Encyclopaedia* continued, "there has been no great opposition to Masonry in the Church. On the contrary, many of the leading Churches' bishops and elders have been also leaders in Masonry."[15]

During the last decades of the nineteenth century, ministers began to join the orders in large numbers. Of the 52 ministers for whom there was information about affiliations, 23 belonged to at least one fraternal order. Membership was more common among ministers who were licensed later in the century (Table 7.3). After 1890, over half the ministers licensed joined the orders.

The Free and Accepted Masons were the most popular group among the ministers with 16 members. They were followed by the Elks (10 members), Odd Fellows (8 members), and Knights of Pythias (6 members). The True Reformers and Good Templars each had one minister as a member. The increased participation of ministers in the orders indicated the extent to which the ministerial role had become more explicitly political and had deviated from the ideal of detachment and mediation within the congregation. Robert J. Williams's establishment of a group of Free and Accepted Masons at Mother Bethel, for example, was most probably a political act that, through the order's secret bonds, helped him solidify his support within the church.

Ministerial Crisis

Every aspect of pastoring was considered in the A.M.E. Church *Review*. In 1913, the new editor, Reverdy C. Ransom, believing that the church

Table 7.3. Ministers' Membership in Orders by Licensing Date

	Members	Nonmembers	% of Members
1845–1869	1	5	16.7
1870–1889	4	12	25.0
1890–1909	10	7	58.8
1910–1919	8	6	57.14

needed theological and organizational direction, published a series of articles focusing on the state of the church and the need for changes. He
shared with others a sense of crisis in the church that well-trained and
well-organized pastors, supported by laymen and women, could overcome. From these articles it is possible to gain a clear view of what the
ideal qualifications for the ministry were and what the reality of the
situation was increasingly to become.

The ideal qualifications of African Methodist ministers resembled
those for ministers of white Methodist churches. J. A. Walker asserted
that the minister must have had a conversion of the heart (i.e., been
"born again"), must have a divine call to the office, and must undergo
physical, intellectual, and spiritual preparation. The result would be a
minister of the following description:

> 1. Like his Lord, he will speak and preach as one having authority. Not
> with egotism, but from a heart conscious of authority from God. . . . 2.
> His teachings will be placed within the reach of his hearers; not a
> barbarian speaking in an unknown tongue. . . . 3. Like his Master, he
> goes about doing good. Here the following Scriptural quotation should
> have full play: "For the Son of Man came not to be ministered unto, but
> to minister, and give His life a ransom for many." . . . 4. Like his Master,
> he will have love for all men for the salvation of their souls. . . . 5. He
> will feed the flock of Christ with that which nourishes; not the husks of
> stale food.[16]

Besides these Christ-like qualities, the minister was also supposed
to be a man of the world. People like Carpenter found it difficult to
balance the sometimes contradictory requirements. The pastor must
know the "modus operandi of organizations," Rev. P. A. Nichols wrote.
He should know his people so well that he is able "to organize them into
groups and clubs according to age, temperament, vocation, and social
standing" without creating any friction in the organization's operation.
"He must," Nichols concluded, "know how to keep these different organizations intact, and how to infuse new life in them, when necessary,
without usurping the authority of officials."[17]

After performing such miracles the minister must have felt that he
was not being paid enough,[18] Added to this, though, he had to be a
businessman and a social director. Properties had to be bought and sold
and mortgages secured. Large sums of money therefore passed through
his hands. According to C. H. Stepteau: "Even where he is fortunate
enough to have officers who have the time and knowledge to attend to

all the details of the Church, the Minister should nevertheless know how. . . . This is the Minister's life work, his task, his living, herein is involved the comfort of his home. In his ability to manage and to do the work of the church lies his future."[19] Since, as we have seen, many ministers had experience in the banking world, handling finances was not usually beyond their capabilities, and often there were several trustees with financial and legal experience of some kind. However, when a church fell into financial difficulties it was the minister who had to bear the responsibility for failure, and if he was unsuccessful he might be appointed to a pastorate at a small African Methodist settlement, where he might be unable to support his family.

The minister was also required to provide social diversion for members of his congregation, and at the same time avoid the taint of commercialism. "When entertainments are arranged for churches the real purpose should be, not financial results alone," Rev. A. L. Gaines wrote, "but that the church may take its rightful place in directing the minds of the young along the lines of literary, dramatic and musical art; and not, therefore, yield to the theatre and club room in its attractiveness and training power." Diversions were for the "uplift" of members, not for their entertainment. "The physical, hygienic and spiritual idea must be prevalent," Gaines continued. Diversions "should be stamped with the approval of the church by being lifted far above similar diversions and games conducted by the world and contaminated by gambling influences."[20] Such requirements increased the difficulties of the minister's job markedly. While the new games and entertainments developing in urban America provided him with new schemes for bringing people into the church, many of them, like the movie houses and baseball parks, competed with the churches for the same audience.

This competition was clearly articulated in a *Philadelphia Tribune* editorial entitled "The Churches and the Moving Picture Shows." The writer described a Sunday service at one of the large churches in Philadelphia:

> Recently we spent an hour in a big church, and listened to a long and rambling sermon on the rewards and punishments of the future life, when the things that worried us were the hard labor, small rewards and many aches and pains that bother us now in this present life. Half an hour more was spent listening to mournful music and earnest appeals for money to keep the Lord's work going. The whole business made us restless, dull, and heavy.

After the service, the writer "felt so down in the mouth from the solemnity of the church experience that [he was] in no humor to go home to bed, and possibly to ugly dreams." He therefore went into a moving picture show where he "spent another hour and a half listening to good music, full of snap and go, and seeing people do things, sad and gay, that were natural to say and do." Leaving the theater with "the good impression of the show full upon us," he wondered why the churches could not "give us better music . . . and teach us more about the philosophy of living and less about the dogmatism of dying."[21]

By the second decade of the twentieth century there was considerable confusion, due partly to the pressures of outside competition, about the path that ministers should take in their preaching. The black preacher of "education, refinement and culture," described by William Creditt as the product of white teachers, no longer seemed to make any headway with his audiences.[22] Rev. J.T.S. White, editor of the "Homiletic Section" of the *Review*, complained that the preaching function was becoming less and less important in the church of his day. "I do not believe it can be said," he wrote,

> that we have produced a single educated man in the last twenty years of
> the race's freedom who through his sermons has been able to touch the
> people at all points as squarely, and to hold them as securely, as did the
> preacher of slave times, or his untutored successors immediately after
> emancipation. People no longer travel miles and miles just to hear a
> sermon as they did in those days. In but few places, if any, in our
> religious commonwealth, can it be claimed that the pulpit is the chief
> drawing card of the church. Music, vested choirs, organizations, catch-
> penny sensational subjects are resorted to in order to get the people out
> to church.[23]

The waning power of the pulpit noted by White was also detected by the A.M.E. bishops. At the Twenty-fifth General Conference, held in St. Louis in May 1920, they called for an "awakening in evangelism," wanting "each minister of the A.M.E. Church [to] become an evangelical flaming torch, lighted from heaven's burning and holy altar, scattering live coals from between the wings of seraphim, who stand on either side of heaven's throne of unexcelled beatific whiteness, in this antiphonal chant."[24] On the whole, however, African Methodist ministers had not been trained to be flaming torches of evangelism. Among those who were able to put aside their training and to develop more theatrical, less

ponderous forms of preaching, some reaped benefits in the form of extremely devoted followings that could be manipulated for political purposes.

Few African Methodist preachers met the ideal qualifications for
the position in their entirety, though many pastors fulfilled some of
them. "The danger signal that we see here and there cropping out," the
minutes of the Philadelphia Conference of 1897 read, "which is calculated to bring discredit upon the Church of Christ, is the unholy ambition for place and power. The means ofttimes used to bring about the
desired results, cause the blush of shame to tinge the brow of Christian
manhood." The conference minutes also noted that "several incompe-
tent men have found their way into the ministerial ranks; men who can
neither manage the financial nor spiritual interests of any church or bring
success along any line, who are continuously on the wing from one conference to the other."[25]

For Spencer Carpenter, the ministry had become too political and
its members too preoccupied with pulling crowds in to their services.
There was also too much infighting among these men as they sparred to
increase the size of their congregations at the expense of others. The
time had come, he suggested, "for petty jealousies and strifes to be put
down in the ministry." He continued, "Not all ministers can preach so as
to draw the crowds, but every consecrated man in the pulpit can preach
that Christ was crucified for a sinful world. Let the crowd go where it
will!"

Besides this problem, the minister often found himself at war with
members of his congregation. Carpenter believed that things were so bad
that it was necessary for ministers to establish a "big brotherhood" to
protect each other from "the assaults of that class of church membership
which believes, not so much in following Christ, but in watching the
minister and embracing every opportunity to slug him with stones." He
described an incident that reveals the type of conflict that could develop
within the churches. A pastor objected to having his desk moved to
make way for entertainments. The officers and most of the members of
the church, according to Carpenter, supported the pastor's objection and
agreed with him that the vestry and not the auditorium was the place for
church entertainments. But a segment of the congregation disagreed and
argued that the pastor was overstepping his authority by refusing "to
allow his pulpit to be used for a concert stage." Carpenter continued,

> At the time when those who opposed the pastor were striving to muster a
> display of strength and fight him in his stand for at least one sacred place
> in the church, one of our Bishops, a man whose heart is running over
> with big brotherhood, visited that church, and without the pastor's
> knowledge, and in the pastor's absence, openly congratulated the church
> for having a pastor who stood firmly against having his pulpit desk
> removed. "Thank God he is one minister I know who insists that his
> pulpit is not the place for cantatas, entertainments, and such things."
> That declaration of the Bishop silenced completely all opposition to the
> pastor.[26]

Had the bishop not stepped in to aid his subordinate, however, the outcome might have been different. Yet the fact that the minister felt it was
his role to challenge those members who had moved his desk and to
"overstep his authority" perhaps showed an increase in the political
power of the pastor within the denomination. At an earlier time, the
pastor would possibly have suffered the indignity in silence and hoped
that his next appointment would be more to his liking. Clearly, the minister's work had become more complicated and more political than the
preaching of the gospel alone.

As noted earlier, the role that pastors played in mediating between
different groups in their congregations was made possible largely by the
system of itinerancy enforced throughout the denomination. During
most of the nineteenth century pastors seldom stayed at a church more
than two years, or one term. In Bishop Turner's mind there was good
reason for keeping pastorates brief. "Some of the big churches have been
quite disappointed and some have become quite indignant at the Bishop
for changing their pastors at the end of two years," he wrote, in 1910.
"But the Bishop says forty-nine out of every fifty of our ministers preach
all they know in two years, and besides if a church has a good thing, they
ought to be willing to pass it around and give someone else a little of it."[27]
By the end of the century it became more usual for pastors to spend two
terms at each church, and by the second decade of the twentieth century
pastors remained at the same location for three, and sometimes as many
as four, terms. By 1935, William H. Heard, bishop of the First Episcopal
District, defended the notion that five or six years was enough for a
single pastorate. "It is now time to make complete changes," he wrote.
"It is not good for a minister to remain in one place for more than five or
six years, for the effect of his work has begun to deteriorate by that
time."[28]

Between 1870 and 1949, the mean number of years in the pastorate climbed from 2.5 (or a little more than a single term) before 1890, to nearly 5.5 (or almost three full terms) after 1930 (see Table 7.4).[29] The minister's success at a church became increasingly dependent on his ability to gain the support of his congregation. If members of the church decided that they did not like the pastor, he was replaced. If the opposite was the case, then the pastorate might continue until the pastor was offered a more appealing appointment or, in some cases, died.

Increasing the length of pastorates altered the relationship between the pastor and his congregation. Previously, the minister knew that his stay at a church would be brief and that his best course of action was to deal with financial difficulties and to raise money for the missionary work of the denomination (largely by inspiring women members of the congregation). Increasingly, after 1900, the minister realized that by working for or overturning an entrenched male elite within his congregation he could remain at a particular church for many years, biding his time until a better position came along.

As Reverdy C. Ransom recognized, the change in length of pastorates was partly the result of the movement of the black population into northern cities. "As the great cities of our nation expanded the Negro population into the number of hundreds of thousands of Negroes," he wrote, "it created both an appeal and an opportunity for individual ministers and bishops to endeavor to establish little ecclesiastical principalities in many cities and states throughout the country."[30] As we shall see, Robert J. Williams was thinking along these lines as he responded to the influx of migrants into Mother Bethel.

Pastors had several reasons for supporting the migration and for

Table 7.4. Mean Number of Years Served by Pastors at Churches to Which They Were Appointed between 1870 and 1949

Years	Mean	Standard Deviation	Cases
1870–1889	2.50	0.94	14
1890–1909	3.36	1.82	45
1910–1929	3.68	1.55	37
1930–1949	5.43	3.62	37

wishing to help the former Southerners. First, there was the idealism associated with their training as Christian ministers; they had been directed to help the person in need just as the Good Samaritan had done. Second, many of them had pastored in the South; they knew the problems in that region and could empathize with those arriving in a big city for the first time. Third, the pastors were professionals, and like all professionals within the black community, they stood to gain from the expansion of the black population in the city. Pastoring a large church or increasing the size of a small church placed a minister in a strong position when new appointments were made. The higher up the hierarchy the individual climbed, the more financially secure he would be. Just as the business person or other professional wished to be more secure, so also did the minister, and for some, the newcomers were the ticket to this security.

However, the increasingly political character of both the pulpit and the pew suggests that it was not easy for the pastor to unite his congregation behind the cause of helping migrants. Indeed, the African Methodist churches that newcomers from the South joined were not places noted for being pacific. As a result, rather than creating new problems, migrants exacerbated those that were already evident within the congregations.

PART III

The "Great Migration"

Previous Page

Migrants in Jacksonville Union Terminal Colored Waiting Room, 1921.
Courtesy Florida State Archives

CHAPTER 8

Many "Promised Lands"

*Mother Bethel is happy to say that at least four hundred of our
brothers and sisters from the South land are safely within our fold.
And among them some of the best blood of the South. Men of
means as well as character.*

REV. ROBERT J. WILLIAMS, JR., 1917

Commentators and historians have written that many of the newcomers
to Philadelphia came in search of the Promised Land, and, indeed, the
image of the Exodus of the Israelites from Egypt was continually in-
voked by black religious leaders and lay people alike. However, the
Promised Land meant different things to different newcomers. For migrants with some urban experience in the South, the Promised Land was
a land of opportunity where they believed they would receive higher
wages and political rights, while their children would benefit from better
schooling. Rural migrants also wanted these "perquisites of American
society," to use James R. Grossman's term,[1] but their main concerns
were far more immediate. For them, the Promised Land was a haven
from both the bondage of debt associated with cotton farming and the
terror of the lynch mob.

This chapter examines two different sources of information about
the migrant population: the Philadelphia Housing Association study of
1924, and the letters of transmittal held at Mother Bethel A.M.E.
Church. What these sources reveal, above all, is the diversity of backgrounds from which the migrants came. This diversity has been over-

looked in the historiography of the "Great Migration," some historians describing the Southerners exclusively as "refugees" or "mudsills" and others referring to them as well-prepared "migrants."[2] Once we discard the idea of a uniform migrant population, we may discover other reasons the North was a land of hope and become more sensitive to divisions existing within churches and other institutions that acted as pillars of African American communities.

The 1924 Migrant Study

Early in 1924, several interviewers working on a policy-oriented social science survey for the Philadelphia Housing Association visited houses in Philadelphia in which new arrivals from the South were known to be residing. Among other things, they wanted to know what these men and women had done before leaving the South and why they had decided to leave. One of the interviewers visited a house at 4312 Fairmount Avenue, in the western section of the city, an area into which African Americans had just begun to move. Here, he found three apartments occupied by four families—a total of thirty-one people altogether. One family came from outside Lawrence, South Carolina; the other three families, who were related, came from near Moultree, Georgia. All four families had been living on farmland in the South, and all had felt compelled to leave because the boll weevil had made it impossible for them "to raise the cotton." The comments of Thomas Williams, aged fifty and patriarch of all three of the families from Georgia, indicate that he did not like Philadelphia and, together with his wife, wished to return to the South. His children, however, intended to remain in the city.

Another interviewer visited a row house at 1315 Locust Street, in the heart of Philadelphia's old black community. In the first-floor apartment he found two families of former Southerners. The first, Wardell and Betty McVey, were very different from Williams and his family. They had moved north from Charlotte, North Carolina, which in the early 1920s was a city of almost fifty thousand inhabitants. The McVeys were young, Wardell twenty-six and Betty twenty-four; Wardell had been an unskilled laborer, while Betty had been a cook; they had no children and, they told the interviewer, had moved north "to make more money."

The Simpsons, a family of three who lodged with the McVeys, hailed from a farm near Newberry, South Carolina, a small city of less than six thousand inhabitants. They had been tenant farmers who had paid their rent in bales of cotton. Like the Williams family and most other former cotton farmers interviewed by the Housing Association, the Simpsons had left their farm because the boll weevil had made it impossible to pay rent and still have cotton left over to sell at a profit; and, like Thomas Williams and his wife, they were relatively old, Lawson forty-one and Lydia forty. Unlike other former farmers, however, the Simpsons had with them only one child. This was sixteen-year-old Fannie, who attended sixth grade (several grades below her age group).[3] While the young McVeys were happy in Philadelphia and intended to stay, the Simpsons were finding life difficult and wished to return south.

The diversity is made even more apparent by a statistical analysis of the survey from which these interviews were taken. The survey was undertaken by William D. Fuller, a white sociology student from the Wharton School who was hired in 1924 by the Housing Association to survey African Americans recently arrived in Philadelphia from the South.[4] Governor Gifford Pinchot had become concerned about the social problems arising from an influx of southern migrants and, like other social science–oriented Progressives who felt that effective action was impossible without a base of information, he commissioned a survey.

Fuller and his associates personally visited 435 residences known to house migrants; of these, 87 (which housed 114 families and 31 single individuals) were included in the survey. The extremely detailed survey elicited a wide variety of information, such as the size and number of rooms occupied by the migrants both in the North and in the South, the reasons for the move north, whether or not work was found on arrival, wages earned before and after moving, and membership in fraternal and religious organizations.

In spite of the wealth of information available in "The Negro Migrant in Philadelphia," Fuller's report made no significant impact on policymaking, partly because the rate of migration had slowed, and the problems seemed less pressing. Moreover, Fuller's conclusions merely supported the widespread belief that the migration witnessed the movement of people from the rural South to the urban North. Not attuned to any diversity within his sample, he made no attempt to differentiate among migrants according to their backgrounds except on the basis of state of origin (showing only that large numbers of migrants were from Georgia, the Carolinas, and Florida, whereas their predecessors had come mainly from Maryland and Virginia).[5]

More recently historian Fredric Miller has examined the data; although migrant diversity is not his focus Miller points to diversity in the motivation underlying the move north, arguing that the decision-making process was not dependent upon a push/pull process.[6] Some moved, he maintains, because they felt they had no other choice; others moved because they learned that they would have better opportunities elsewhere. The push/pull process cannot be dismissed entirely, for those who were being pushed off the land had to decide where they would go, and those being pulled north were attracted by things they lacked at home. While Miller determines that migrants came from both urban and rural backgrounds, he does not attempt to link background and reasons for migrating.

To shed light on the characterisitics of the two groups being either pushed or pulled north, I have examined differences between families from rural and urban backgrounds.[7] I classified the two groups by population of previous community and by previous occupation. The rural group consisted of families that either had come north from a place with fewer than twenty-five hundred inhabitants (that is, from a place defined as rural in the U.S. census) or had as head of household someone who had been working in a specifically rural occupation such as farming. The urban group included those families coming from places with a population of more than thirty thousand (provided they had been employed in nonrural occupations). Eighteen families were omitted from the rural–urban comparison because it was unclear whether they were urban or rural. Single individuals were also excluded because, owing to their transience, they were seriously underrepresented in the survey.

This classification revealed a migrant population made up of sixty-five rural families and thirty-one urban families—roughly reflecting the proportions of rural and urban population throughout the South, and indicating at the outset that both groups must be recognized in any history of the northward migration. Further analysis showed each group to have different reasons for leaving the South and differing levels of preparation for their new environments. It makes sense, then, to divide the migrant population into two ideal types: "migrant families," who generally set out from urban areas, and "refugee families," who generally came directly from rural areas. The migrants were people in search of upward mobility—both economic and political. Attuned to opportunities outside their own community that might offer them a better standard of living, they were usually prepared for the move to their new home. The economic and political refugees either had been pushed off the land because of the boll weevil's destruction of the cotton crop or had been terrorized into fleeing a harsh racial climate.

Of course, Philadelphia's new arrivals did not all fit into one or the other of these two ideal types. Rather, a migration continuum encompassing all of them stretched between the urban migrant and rural refugee groups. Generally speaking, people at the migrant end of the continuum had spent some time in a southern city, while those at the refugee end tended to be sharecroppers or tenant farmers who had little economic power owing to the control of their livelihoods by merchants and landowners. The refugees were more likely to be victimized by the white mob. Near to this latter group on the continuum were some wealthy farmers whose success brought hostility from the surrounding white community and who had to flee the South. Commitment to the land and lack of experience of urban environments kept these people outside the more advantaged migrant group, while their relative wealth (if they did not, like so many, lose their savings soon after arrival in the city) and their access to resources through their social position placed them on the margins of the refugee group.

Placing women on this continuum requires special care. In many instances, women can be positioned according to their families' backgrounds. Particularly when a woman was traveling alone, however, this might not be the case. Migration of young women into service jobs in the cities might be a strategy to enable a family to hold onto its land and remain where it was. In such cases, whatever experiences occurred after arrival in the city, the familial connections with her home (such as children left in the care of a mother) would have placed considerable restraints on a woman and would have made her ambivalent about life in her new surroundings. Near to such a woman on the continuum would be the individual who, according to historian Darlene Clark Hine, wished to escape from a condition of domestic violence.[8] Such conditions were exacerbated by the breakup of the sharecropping system and tensions arising from the process of migration itself, and so were in many ways linked to the difficulties that all refugees faced in coming to terms with a changing patriarchal system. Once these women arrived in the city, however, they might act very differently from the women who maintained connections with their homes and who might wish to return. These refugees from domestic violence might have seen the migration as a truly liberating one, even though the urban experience, given the marginal position of so many people, might not have been very different

from what they had been used to, at least in terms of the relations between men and women. Finally, women who came north after experi-
encing life in a southern city, perhaps working as a teacher or even in
service work, and who gave as their reason for moving north the opportunity to earn better wages and get better benefits should be placed at
the "migrant" end of the continuum.

Clear differences are evident between urban and rural groups in
terms of motivation underlying the migration. Each household head gave
the interviewers his or her main reason for leaving the South. These fit
into three groupings: positive reasons (things that were attractive about
the North); negative reasons (problems in the South); and family connections in Philadelphia.[9] The last grouping was kept separate from the
"positive" grouping because it explained more why the migrants selected Philadelphia as opposed to another northern destination, not why
they wished to move in the first place. Similar percentages of both
groups had family connections in Philadelphia, but the rural group was
heavily weighted toward negative reasons for moving, while members of
the urban group tended to give more positive reasons (see Table 8.1).
Rural people more often moved north reluctantly, believing, as so many
rural African Americans did at the time, that their proper place was on
the land.[10]

The rural and urban migrants also tended to have different patterns of migration. While the flow of urban migrants into Philadelphia
was fairly regular, the rural group had a more dramatic increase in migration during the heaviest months of the 1923 migration (Table 8.2). This

Table 8.1. Reasons for Moving North by Rural and Urban Groupings

| | Rural | | Urban | |
	No.	%	No.	%
Negative	34	52.5	8	25.8
Positive	15	23.1	13	41.9
Family	16	24.6	10	32.3
Total	65	100.2	31	100.0

Note: Contingency coefficient, .26; significance, .04. The coefficient is low because the family category is
included. Moreover, the statistics show a pattern more like a continuum than a clearcut division between
rural and urban people.

Table 8.2. Date of Arrival of Head of Household by Rural and Urban Groupings

	Rural		Urban	
	No.	*%*	*No.*	*%*
Summer 1922	9	13.8	8	25.8
Oct. 1922–Feb. 1923	13	20.0	6	19.4
Mar.–July 1923	31	47.7	9	29.0
Aug. 1923–Jan. 1924	12	18.5	8	25.8
Total	65		31	

finding confirms reports indicating that most of the rural people arrived in the city between March and July of 1923.[11] It also suggests that families with urban backgrounds came throughout the year, whenever they had made their preparations, while rural families came in a large wave when the migration propaganda was at its highest or when they had determined that they were sitting on another failed cotton crop. In either case, the likelihood is that they were less prepared for the city than their urban counterparts.

Once in Philadelphia, rural household heads generally had greater difficulty getting work than their urban counterparts. While more than half of the rural migrants said they had had difficulty getting a job, the corresponding figure was 40 percent for the urban group. The important factor in this disparity was age; being younger, the urban migrants found work more easily than rural migrants. Indeed, age of household head was one of the crucial differences between the two groups, the rural group having a mean age (35.4, $n = 64$) five years higher than that of the urban group (30.2, $n = 27$).[12] This age difference adds to the impression that migrants from the cities were younger people in search of better opportunities. The older rural migrants would have been more settled in their former residences and unwilling to move but for the fact that circumstances forced them to do so.

The size of families of both groups also seems to confirm the more settled character of rural people prior to their migration. Not surprisingly, given that the heads of the rural families were older, these families had more children than those from the large cities (Table 8.3).[13] Of 34 families with 3 or more children, only 2 were from the urban grouping. It

Table 8.3. Mean Number of Children per Family by Age Groups and Rural and Urban Groupings

	Mean	Standard Deviation	Cases
Rural	3.0	2.6	62
Under 25	1.7	1.3	11
25–29 years	1.8	1.5	11
30+ years	3.7	2.9	40
Urban	1.0	1.1	27
Under 25	0.8	0.8	5
25–29 years	0.6	0.8	10
30+	1.4	1.4	12

seems a fair supposition that people with larger families would be more reluctant to move, especially to a city, than those with smaller families. While a large number of children represented a boon for a farmer, since there would be laborers to help on the farm, so many children were a serious hindrance in the city. Controlling the two populations for age confirmed the existence of a clear difference between them. While the average number of children per rural family tended to increase greatly with the age of the head of household, it did not vary to such an extent for urban families.[14] This suggests, perhaps, that members of the latter group limited their reproduction in some way. After living in a city in the South, they perhaps realized that a large family did not improve one's standard of living.

Since rural parents were generally older, so also were their children. The average age of the eldest nonworking, school-age child in each family was 9.2 years for the rural group, while for the urban group the age was only 5.4 years. This age difference was particularly important because it meant that many more of the children from rural backgrounds had missed out on education. The desire for education seems to have been very strong in the minds of all migrants, and they seldom failed to take advantage of education when it was offered to them. However, because of poor schooling in southern states, over 75 percent of the oldest school-age children in each family were three grades or more behind their age group when they entered Philadelphia schools. Fifty-eight percent were between five and eight grades behind. The number of urban children in school was insufficient to determine whether they had been better educated than the rural children; the important question here is whether the children entered schools in their new city at an early enough age to reap the benefits of better-funded education. Looking again at the eldest child in each family, it is clear that many rural children were too old when they came to Philadelphia to get the most possible benefit from the city's schools. Of the 50 children with rural backgrounds 36 (or 70 percent) were already of school age, while only 6 of the 15 children with urban backgrounds (or 40 percent) were in this age group. Rural households, then, were often disadvantaged by the older age of their head of household, by their larger number of children, and also by the older age of their children.

Again not surprisingly, rural families in their new homes had to contend with higher residential densities than urban families; the mean number of individuals per room for rural families was 2.5 ($n = 65$), while for urban families it was only 1.8 ($n = 31$).[15] Besides being less comfortable, the rural families were more exposed to diseases, which spread more easily in overcrowded conditions, and were less likely to have a spare room to rent for supplemental income. When they did sublet rooms, rural migrants often severely increased their overcrowding. And because their families were large, they had to spend on average more than $2.50 per month more on rent than their urban counterparts.

Moving north from a southern city often meant that a family head either had some kind of skill or at least some industrial experience. Unfortunately for migrants, however, such backgrounds did not translate into skilled jobs in Philadelphia because very few firms employed black people in skilled positions during the 1920s. Only 9 household heads from the 1924 sample were definitely employed in skilled positions; of these, 5 had come from large cities, 2 from small urban areas, and 2 from rural areas (see Tables 1.1 and 1.2). Nevertheless, the urban group seemed to fit a more traditional wage structure, with the youngest earning the least and the oldest earning the most, while the rural group's mean wage was made high by the anomalous mean wage of its youngest members (Table 8.4). Perhaps younger rural migrants were able to adjust to urban life more readily than older rural migrants. However, this would not explain why they earned more than members of the urban group. It is possible that while members of the urban group secured mainstream unskilled industrial jobs, the younger rural migrants were doing odd jobs and moonlighting.

The small size of their families allowed urban heads of households

Table 8.4. Mean Wage of Household Head by Age Groups and Rural and Urban Groupings

	Mean ($/Week)	Standard Deviation	No.
Rural	20.3	9.5	64
Under 25	24.5	6.1	11
25–29 years	19.6	11.1	12
30+ years	19.4	9.6	41
Urban	17.3	12.2	27
Under 25	11.6	12.1	5
25–29 years	15.2	10.9	10
30+ years	21.5	12.8	12
Total	19.6	10.0	102

to spend on average a little more money on each family member. Although total family income was greater for the rural group, owing to the greater number of wage earners in rural families, income per family member was actually $1.50 per week less for rural than for urban families.[16]

With respect to the friends and relatives that members of each group had in the city prior to arrival, the two groups were fairly similar. A large proportion of both groups had connections with people in the city prior to arrival, though for the rural group this figure was higher (89 percent as compared to 68 percent). A few rural migrants went to places where they knew absolutely no one, but on the whole they were less likely to do so than members of the urban group. Urban life in the South may have made urban blacks more used to living apart from family and friends, or more confident that they would be able to make connections when they arrived in the city.

Another apparent similarity between the groups was their church membership in Philadelphia.[17] In the South, church membership levels were fairly even between the two groups—about 87 percent of both groups were church members before leaving. In Philadelphia, the rural group seemed a little more reluctant to become affiliated with a church. While 37 percent of former churchgoers among the urban group had already attached themselves to a congregation, only 28 percent of the rural migrants had done so.[18] This difference is magnified by the fact that more elite churches (Protestant Episcopal, Presbyterian, Methodist, and some Baptist) had more stringent requirements for membership than the more democratic churches (mainly Baptist and Holiness). Many members of the rural group would have been looking for a congregation in which they felt comfortable or trying to establish their own church with friends and relatives from their former community.[19]

The desire to return to the South among migrants is difficult to interpret. On the one hand, people who came north because they felt they had little choice would have been unlikely to go home unless things were extremely bad in their new home (although some returned south without going home). On the other hand, those people who came north full of high expectations might have desired to return home at the slightest disappointment. Even so, rural migrants more often expressed a desire to return. Almost 30 percent had definitely decided to return as compared to only 16 percent of the urban group. A further 37.5 percent of the rural group were either undecided or thought they might return; for the urban group this figure was 32 percent. Since a larger proportion of the rural group had felt compelled to leave the South in the first place, these figures suggest that this group was more disaffected from the new urban environment than was the case for migrants who had experienced some city life in the South.

Migrants who had had prior urban experience clearly did not always fare better than their rural counterparts. In terms of income, for example, the sample included a group of young rural migrants who were able to earn higher wages than the rest of the former Southerners. Nevertheless, the analysis suggests that experience before migration was important. The higher age of members of the rural group, their larger number of children, their more negative reasons for coming north, and their more frequent desire to return home, all suggest that they were less prepared to face life in a northern metropolis.

What this analysis suggests is that historians need to give greater consideration to the southern city as a destination for black migrants leaving rural areas and as a preparation ground for the larger metropolitan areas of the North. James Grossman's dismissal of the southern city as a significant part of the Great Migration story, derived from a northern bias found in both the original documents associated with the migration and in the historiography generally, is typical. Historians and commentators alike have assumed that the only land of hope was in northern states. In Grossman's narrative, therefore, when migrants "tarried in a southern town or city" they did so "because they could afford to go no farther." The southern city was no more than "a convenient stopping place, either to earn enough to continue north or to learn the ways of the city and acquire some urban job skills." And should it be imagined that migrants who "tarried" for extended periods in the southern city might have learned some important city ways helpful to them when they reached their "final destination," Grossman adds that "even in the larger cities in the South, blacks often lived amid what Monroe Work described as late as 1923 as 'country conditions.'"[20]

However, Work's main point in the article, "Research with Respect to Cooperation between Urban and Rural Communities," was that the migration was a national phenomenon from rural areas to cities, not a sectional one from south to north. Work wrote:

> The migration from the rural districts of the South directly to the cities
> of the North has not been as great as the movement from country
> districts to cities; even the migration of 1916–1920 was for the major part,
> a movement of Negroes from the country districts to cities. This included
> for the most part, migration to the North from cities of the South and
> migration from country districts of the South into Southern cities to
> replace those who went North.

Work did describe the "country conditions" of some southern cities, but he made it clear that he was referring only to housing conditions. "That is," Work wrote by way of qualification, "although . . . in towns, [a large number of the urban Negroes'] houses are not provided with city conveniences, such as water, electric lights, and sanitary provisions."[21] Such housing problems were, in fact, similar to those found in northern cities where such "city conveniences" were either not supplied or were woefully inadequate owing to overcrowded neighborhoods.[22]

Even while housing conditions in the southern city might be "countrified," people living there could still gain important experience that would help them if they moved to the northern metropolis. "Take for example, the problems of family-life," Work wrote.

> There are in the rural districts forces which operate to a considerable
> extent to maintain the family unit. . . . When this family migrates to the
> city, new forces begin to operate; the tendency is for various members of
> the family to engage in various kinds of occupation; each is probably
> working for a different employer; this tends toward the disintegration of
> the family.[23]

If the process of migration brought to bear new forces leading to family disintegration, then it may have been easier for migrants to deal with some of the tensions arising from this situation in the smaller, "countrified" southern city than in the northern ghetto. Further, if a family then moved on to the larger city after surviving its first urban encounter, then perhaps it had a very important resource that a family making the move straight from the field to the large city did not have. In short, most migration stories fail to recognize the southern city as a land of hope and possibility in the minds of black Southerners.[24]

While there were differences among the migrants (analogous to those, for example, between more urban European Jews and rural southern Italians), this does not mean that some people carried with them a "culture of poverty" that made their transformation into urban people difficult. Given time and opportunities, all rural migrants either adjust to city life or adapt the city to their own ways. But assimilation into the existing black communities was difficult because these people were deemed foreign by the urban community. Philadelphia's black communities were organized around people who had become urbanized over a long period of time, their institutions were supported by white and black elites who had a cosmopolitan outlook, and many of the "migrants" who came north prior to the Great Migration had begun to acquire an urban culture in the South. Consequently, no feeling existed in these communities that they would have to change to make room for rural people. Instead, a form of "culture of poverty" thesis was generated by longtime members of the community to explain the "failure" of newer, rural migrants and their unwillingness to assimilate into the institutions of black Philadelphia.

"Mother" Bethel's Southern Migrants

Migrants who came to Mother Bethel A.M.E. Church in Philadelphia, like the diverse general population of migrants, were not just peasants, nor were they always poor. Many of them bore characteristics likely to appeal to northern urban black churchgoers who wished to increase the size of their congregations and to welcome the newcomers at the gates of their cities.

African Methodists moving north often brought with them letters of transmittal generally written by the pastor of their former church and testifying to their good character.[25] One hundred ten such letters brought to Mother Bethel between 1916 and 1918 remain at the church to this day and provide a fairly clear sense of the origins of many of its newcomers at that time.[26]

Bethel's newcomers during the war years came predominantly from three Southern states: South Carolina ($n = 21$), Georgia ($n = 32$), and Florida ($n = 34$).[27] There were several reasons for this. First, states west of Georgia were not heavily represented among the new arrivals mainly because African Americans from states like Mississippi, Alabama, and Louisiana tended to migrate to midwestern cities.[28] The absence of people from Virginia ($n = 2$), Maryland ($n = 0$), and North Carolina ($n = 1$) is less easily explained; as mentioned earlier, large numbers of migrants came to Philadelphia from these states, and yet very few of them made their way to Bethel. The explanation is rooted in the history of the A.M.E. denomination. In the South, Georgia and South Carolina were the strongholds of Richard Allen's denomination. Maryland and Virginia had many black congregations linked to the Methodist Episcopal Church, while North Carolina had become the stronghold of the A.M.E. Zion Church. As a result, Marylanders of the Methodist faith headed for a church like East Calvary Methodist Episcopal, whose pastor, Charles Albert Tindley, was born in Berlin, Maryland. Likewise, Methodists from North Carolina headed to A.M.E. Zion Churches like Varick Memorial, pastored by James Walker Hood Eason, a native of North Carolina and son of a famous southern minister.

In fact, though, Mother Bethel also had strong connections with Maryland prior to the Great Migration. Linking the membership records for 1916 to the 1910 census shows that a large proportion of Bethel's members were either born in Maryland or had parents who were born in Maryland. Delaware and Virginia were also heavily represented as birthplaces for the 1916 members. This is important to remember because the Great Migration represented not the beginning of black migration from the South but an increase in the migratory flow and a change in the sources of migration. Delaware, Maryland, Virginia, and to a lesser extent North Carolina were the origins of most of the earlier migrants to Philadelphia; during the Great Migration, with the reduction in transportation costs, South Carolina and Georgia predominated as origins for the migrants.[29]

The three states that provided so many of Mother Bethel's members, Florida, Georgia, and South Carolina, were clearly different in many respects. Florida was more urbanized than Georgia and South Carolina, with the last being by far the slowest to urbanize between 1900 and 1920.[30] In Florida, a black person was as likely as a white person to live in an urban area. In Georgia, he or she was a little less likely, and in South Carolina, much less likely to live in such areas.

By 1919, Florida's farm production was very different from that of the other two states. While Florida farmers, like those in Georgia and South Carolina, had been committed predominantly to cotton and corn in 1899, between 1909 and 1919 they halved their cotton acreage and increased their hay and forage crops. As Florida's supervisor for the agricultural component of the Fourteenth census wrote, "There is but little cotton produced in this section now, and has been but little for the past several years on account of the boll weevil."[31] This insect struck Florida earlier than South Carolina and Georgia, causing "the permanent abandonment of farms" in this most southern state earlier than elsewhere. Meanwhile, Georgia and South Carolina farmers remained committed to cotton (though South Carolina began to grow more tobacco). The new Florida farm production was less labor intensive, however, and farm laborers in Florida began to experience displacement earlier than those in the other two states. Consequently, large numbers of former farm laborers began to move into Florida cities many years before the northern opportunities opened up; this migration accounted for the earlier tendency toward urbanization in the state and the dramatic growth between 1900 and 1920 of cities like Jacksonville and Tampa.

The different rates of urbanization among southern states resulted in a very diverse group of migrants making their way to Philadelphia. Letter bearers who arrived from Florida and Georgia had a more urban background, on the whole, than those from South Carolina (Table 8.5). Of those who came from Florida, 76 percent came from large cities like Jacksonville, Pensacola, and Miami; a very large percentage (65 percent) came from Jacksonville alone, the largest city in the state. Likewise, 69 percent of those from Georgia came from cities such as Savannah and Atlanta. By contrast, very few South Carolinians (16 percent) came from a large city, and most arrived from small towns in rural counties, of which Greenwood was the most common place of origin. The supervisor of the agricultural census in South Carolina noted the sudden decrease in farm laborers in that state, and it is likely that the South Carolinian migrants arriving at Bethel came straight from their farms. Their Floridian and Georgian counterparts had generally moved first to a local city before

Table 8.5. Type of Place of Origin of Letter-Bearers from
Florida, Georgia, and South Carolina

	Florida		Georgia		South Carolina	
	No.	%	No.	%	No.	%
Village (<2,500)	5	15	1	3	2	11
Town (<10,000)	2	6	3	9	12	63
City (<25,000)	1	3	6	19	2	11
Large city (>25,000)	26	76	22	69	3	16
Total	34		32		19	

migrating north.[32] For such people the move north may have constituted just one part of a process of migration; it was unlikely to be the only move they made in their lifetimes, and if they themselves did not move again, their sons and daughters probably would.[33]

In terms of place of origin, Bethel's letters of transmittal show that this church's newcomers fall very largely into three groups, two urban groups from Florida and Georgia and a rural group from South Carolina. It seems appropriate, therefore, to focus in closer detail on three communities—Savannah, Georgia; Jacksonville, Florida; and Greenwood, South Carolina—because these three places account for fifty letter-bearers, nearly half the total number.

Savannah, Georgia

On Monday, April 2, 1917, three members of St. Phillips A.M.E. Church of Savannah, Georgia—Margaret Mason, B. W. Brinscombe, and Benjamin Johnson—asked their pastor, Rev. Richard Henry Singleton, to write them letters of transmittal that they could carry with them to Philadelphia.[34] Singleton had already written several such letters on the church letterhead. Even his assistant pastor, Rev. C. P. Perry, was thinking of leaving Savannah.

He also knew that since these three members were heading to the City of Brotherly Love, it was likely that they would be heading to Mother Bethel. Singleton knew the city well. Earlier in the year, he had led his delegation in the Georgia Conference to the Centennial Conference of the A.M.E. Church, which was held at Mother Bethel. He had lodged in the city with African Methodists and had felt most welcome in the North. He had also corresponded with Richard R. Wright, Jr., when he was contributing articles to the *Christian Recorder*.[35] Wright's father, Major Richard R. Wright, Sr., president of Georgia State Industrial College, was one of the most prominent members of Singleton's congregation (until persuaded by Wright, Jr., to move his family to Philadelphia to establish a bank).[36] Added to these connections, Singleton had just recently received a leaflet from Mother Bethel sent by the pastor, Rev. Robert J. Williams, and the church's Reception Committee. Bethel was obviously well prepared to receive new arrivals, and he knew that his members would welcome support when they arrived at their destinations. Singleton anticipated that, since the leaflets made a strong case for moving north by outlining economic, political, and social reasons for leaving the old Confederate states, many more would leave his congregation in the coming months. Before the end of his pastorate, in 1920, Singleton had signed more than twenty letters of transmittal for Mother Bethel alone.[37]

The Rev. Singleton most likely did not try to dissuade his members from leaving Savannah. For one thing, he had brought more than twenty-three hundred new members into the church himself, and his congregation, with more than twenty-five hundred members in 1916, was large enough that he did not need to worry about its depletion.[38] Indeed, the congregation was as large as any found in Philadelphia's A.M.E. churches and included many of Savannah's leading black families. While he did not wish to lose members who contributed large amounts of time to the church, Singleton realized that others would take their place. The migration north was one part of a larger migration of African Americans from rural areas into cities contributing to the growth of such places as Savannah. And because that city was on the Savannah River, many who wished to go north from South Carolina and Georgia stayed there for a while before leaving on a northbound steamer.

Being pastor of a large urban church, Singleton was in a better position than some African Methodist preachers assigned to rural districts. In one Georgia conference of the A.M.E. Church membership had dropped from eleven thousand in 1915 to five thousand two years later. Consequently, at a session of this conference,

> men who had been pastors of these people stood on the conference floor with tears in their eyes and sobs in their throats pleading to be allowed to go with their congregations. "Not that we want to go for our own sakes,"

they said, "but for the sake of our people. We know it means suffering and hard living, but we will work with our hands for our support, that we may minister to our people, may keep them together that they may not drift and be swallowed up in the great cities of the North with no spiritual or moral guidance to keep them from the downward path."[39]

Singleton, at least, did not face such a dramatic drop of membership at St. Phillips, and he could be more optimistic about the migration because he had been dealing with former rural dwellers for many years.[40]

In any case, it probably would have been pointless to try to persuade members who asked for a letter of transmittal not to leave. One white commentator described the sentiment of most African Americans toward migration thus:

> The feeling among the more intelligent negroes is . . . that things will have to take their natural course and that while there may be a large sacrifice of lives, health and individual positions, still the ultimate end will be for the benefit of the greater number and that since nothing can be done to prevent their leaving, no action can be taken. I do not, in fact, think that the men with whom I have conversed regarding this subject from time to time are inclined to do very much to prevent this emigration and I doubt that if they did attempt to do so whether it would have any effect.[41]

Singleton probably favored the migration anyway. He would have heard that many migrants had written to their families and friends in the South that conditions were much better in the North. He also had received the journals of the denomination, which strongly supported the migration. Even the *Southern Recorder* had suggested that the best thing for black people to do was to move north to reap the benefits of political rights, higher wages, and greater social equality. Further, these arguments were not matched by credible counterarguments. Booker T. Washington, who had argued throughout his life that blacks should remain in the South, had died two years previously without leaving a successor of any stature. Those who opposed the migration were southern whites, and their arguments were clearly specious and self-serving. It is unlikely that Singleton shared the northern black view that the migration was a modern Exodus, a way for God to show a new chosen people the way out of Egypt toward "the Promised Land." But, after the pessimism resulting from disheartening developments for "the race" in the first decade of the twentieth century, the increase in lynchings, the systematic segregation, and the Atlanta race riot, he probably inclined toward the view common among southern black commentators that the migration would produce improvements in the South for those who remained.[42]

This view was summarized by a Georgia colleague of Singleton, Rev. W. D. Johnson, in an article in the *Recorder*.

> I am of the opinion that the migration of our people to the North will benefit the Negro, because of the school facilities to be had in the North, and while I think that, I also think that [the] Negro who stays in the South will be benefitted for the white man will become more appreciative of the services of the Negro and will pay him better wages and will provide better school facilities for Negro children.

Even in the face of white oppression, many black Southerners still retained a strong commitment to their region and hoped that "the white man" would change his ways. This commitment was clear in Johnson's article: "[T]he Negro loves the southern white man," he wrote, "and even though he has gone North by the thousands and many more are still going, he loves the sunny South and the southern white man as the dog loves the kennel and as the dove loves her mate."[43]

The level of violence in Georgia clearly troubled members of the black population and was an important cause of the wartime migration. Mary Debardeleben, a southern white member of the Methodist Episcopal Church, South, described many instances of racial violence directly linked to the migration. A friend of hers, she wrote, talked to a black man who was leaving his home with his family to move north. Her friend asked the man why he was leaving.

> The old man, with trembling fingers, drew from his pocket a crumbled paper and spread it out before them. At the top of the sheet was crudely drawn a skull and crossbones; below was written: "You are hereby warned that you and your entire family must be gone from this community within 48 hours. Your attention is called to the symbol at the top of the notice." In the community in which the man lived a woman had been burned at the stake a few months before. Her crime was due to the natural impulse of motherhood. She had dared to protect her child from the blows administered by a white man. And so the old man fearing for his life was fleeing in the dead of the night.

Debardeleben had other horror stories. In another Georgia town, for instance, "four innocent Negroes were foully murdered in the usual way— by an insane mob." And she continued:

> The father of the family was lodged in jail for an assault on an officer who came to arrest him. The mob therefore seized the family—the

mother, two daughters, one of whom was soon to become a mother, and a ten-year-old boy. I cannot go into the revolting circumstances of it all. Suffice it to say that little white boys saw it and hence seeds of brutality, hatred and revenge were planted in their young hearts. Many Negroes are leaving that section. Just what portion are leaving, I cannot say, but such outrageous violation of law is certainly playing its part in the exodus.[44]

Not all families who made the move north were actually threatened, but reports of lynchings were so widespread that all migrants from the regions in which they were occurring had cause to fear for their lives and their families' well-being.

Almost two weeks after the four members of St. Phillips approached their pastor, Helen Cinnamond, the general secretary of the Associated Charities of Savannah, wrote a letter to the Armstrong Association in Philadelphia in response to its request for information about the number of migrants leaving Savannah. Cinnamond noted that Savannah was "a kind of clearing house" for blacks coming from the South; around three thousand blacks passed through the town. Cinnamond wrote, "Passage on Ocean Steamship Company's boats is being engaged to their utmost capacity and I am informed are taking one hundred or more Negroes every trip." She then commented on the kinds of people that were beginning to move north:

Last winter your cities of the North met with many difficulties and it is thought that you drew the riff-raff, so to speak; those who left merely upon suggestion and without preliminary preparations. At this time, however, they appear to be planning to sell their household and other property and to be going with a small amount of money at any rate in their possessions.[45]

Whether Cinnamond's assessment was correct and whether these people were in fact better off than their predecessors is questionable.[46] It is likely, though, that they were indeed more organized than the so-called riff-raff, having had at least a winter to consider the move. The first waves of migrants had left during the previous spring, summer, and fall.

Jacksonville, Florida

In many respects the situation at Mt. Zion A.M.E. Church in Jacksonville resembled that at St. Phillips in Savannah. Mt. Zion had been pastored between 1910 and 1915 by Daniel Minort Baxter, a very successful minister who, like Singleton, had many connections with the North. He had contributed several articles to the *Christian Recorder* and the *A.M.E. Church Review*, both published in Philadelphia, and was a prominent member of national organizations like the Free and Accepted Masons Progressive Order of Men and Women, the Good Templars, and the Republican Party. Also like Singleton, Baxter was a member of the Centennial General Conference of 1916. When he returned from Philadelphia to Jacksonville after the conference, Baxter retained his strong ties with Mt. Zion by becoming presiding elder of the North Jacksonville District, and no doubt assisted James A. Long, the new pastor of the church, in advising the many members who were deciding whether or not to leave Florida for the North.[47]

Baxter himself moved to Philadelphia in 1920 to take up the appointment of business manager for the A.M.E. Book Concern, a position he held for sixteen years. He maintained strong ties with former congregants from Mt. Zion who attended Philadelphia's A.M.E. churches. No longer tied down to a single congregation, Baxter was able to provide assistance to his scattered flock.[48]

Mt. Zion Church was like St. Phillips in many respects. It was located in a growing city and in an area in which the A.M.E. Church was very strong. According to the *Centennial Encyclopaedia*, Duval County "was the great A.M.E. stronghold" in Florida (p. 309). Just prior to the Great Migration, during Bishop Heard's administration, the denomination experienced a period of great activity. It was believed that the period would be considered a "golden age, . . . for in all departments of the church there were marked increases and greater activity than ever" (p. 310). Mt. Zion Church, itself, underwent considerable growth. During his five-year pastorate, Baxter had completed Mt. Zion's edifice at a cost of $4,000 and lifted mortgages amounting to more than a thousand dollars. He had also added 2,020 people to the church rolls. The church prospered, not least because many of the members themselves were prosperous. Baxter had collected $26,000 from the stewards alone and $36,000 from the trustees during his pastorate. Like St. Phillips, Mt. Zion did not face the pressures that many smaller rural churches faced and its leaders could respond favorably to the desires of many members who read the leaflets sent out by churches like Mother Bethel and wished to go north.

Besides the Bethel leaflets, Jacksonville migrants probably read other pamphlets and notices, such as the pamphlet issued by the Rail Road, Mining and General Constuction Works of America in October

1916 entitled "Advice to Negroes Migrating from the South to the North, East and West."[49] This pamphlet, written by Rev. Frank W. Lancaster, a black man who held the peculiar position of general missionary secretary for the Jacksonville company, is worth considering at length as it confirms the suggestion that the people moving north from Jacksonville were indeed predominantly "migrants" rather than "refugees." The pamphlet is particularly revealing because it appears to be written with a certain audience in mind. At no point does it explicitly mention the hardships of the South, economic, political, or social, as might be expected of a pamphlet encouraging people to leave a place of oppression. Rather, it reads like an advertisement for industrial areas throughout the country. For example, the first section outlines industrial opportunities:

> Without doubt, you have been impressed with the advanced industrial opportunities to you here over those that obtained where you were formerly located in the south, and we congratulate you upon your wisdom of choice and change. It stands without question, that the vast demand for labor in this and other northern, eastern and western sections of the country are such, that the employers will hail with peculiar delight your coming and do everything possible to make you feel at home and free, thereby assisting you to make good and be content.

The language indicates that the author wished to appeal to migrants. Further, it indicates that he believed that these people had come to Jacksonville primarily for the economic opportunities that the city provided. He seemed to believe that a migration system existed, of which the move to Jacksonville was just one part. The suggestion in this passage (and elsewhere in the pamphlet) is that migrants who came in search of opportunity in Jacksonville would move on to other places if better opportunities presented themselves.

"You will allow us to call to your attention the fact," Lancaster wrote, "that your coming to these parts is purely a business proposition." The pamphlet proceeded to treat the whole process of migration in this light, providing advice for migrants about how to present themselves to employers and how best to improve their job prospects. At one point, Lancaster told his readers to "Adopt Business Rules:"

> Now that you are in the north . . . settle down to the fact that we too must adopt business rules and stand by them. Figure everything from a business standpoint. If you are valuable to your employer, he needs you and will keep you, if not he does not need you and will not keep you. Be an asset to your employer, and thus make your employer an asset to you.

Pay your honest debts gladly and expect those in debt to you to do likewise.

Other advice included warnings about "sharpers and grafters," who would try "to relieve you of your hard-earned savings." Lancaster clearly assumed that the migrants had savings, something that was often not the case for migrants from other districts.

Lancaster's description of the Jacksonville migrants is very different from the more common depiction of the migrants as refugees moving north to "the Promised Land" to find a safe haven from oppression. These migrants had more human resources (training and experience) appropriate to the urban environment than those moving straight from their farm land to the northern metropolis.

Greenwood, South Carolina

South Carolinian migrants tended to come from a rural background. In *One More Day's Journey*, Allen Ballard focuses on people he describes as "refugees" who made their way from Greenwood and Abbeville Counties in South Carolina to Philadelphia. Mostly they were farm workers who left their homes because of the boll weevil or because of the lynching in 1916 of Anthony Crawford in Abbeville's town center.[50] Ballard tends to overlook the boll weevil and concentrate instead upon the violent oppression of black Southerners. Nevertheless, paying closer attention to the plight of cotton farmers would not bring his "refugee" characterization into question. One of the key sources for his work, Hughsey Childs, a Baptist, clearly was a refugee who but for the collapse of the cotton crop would probably have remained in South Carolina. In an interview for the oral history project, "Goin' North," Childs said:

> In 1916 I made sixteen bales of cotton; 1917 that was cut in half. And the next year was nothing. People that used to have eighteen and nineteen bales of cotton were lucky to get three. So you see, what you going to do? Because in the South at that particular time, the only thing we had to make money was with the cotton. That was the only commodity we had. That's where we got our money from. But the boll weevil came in, and that's what started people comin' here, because the farmer he didn't have no other place to go.[51]

Yet, even in South Carolina, not all northbound African Americans fit the refugee description. Many people had more resources available to them and were moving north not to escape oppression but to take advantage of opportunities. In March 1917, for example, Margaret Laing, the general secretary of the Associated Charities of Columbia, South Carolina, responded to a request for information about the migration from the Philadelphia Housing Association. She outlined the situation in Columbia, a city in the center of the state that many of the migrants would have passed through on their journey north. She wrote:

> We cannot give any definite report as to how many have left this community, but this Spring a year ago, when one of the Public Institutions advertised for laborers, there were a great many applications by colored men, more than was necessary. This Spring the same institution advertised for laborers, but only twenty applied. We believe that this small number of applicants was due partly to migration.

Clearly, then, many migrants from South Carolina had had the choice of accepting a job in a nearby city or moving north for a better-paying job. The diversity of the South Carolina migrant population is confirmed in the remainder of Laing's letter:

> We should say possibly three hundred laborers, trades people and artisans plan to go north to Philadelphia, during this spring. A large number of these will probably be whole families, but there will be some single men and single women. We do not know of, and do not believe that any whole groups or congregations will go from this community. It seems that those who are planning to leave here are of pretty good moral average, some of them own small homes and businesses. We know of one wealthy colored man, worth approximately $10,000.00 who plans to go. He is a skilled worker.[52]

Those who moved north were obviously not just an undifferentiated group. Men and women as respectable as the skilled worker mentioned by Laing would definitely appeal to members of a congregation like Bethel on the lookout for new members. Some of his fellow migrants, needless to say, would not.

Greenwood was a cotton farming county in northwestern South Carolina. It had a population of 34,225 in 1910, of which 49.4 percent were African American. In 1920, the population grew to 35,791, and the number of black people in the county actually increased in spite of the migration. African Americans now made up 52.8 percent of the population, and 69.4 percent of the farms were run by black farmers. Of the 2,778 farms run by African Americans, however, only 277 were actually owned outright.[53] While less than 10 percent of black people owned their farms, nearly 60 percent of white farmers owned theirs. Class division in the county seems to have closely followed racial division. The large majority of blacks were sharecroppers facing similar economic circumstances—the need to borrow money for seed and supplies until harvest time, when a portion of the crop would go to paying off the debt. Some farmers were more successful than others and some farms were better situated than others, but on the whole the black community did not have the social divisions that characterized more urban black communities.[54]

The strength of the A.M.E. Church in South Carolina was unusual because of the rural nature of the state. Founded in Philadelphia, the denomination tended to have an urban following except in South Carolina. The church's strength in this state dates back to the antislavery work of the denomination. The connection between Morris Brown and Denmark Vesey's slave rebellion in South Carolina did much to promote African Methodism among black South Carolinians.[55] During Reconstruction, African Methodism spread rapidly under the leadership of people like Bishop Daniel M. Payne, Henry McNeil Turner, and William Henry Heard, who worked closely with the Republican Party.[56]

South Carolina also had strong connections with Mother Bethel. Bishop Heard was a pastor at both Mother Bethel and Mt. Zion A.M.E. Church in Charleston. Bishop Coppin, who maintained strong links with Bethel after finishing his pastorates at the church, was bishop for the district in which Greenwood was located just prior to the Great Migration.[57] As a supporter of the migration and a former migrant himself, he may have encouraged members of Weston Chapel (a church from which many of the Greenwood migrants came) to move to Philadelphia. Such connections between Bethel and Greenwood continued after the beginning of the migration. Those African Americans who moved north did not cut off all links with the South. Usually they returned to Greenwood once a year for the August revivals and for the harvest period. While at home they spread the news about employment opportunities in Philadelphia and encouraged other members of the community to leave Greenwood.

Allen Ballard has described the development of South Carolina enclaves in Philadelphia itself. He maintains that most of the Greenwood "refugees" settled in the northern section of the city in an area bounded by Girard Avenue on the south, Susquehanna Avenue on the north, and between 10th Street on the east and 12th Street on the west. The pattern for settling in this district was for a family to become established in an apartment and then to rent out rooms to other families or individuals from their town. One person, according to Ballard, recalled that he first stayed in a house rented by his sister, in which three families from Greenwood, including the family of an A.M.E. minister, also lived.

Once the Greenwood families were settled in this area they began to create institutions to support themselves and to re-create their old community. Two institutions developed as meeting places for Greenwood blacks. One was George Bailey's store at 1422 North 10th Street. Bailey had been raised in Philadelphia, but he married a woman from Greenwood, and consequently his store became a communication center for Greenwood's black families arriving in the city. The other institution was a bar run by Roosevelt "Buddy" Peterson of Greenwood at 13th and Oxford.

It is unknown whether the African Methodists among the Greenwood migrants shared in the same community development as Baptists from this county. According to Ballard, the African Methodists considered themselves of better class than the Baptists, and this might have militated against their contribution to the transplanted community. However, Ballard also suggests that the class distinctions were not as strong in Greenwood and Abbeville Counties as they were in urban areas, and so cooperation and sharing between Baptists and African Methodists may have been possible. Certainly the desire for community was strong among South Carolinian African Methodists. Those who joined Mother Bethel quickly formed the South Carolina Club, which helped other new arrivals to adjust by enabling them to get to know a small section of the congregation that had similar backgrounds to themselves.

South Carolinian migrants, according to Ballard, were renowned for their propensity toward violence.[58] Among the reasons for this may have been their experiences with the breakup of the sharecropping system, their unfamiliarity with the wage-labor system, and tensions that arose from the changing gender relations within families in the northern metropolis. Unfortunately, the role that this propensity played in the split in the congregation at Mother Bethel in 1920 may never be known. Certainly, though, the animus of longtime members of the congregation toward the new arrivals was directed at the more rural South Carolinian migrants because their rural ways were considered uncouth.

The migrants who brought their letters of transmittal with them to Mother Bethel were a diverse group. To Bethel's members, who had been born in Philadelphia or the urban regions of the upper South, the people from Jacksonville and Savannah would not have appeared very different from themselves. Migrants from South Carolina may have raised a few eyebrows, but it is likely that even they tended to bring resources with them—hence, Williams's satisfaction that Bethel was attracting "some of the best blood of the South."

The letter of transmittal itself was just such a resource. For northern African Methodists, it signified that the bearer had been a member of an A.M.E. church long enough for the pastor to feel comfortable issuing a letter. It also suggested that the person had served the former church well. While a letter did not guarantee that the bearer was economically well-off, it nevertheless suggested that the person had managed in the past to fit in with people who were. And since class divisions were not always economically determined in the black community, it may have been as important to "fit in" culturally as to have the material possessions that usually help define class. As long as the newcomers brought letters with them and a probationary period was adhered to, then, within certain limits, northern African Methodists could feel fairly confident that they would know how to comport themselves in their churches. Indeed, as the next chapter discloses, they may have known too well how to comport themselves politically.

CHAPTER 9

The Earnest Pastor's Heated Term

*The latch string of Mother Bethel hangs on the outside. We know of
no North, South, East or West. We must unite our forces in
working out our common destiny; husband our means, buy homes,
educate our children, live right before God, and man; and by so
doing we will compel men everywhere to acknowledge the
Fatherhood of God and the Brotherhood of man.*

REV. ROBERT J. WILLIAMS, JR., 1917

On Wednesday evening, April 21, 1920, a thousand members of the
Bethel African Methodist Episcopal Church congregation sat in their
pews impatiently awaiting the arrival of their pastor. The Rev. Robert J.
Williams was late on account of another meeting concerning repayment
of a loan. As the church members waited, they began to discuss Williams's shortcomings. Some claimed, according to a *Philadelphia Tribune*
reporter present, that they had lent him money and had not been repaid;
several women, whom Williams had allegedly tried to remove from the
church, spoke of his immorality; and a man asked how much the pastor
had received for helping someone obtain a liquor license in Chester.
When Williams finally arrived, he opened the meeting with his usual
prayer and song. After these, he started employing the "steamroller
methods" for which he was renowned, ruling against his opponents and
denying all allegations made against him. But the pastor soon found that
he had lost his support within the congregation. The consensus of the
meeting, the reporter believed, was that Williams should attend a revival

somewhere to be converted to Christianity.[1] Thus ended a pastorate that had appeared four years earlier to be one of the brightest in the Philadelphia episcopal district.

Williams's downfall resulted from a turbulent conflict between the pastor and the longtime members of the Mother Bethel congregation. The conflict reveals, at the level of the congregation, how the influx of southern migrants could lead to instability in Philadelphia's black churches when the newcomers asserted their rights and challenged established members for control. Besides the insight the conflict gives us into the problems facing all churches at a time of changing residential patterns, financial difficulties, and massive in-migration, it also brings Bethel Church to life. It shows how a pastor with a forceful personality and clearly defined aims could reform both the structure of the church and its forms of worship and, at the same time, generate such positive and negative reactions among his communicants that his congregation would break apart.

Robert J. Williams had been born in Philadelphia in May 1871, the oldest child in a family of eighteen children. He was brought up in Berlin, Maryland, and received the rudimentary education typical of southern public schools, which were open only during the winter months. When Williams underwent conversion at the age of twelve, he joined the Methodist Episcopal Church, which was the dominant Methodist denomination in Maryland and had numerous black congregations. He returned to Philadelphia in the early 1890s and finished his education by enrolling at the Institute of Colored Youth, whose principal was the prominent African Methodist, Fanny J. Coppin. It is likely that Williams came into contact with many African Methodists at the institute; even so, in 1897 at the age of twenty-six, he became licensed in the Methodist Episcopal Church and went to serve in Delaware. Five years later, he joined St. Paul's A.M.E. Church in Harrington, Delaware, and was quickly appointed to a pastorate in South Wilmington.

Williams served at several churches in the Philadelphia region before he was appointed to the pastorate at Bethel, and he made a lasting impression at nearly every one. At Grant Chapel, in South Wilmington, "he saved the church from the sheriff's hammer, and added fifty members." At Payne, in Philadelphia, "he met the sheriff again, but saved the church" during his one-year tenure. At Kennett Square, Pennsylvania, where he served for three years, he remodeled the church, added 70 members, paid off the debt, and left $460 in the treasury. Then in two years at York, he again remodeled the church, erected a hall at a cost of $600, added 120 members to the church, and reduced the mortgage by $400. Finally, in five years of service at Murphy A.M.E. Church in Chester, he pulled together a divided congregation, attracted 203 new members, and substantially reduced the church debt.

In 1914, Williams was appointed presiding elder of the West Philadelphia District, and during his two years in this position he helped to establish Tyree A.M.E. Church, named after the bishop of the First Episcopal District.[2] In 1916, he was one of the leading members of the Pennsylvania delegation at the Centennial Conference of the African Methodist Episcopal Church, which was held at Mother Bethel.[3] Along with these feats, Williams's leading position in the Pennsylvania Masons earned him a great reputation among Philadelphia's African Methodists.[4]

This reputation and success derived in part from the pastor's style in the pulpit. Williams was a very charismatic preacher who approached church services with an evangelical fervor. Unlike most other African Methodist ministers in Philadelphia at the time, he had not been educated at a theological seminary, and his preaching method was not restrained by formal theological training.[5] Indeed, his style of preaching was still foreign to most of Philadelphia's black churches at this time, whose pastors' sermons usually resembled those of their white counterparts.[6] Williams often included songs in his sermons and composed hymns for his congregation, enhancing his popularity as a preacher.[7] In all likelihood, Williams modeled himself on his uncle, Charles Albert Tindley, minister at East Calvary Methodist Episcopal Church. Both men possessed an evangelical fervor and both composed and sang their own gospel hymns. Tindley, also born in Berlin, Maryland, and self-educated, was about fifteen years Williams's senior.[8]

Williams was appointed to Mother Bethel in 1916 partly because Bishop Evans Tyree wished to reward him for services rendered (Bethel was considered a major step up from the small churches outside Philadelphia), and partly because the bishop felt that Williams would be able to deal with the church's financial predicament. During the first decade of the twentieth century Bethel had been in poor financial and spiritual condition. The congregation had never managed to repay mortgages taken in 1890 to build a new church edifice when Bethel was one of the

leading churches in the A.M.E. Connection. By 1899, during the pastorate of Levi J. Coppin, church members were expressing considerable
concern about the financial situation:

> We have taken a census of the membership of the church and we find
> we have only 924 actual members although it is often reported that we
> have 1500. . . . Something must be done if we expect to pay for our
> church and we the members should do it and depend entirely on
> ourselves and stop begging our friends and the public.[9]

The church debt had not diminished during the first decade of the new
century, and a split in the congregation in 1910 along with dwindling
membership had made it even less likely that it would be paid.[10]

In April 1912, a financial revival began at the church with the election of a new corporation president, Colonel Philip H. Edwards. In the
next four years the trustees collected about $19,000. However, Edwards
initiated a building program, replacing old frame buildings next to the
church with two modern houses costing $16,000 and renovating the
church. Consequently, the church debt still had not been reduced substantially, and the bonded indebtedness remained $11,997.[11] As the Rev.
Williams had triumphed over many similar difficulties at other churches,
he was considered the perfect choice for the pastorate at Bethel to complete the renaissance.

One way to deal with Bethel's financial problem, Williams realized,
was to increase the pool of people from which money could be collected.[12]
His appointment came at a time when preparation for war created an
economic boom, thus increasing the demand for labor in Philadelphia. As
a result, black migrants began to enter the city in large numbers, and
these men, women, and children needed assistance in finding housing
and jobs. Williams believed that by helping these people, and by persuading more to leave the South, his church could provide a valuable
service and at the same time attract many new members. Soon after his
appointment, therefore, he established an information bureau to print
leaflets advertising Bethel, which were distributed at African Methodist
Churches in the South. These leaflets encouraged African Americans to
come North to join the "mother" church of the denomination.[13]

Established church members at Mother Bethel also supported the
induction of migrants into the church, partly because many of the denomination's leaders had been urging them to welcome the newcomers

but also to ease their financial burden. Problems in repaying the large mortgage had been increased by population movements during the first fifteen years of the century. Roughly 62 percent of Bethel's members had been working class in 1897. Half of them had lived and worked as domestics in the houses of white upper-class residents of the Seventh Ward, in which the church was located. As middle- and upper-class white people left the area and were replaced by Jewish immigrants, working-class members of Bethel needed to seek employment elsewhere. Many had left the area by 1916, moving west of Broad Street and across the Schuylkill River into West Philadelphia. Consequently, the church required support from new members. According to one older member, the people from the South saved the church from extinction as "we were barely able to hold on financially."[14]

This member exaggerated the problem a little; after all, Edwards had already done a considerable amount to turn the church around financially. But it seemed clear to established members that the new pastor's intentions complemented their own and that his plans did not depart dramatically from the course of action already embarked upon by the church's corporation. The minister and members were brought yet closer together by the mutual desire that Bethel once again become a leading church in Philadelphia's black community. It was not surprising, therefore, that when migrants started to flood into Mother Bethel and it became necessary to establish an organization to help them, Colonel Edwards accepted Williams's invitation to become chairman of the Reception Committee.[15]

In order to attract new members to Bethel, Williams portrayed the church in a light that would appeal especially to migrants. This is evident in the leaflets he distributed in the South. On the top lefthand corner was a picture of Williams giving a welcoming salute as if he were coming forward to greet a new arrival. Below it were various short prayers and poems written by the pastor. Each of these was calculated to appeal to the migrant. The theme of the church as home resonated in each appeal, as in the short poem, "Let This Be Your Home":

> *Beloved, let this be your home*
> *Even if your stay is short.*
> *To all, I say, never roam.*
> *Heaven loves a contrite heart.*

Enter Bethel, enter now,
Let the spirit teach you how.

To the "City of Brotherly Love"
you are welcome;
At Mother Bethel you
will be at home.

Below this, Bethel was described as: "The home for the stranger; the pride of the Connection; the center of attraction; the house of God."

On the reverse side of the leaflet Williams provided reasons for black people to come North. The last passage on this side also was designed to appeal to the migrant:

THE CHURCH THE HAVEN
Civilization is founded on Christianity. The Church is the organized agency of Christianity. When you go into a strange community, the first thing you should do is to find a church. To be satisfied, you should find the church of your choice, and when you find the church of your choice, join—connect yourself with the church.
    The church is the haven of safety. The tents of wickedness are on every hand. Satan is busy. His forces are organized. To keep out of his clutches you must keep in the ranks of God's army.
    Mother Bethel sends you these greetings, and if you come to Philadelphia we invite you to come within her fold. The members of the Mother Church of the African Methodist Episcopal Connection will do everything in their power to help you, and to make you welcome to their church and their homes.[16]

Words such as "haven," "home," "fold," and "safety," juxtaposed with "the tents of wickedness" and the fears of Satan's "clutches," gave "Mother" Bethel great appeal. These leaflets played upon the migrants' fears and their desires to join a group for protection while they adjusted to their new city environment.

Church services at Mother Bethel were altered so that they might appeal to migrants. Williams departed from the more traditional forms of worship and employed evangelical aspects, talking in his sermons about problems facing his communicants and putting more "snap and go" in the church music. In one of his sermons, for instance, Williams "eloquently discoursed upon the Scriptural selection of the service and closed with an acrostic on the word 'home.'" "H" stood for hospitality, "O" for opportunity, "M" for militant, and "E" for elevation. Another sermon was called "No Cross, No Crown," suggesting to his congregants that their hardships would someday be compensated.[17]

Chanting and "shouts," forms of worship incorporating call and response so familiar in black churches today, were not new to Bethel, but Williams employed these more frequently and gave them a special twist by making the ritual more personalized.[18] Services began with hymns that the pastor had composed, such as the "Bethel Battle Song," and a special salute called the "Ta-wawa," was used to welcome the pastor as he climbed onto the pulpit. After being greeted by this salute at one service, Williams proclaimed, "I'm happy, are you?" Whereupon a loud "yes" resounded through the church. In keeping with this personalized ritual, he presented a picture of himself to Mrs. Mayme F. Bell at one Sunday service.[19]

By personalizing both the services and the purpose of the church, Williams used his charisma to turn the focus of attention toward himself. This allowed him to equate the success of the church with his own success, helping him to pull the congregation closer together behind his leadership, and also to appeal to migrants. At first he was successful both at unifying the church and increasing membership. After he had received his hundredth new member into the congregation, the *Tribune* (later one of Williams's detractors) published an article entitled, "Earnest Pastor Works during Heated Term," in which it noted: "Bethel is going forward, peace prevails in every department."[20] A few months after this, in May 1917, one of the pastor's supporters compared him to Richard Allen. "Dr. Williams's pastoral relations with the mother church are much like that of the Brother Allen, who was the founder of the Bethel Church and was pastor at the beginning of the first century," the supporter pronounced. "Williams is pastor at the beginning of the second century, and the great work he has done shows that he is the right man in the right place."[21]

The Information Bureau's leaflets and Williams's style of preaching attracted large numbers of new members to Bethel. At almost every weekly service several men and women were converted or welcomed by letter into the church.[22] Indeed, between July and December 1916, 165 new members were received into the church, increasing the congregation by as much as 20 percent in the space of five months.[23] Most of these people had recently settled in Philadelphia. As discussed in the previous chapter, Bethel attracted migrants mainly from Florida, Georgia, and South Carolina, with the majority from Florida and Georgia. These must have been the places where Williams's propaganda was most effective, or where the pastor concentrated his leaflet campaign among particular Af-

rican Methodist churches, since many of the newcomers to Bethel came
from the same churches.

The large influx of migrants into Bethel, which was reported extensively by the *Tribune*, increased Williams's reputation and added to
his prestige among local churchmen.[24] He became a leading figure not
only in the A.M.E. Church but in black Philadelphia generally. Not long
after arriving at Bethel, he was invited to join the Interdenominational
Ministerial Alliance,[25] and in May 1917, he was given a reception in recognition of his "valuable services and intense devotion to racial interests."[26] The following year, he organized the Richard Allen Lodge of the
Free and Accepted Masons[27] and was elected vice president of the Colored Protective Association, established in response to the Philadelphia
race riot. The list of the C.P.A.'s leaders included black Philadelphia's
most prominent ministers, and the fact that Williams was given such a
prestigious position, with no churchmen placed above him, attests to his
influence at this time.[28] This was definitely the high point in Williams's
career.

He may have been too successful. By bringing a large number of
migrants to Bethel he made many of the established members of the
church feel insecure about their own positions, and the low opinion the
latter had of the newcomers only increased tensions. Recruiting new
members was all very well, these people thought, as long as they came
from recognized A.M.E. churches in the South with a letter from their
former pastor confirming their upstanding moral character. Once Williams began welcoming into the church people who established members thought were of dubious character, who came without letters, and
who were accepted on only a declaration of faith, then he had gone too
far.[29]

The congregation soon became divided. Williams's supporters
were mainly those members of Bethel who had recently arrived in Philadelphia; his opponents tended to be established Philadelphians who
wished to maintain control of their church. Although the pastor manipulated this division in an attempt to seize control of the governing bodies
of the church,[30] the division was nevertheless founded on animosities
between newer and older members; Williams could not create a conflict
out of nothing. The Bethel Corporation was a key body in this division.
Along with the board of trustees, this governing organization was independent of the A.M.E. episcopacy, and the pastor was excluded from its
meetings. It represented the interests of the established churchgoers
who had elected its officials. While the church had been incorporated for

the democratic purpose of securing power for the congregation against
the threat of white Episcopalians and Methodists, by 1890 the corporation had become a conservative body sustaining the power and prestige
of a minority within the congregation and often opposing change.[31]

In particular, Williams threatened the power of Colonel Edwards
and a small group of his supporters who were all entrenched in their
positions as trustees. Most of these men had been elected to the board
during the first decade of the century.[32] At the corporation election of
April 1912, they had rallied around Edwards to depose the previous president of Bethel, John R. Powell. It is unclear whether or not a conspiracy
was involved, but the manner in which Powell refused to accept the
gratitude of the congregation for his years of "unstinting service" suggests the possibility of some underhand dealings between the new president and his supporters.[33] Certainly, though, Edwards guarded his power
jealously, and when Williams's efforts to increase church membership
began to appear threatening to him and his coterie, he opposed the pastor, whose plans he had previously endorsed.

Soon after Williams's installation, a number of church officials began to believe that he wished to use the migrants' loyalty to make himself president of the corporation and to bring the church completely under his control. A number of established church members would have
lost their prestigious positions to new members—positions such as
trustee, steward, usher, class leader, Sunday school official, and historical
commissioner.[34] Realizing, therefore, that Williams's motives might be
inimical to their interests, these established members began to take mea-
sures to secure their positions. In October 1917, the corporation
amended its bylaws so that "no member shall be eligible to either of the
said offices [treasurer and member of the board of trustees] who shall not
have been a member of the African Methodist Episcopal Connection in
the United States for at least three years and a member of this church for
at least two years previous to his election." This resolution, adopted
unanimously, aimed to limit the power of newcomers to the church and
to restrict control of the corporation to established members. It complemented other bylaws that restricted voting for corporation officials to
members who had joined the church "by letter" and who had been
"publicly read into membership."[35]

A brief look at the Sunday School Board reveals the kind of turmoil
that was beginning to occur in the church. Just prior to Williams's arrival
at Bethel, the Sunday School Board consisted of thirty-three officers who
by their attendance record appear to have been extremely committed to

their work. No doubt, they were inspired by Superintendent D. James Mason, who had served in this position for more than twenty-one years. During the first half-year of Williams's pastorate, the board maintained an 82 percent attendance record, which, considering that Anna Gilbert fell sick and others had to be "distant" from the city, was remarkable. By 1917, however, congregational growth necessitated an increase in the number of Sunday School officers, and twenty more officials were appointed. Some of the new appointees, like D. A. Hart, William Glenn, and Mr. and Mrs. Tooks, had only just arrived from the South. Attendance levels started to drop, though it is uncertain for what reason. In 1918, there was a considerable shake-up in the Sunday School Board. Having served as superintendent for twenty-three years and still only in his fifties, Mason was replaced by Sydney E. Purnell. Likewise, the secretary, Charlotta D. Reynolds, was replaced by Mrs. Millie Williams, the pastor's wife. Another nineteen members of the school board had their names deleted from the roll, and the board was returned to its premigration number.[36]

By March 1920, Williams had developed a plan with William H. Thompson, his attorney and a new arrival at the church, to take over the corporation.[37] A committee of one hundred was formed, and nominees were selected for the corporation election to be held early in April; all of them had arrived at the church after 1916.[38] The implications of this replacement of corporation officials were revolutionary for Mother Bethel. The new men demanded sweeping reforms: an end to church debt, a reorganization of the corporation that made the pastor chairman ex officio of all boards, voting rights for women, and a relocation of the church.

Mother Bethel's debt would be paid off by relocating the congregation. The church and its real estate holdings were believed to be worth more than $150,000, and since the church debt was still about $30,000, it was estimated that the church could be sold, the mortgage paid, and a new church bought and that the congregation would have a profit of approximately $85,000. Bethel was (and remains) located at 6th and Lombard Streets. Williams and Thompson reasoned that if the congregation moved farther west, it could purchase a building inexpensively from a white congregation moving to the suburbs.

The reorganization of the Bethel Corporation was an important consideration for Williams. During the 1890s a number of local A.M.E. churches became incorporated while the denomination itself remained unincorporated. As Hightower H. T. Kealing complained in an editorial in the *Review*, this meant that the local churches had a legal existence that the general church did not have. Consequently, any congregation's refusal to be governed by the discipline of the church would be upheld by the civil legal system. A number of churches, Bethel included, used the power incorporation gave them to deny the right of the pastor to preside over meetings of the board of trustees, even though this right was "explicitly set forth in the Discipline of the Connection." Moves were made to incorporate the connection, but for the general church to regain control of the recalcitrant churches, the churches would have to surrender their charters and agree to new ones dictated by the general body.[39] By reorganizing the corporation and board of trustees at Mother Bethel, Williams would be bringing back into line perhaps the most important church in the A.M.E. Connection. The pastor believed, therefore, that if he executed this takeover successfully he would be elected bishop at the A.M.E. Church Convention in June of 1920.[40] This would have made him one of the most powerful black churchmen in the country.

Williams was playing with fire. Many members of the congregation were bound to be upset by the amount of power that he wished to concentrate in the hands of the pastor. In addition, the idea of voting rights for women was still very difficult for many members of the congregation to accept. Williams might have supported the vote for women from a conviction of its justness, but it cannot have escaped his attention that women had always constituted a majority of Bethel's membership. If Williams gained control of the corporation with the migrants' votes, he may have believed he could retain that control with the support of women.[41] Another important consideration was the fact that the A.M.E. episcopacy had declared that women should have the vote; if Williams had had aspirations toward the bishopric, he would not have wished to contradict episcopal policy.[42] But while voting power for women was a good long-term policy for Williams, it could not help him in the short term. Men controlled the corporation, and they would be less likely to support the pastor if they knew that this was one of his goals.[43]

Lastly, Williams had neglected to take into consideration the great attachment of members to the church edifice. Since it had been constructed at great expense to church members in 1890, the building had become a shrine for African Methodists, despite the fact that it was now located in an increasingly white residential area.[44] According to Montrose William Thornton, pastor of Bethel between 1907 and 1912, hundreds of tourists annually visited this landmark, often described as the "abbey of African Methodism."[45] They came to see the stained glass windows, which featured deceased African Methodist bishops, important events in the life of Jesus, and symbols from the Masonic Order and the Order of the Eastern Star.[46] Or they came to see the sarcophagus of Richard Allen, the founder of Bethel, which had been placed in a crypt in the basement of the building. Belonging to a revered church bestowed a prestige that members were unwilling to relinquish.[47]

The power struggle came to a head in March 1920, when Williams organized "a special men's conference" to discuss with his supporters plans to gain control of the corporation. The meeting did not go as planned. Some trustees had learned of the meeting and had decided to confront Williams outside his lawyer's office, at 17th and South Streets, before the meeting.[48] As Williams approached the office, several "spotters" came toward him. As soon as he recognized them in the light from the street lamps, the pastor turned on his heels and ran down Kater Street, a side street running parallel to South. He managed to escape, but three hours later he returned and was met by the same men. Another chase ensued, during which Williams boarded a trolley for center city. Unfortunately for the pastor, the trolley moved slowly and one pursuer managed to catch up with it. The "spotter" boarded the trolley and sat down next to Williams, and the two fell into a heated argument during which Williams revealed his plans to wrest control of Bethel from his opposition.

Two Sundays after the South Street chase, on April 12, the congregation met at Bethel Church for the annual meeting to elect a president and other corporation officials. Having learned of Williams's plan, Colonel Edwards was well prepared to thwart the pastor's strategy. When D. A. Hart, one of Williams's supporters, rose to speak, Edwards informed him that he could not be recognized at the meeting because he had not entered the church with a letter and had never been publicly read into the church. Next, Thompson tried to address the president, but he was informed that he could not be recognized for the same reasons. Both Hart and Thompson were asked to vacate the space reserved for members of the corporation. Steadfast in their conviction, however, they remained where they were. Hart had been a member of the church for at least four years and had been chairman of the Information Bureau since its inception in 1917. Likewise, Thompson was a respected member of the church and had attended many previous corporation meetings without objection. After a few minutes of protest Hart withdrew peacefully, but Thompson remained until the sexton called police officers to escort him to the vestibule.[49]

Williams could succeed only if his men were elected to the corporation, but the likelihood of this dissipated once Edwards evoked a seldom used Bethel bylaw. This law decreed that "the names of all candidates for election must be placed in the church thirty days prior to election."[50] Since the conspiracy itself was less than thirty days old, none of the names of Williams's candidates had been placed on a noticeboard in the church, and all were disqualified. Thus, Edwards's men were elected, and Edwards was returned to the presidency.

Discussion at the meeting then turned to the question of how to depose Williams. Edwards made an impassioned speech about the history of the church and all that it stood for. He was ashamed to say that the church was not fulfilling its historic purpose because "there are a few members who have lately come among us who have sectarian ideas about North and South. Had Richard Allen desired that Bethel be like other churches," he continued, "he would not have had it incorporated, for he secured through this medium a guard against white, and possibly some black, devils."[51] Others rose to condemn the pastor. Eugene D. Fennell mentioned several conversations during which Williams had declared his intention to alter the status of Bethel's incorporation and had admitted that his main concern was not to injure his candidacy for the bishopric. The pastor's fate was sealed. A resolution was adopted and sent to the presiding bishop for the Philadelphia District declaring that "under no circumstances do we want Reverend Robert J. Williams returned to Bethel A.M.E. as pastor."[52]

The following Sunday, April 18, Williams sat in the congregation. After a visiting clergyman finished his sermon, the pastor rose to the pulpit and, in a last bid to pull the congregation to his side, proclaimed, "I am going to dismiss the heads of various departments of the church. I have already taken the class books away from some class leaders, and I may take away the license of some of the local preachers who voted against my return to this pulpit." After this threat, he continued, "I am ready to die and go to heaven or hell. I am going to preach the funeral of seven who were against my return. I am going to be returned to Bethel against all opposition." Believing that he had stirred up enough support for his cause, Williams called a meeting for the following Wednesday.

Williams had miscalculated, however. As we have seen, the members of the congregation who gathered for the Wednesday meeting came to dismiss the pastor, not to support him. Consequently, he was not returned to Mother Bethel by the bishop for the district. He left the church with about a hundred supporters in June 1920 and founded a new church, Thrift A.M.E., one month later. The church members made a down payment of $3,000 on a building at the corner of Broad and Christian Streets, but the deal fell through and they lost their money.[53] The *Tribune* then accused Williams of stealing several hundred dollars taken in at the only service held in this building but later retracted the charges.[54] The pastor's difficulties ended finally when another building was bought with the help of a supporter who contributed his entire life savings to Mt. Zion, as the church was now called. Williams ended his career in relative obscurity pastoring this church. He died in 1923 at the age of fifty-two.[55]

As with all political battles, the losing side suffers not only the indignity of defeat at the time of the struggle, it also suffers the vilification of those who record the events. Thus, the *Tribune* strongly favored the trustees of Bethel, treating Williams almost as if he were a megalomaniac. Yet we should not forget the same paper's description of Williams earlier in his pastorate as the "Earnest Pastor." No doubt he did have considerable concern for the welfare of southern migrants, but at some point during his pastorate he acquired a taste for power. Whether it became the addiction implied in the *Tribune* and whether it was greater than Colonel Edwards's own desire for power is another matter. Had Williams been at a Baptist church, where the pastor had more authority in relation to the congregation, or had he been successful in his attempt to gain control of Bethel, his desire for power might have gone unnoticed or have been viewed in a more favorable light. Furthermore, the elite members of the church cannot escape the charges of being opportunistic in their own way, increasing membership for financial reasons, and safeguarding their own power.

It is clear that Williams's personality had had a great impact on Mother Bethel. Once he had departed, Bethel's congregation managed to overcome its problems. Bishop William Henry Heard, the new bishop of the Philadelphia Conference, appointed Harry P. Anderson to Bethel, largely because he felt that Anderson would be able to communicate with both new and established members of the congregation.[56] This was a good appointment. Within a year most wounds had healed, and during Anderson's pastorate Bethel managed to continue its work for the migrants without friction,[57] mainly because Anderson was judicious enough not to challenge Edwards, who remained president long after Williams had departed.[58] Meanwhile, the percentage of newcomers to the city in the congregation increased as established members continued to leave the church in large numbers, the more prosperous ones joining the more elite Episcopal denomination.[59]

Robert J. Williams was not the only Methodist pastor who attempted to use the migrants' loyalty to undermine the position of an established elite in a church; nor was he the only minister who presided over a congregation that split apart. James Walker Hood Eason, pastor of Varick Temple A.M.E. Zion in South Philadelphia, also found himself faced with divisions in his congregation that his political maneuverings had largely created.

Eason was appointed to Varick in 1915, after his predecessor, Sylvester L. Corrothers, had been charged with misappropriating funds.[60] The young pastor from North Carolina was a renowned evangelist who could sweep an audience into a frenzy with ease. "When James Walker Hood Eason rose to his feet he was met with a storm of applause that continued for several minutes," according to the *Negro World*. "He was at his best and filled the body with brilliancy and fervor. He made his audience laugh and weep with him. He filled their emotional souls with visions of peace and tranquility."[61] Under Eason's stewardship, the congregation at Varick grew quickly, mainly because Eason welcomed migrants to the church.[62] He himself had been born in North Carolina, the son of a prominent Zion pastor in Alabama, James E. Eason, and was aware of the problems facing newcomers to the city. He was able to preach to them as one of their brethren.

New members entering Varick were particularly committed to the pastor, and Eason was quick to take advantage of this loyalty. When the pastor endeavored to make the board of trustees subordinate to himself in 1917, however, the established members of the congregation used their superior numbers on the board to expel him from the church. Consequently, the congregation divided. The group following Eason moved to a member's house until it could afford to make a down payment on a building formerly owned by the white congregation of Eighth United Presbyterian. The new church was named the People's Church and was located just four blocks away from Varick Temple, at 15th and Christian Streets.[63]

Shortly after Eason had formed this new church, he joined Marcus Garvey's Universal Negro Improvement Association. Without his congregation's approval, he sold the church building to Garvey's Black Star Line for $25,000 at the end of 1919. It may well be that Eason thought his congregation would follow him into the Garvey movement, but in fact his action caused an uproar among the church members, who filed a civil suit against him. Once the case was settled in favor of the congregation (which regained the church building), the members decided to return to the A.M.E. Zion Connection and changed the name of their church to Metropolitan. Rev. B. J. Bolding was appointed to replace Eason, and members of the Varick congregation agreed to share several services with their Zion brothers and sisters at Metropolitan.[64] As in the case of Mother Bethel, once the pastor concerned had been removed from the picture, the divisions between the conflicting groups were smoothed over. Meanwhile, the estranged pastor left Philadelphia for New York, where he campaigned fulltime for the UNIA. He became extremely popular, so much so that he threatened the power of Garvey himself. Then, in 1923, he was mysteriously assassinated.[65]

The examples of Williams at Mother Bethel and Eason at Varick Temple clearly cannot be used to suggest that established black Philadelphians were implacably opposed to the influx of migrants into their churches and that conflicts between old and new black Philadelphians were inevitable. Certain aspects of the Bethel conflict, for example, reveal that the lines were not neatly drawn between older and newer groups in the city. First, by requiring letters of transmittal and examining new arrivals, members of the church elite were able to attract people who they believed would fit into the congregation, showing that they themselves recognized distinctions among the migrants. Second, established members of Bethel objected to the newcomers only when they began to try to displace members of the board of trustees. The fact that they originally set up a welcoming committee and participated in city-wide efforts to house the migrants shows that they had had considerable concern for the welfare of the new arrivals. Further, after Williams had left Bethel, the church did not "replace the latch on its door" to keep out the migrants, and when the rate of migration increased again in 1922 and 1923, the church contributed to efforts of the A.M.E. denomination to alleviate some of the newcomers' housing problems.

The rapid increase in the size of many congregations, along with the continued high turnover of members caused by the movement of families around the city, led to some instability in these congregations. This instability could be manipulated very easily by ministers wishing to increase their power and prestige (as in the Varick and Mother Bethel cases), as well as by members of the congregations. Nevertheless, the direct cause of this instability was not a sectional conflict between Northerners and Southerners.

The fact that Williams and Eason, both of whom had been brought up in the South, were considered established Philadelphians indicates that lines between older and newer residents of the city were not clear-cut. Important divisions existed, but they tended to be between people like Major Wright, who came north with resources and connections, and those who did not. Both groups settled in Philadelphia into new congregations that were similar to those they had been members of in the South, whether of the older denominations or of the newer, so-called cult organizations.

Often the dividing line fell between migrants who came from urban areas and those from rural districts of the South. The former managed to assimilate into the northern urban community more easily than the latter. Indeed, the very fact that some newcomers were able to compete for control of major A.M.E. and A.M.E. Zion churches in Philadelphia signified that they had assimilated well into the community and had learned how things were run. Ironically, it also represented the openness of the congregations as well as the ability of some newcomers to settle into the institutional life of the black community.

However, incidents at Mother Bethel and Varick also reveal that the good intentions of black churchgoers could be undermined, if only temporarily, by political maneuverings within the congregation. Since blacks were cut off from many avenues for advancement, their churches became places where power and prestige could be secured. Opening the doors of the churches to newcomers created instability. Conflict, or a mass exodus of longtime members, could be averted only if the newcomers did not threaten the positions of more established members. Once a pastor began to manipulate the situation to his own advantage, power struggles were likely. These struggles in turn detracted from a congregation's ability to aid the migrants.

The conflict at "Mother" Bethel was no mere family squabble. It represented in a nutshell many of the dilemmas facing African Americans in Philadelphia during this period. Was it possible for black people to continue making progress toward integration and equality in the city of brotherly love? Would it be possible for "the race" to unite in opposition to oppression? Would black institutions continue to be financially secure and remain the locus of community life, helping to bring about a degree of racial unity? Or would their centrality in black communities be questioned and their efforts to survive foster division rather than unity? Looked at in the light of such questions, the earnest pastor's efforts look less like megalomania than a failed attempt to come to terms with his church's changing position in Philadelphia.

CHAPTER 10

"Let This Be Your Home"

*Wherefore say unto the children of Israel, I am the Lord, and I
will bring you out from under the burdens of the Egyptians, and I
will rid you out of their bondage, and I will redeem you with a
stretched out arm, and with great judgments.*

EXODUS 6:6, quoted on Bethel envelopes

The role of northern black churches in the migration of African Americans from the South has been painted in an unfavorable light. Historians have argued that established black churches were unprepared for the influx of newcomers and that migrants felt compelled to create their own congregations because church members did not show enough consideration toward them and in fact betrayed a good deal of hostility. They have also suggested that because religious organizations created by the migrants were small and unstable, they were not equipped to provide their members with the benefits that larger, more stable churches offered. The established black churches' unwillingness or inability to help change black peasants into urban dwellers is thus seen as a major reason for the subsequent failure of African Americans, in contrast to other immigrant groups, to escape from ghettos.[1]

In fact, however, as we can see from the example of Mother Bethel, the older churches were prepared to receive the migrants. During the period of the Great Migration, many of Philadelphia's African Methodists followed Robert J. Williams's example and advertised their church's "homelike" atmosphere in order to attract migrants and make them feel welcome.[2] Moreover, migration was not a totally new phenomenon for black churches. As early as 1907, Richard R. Wright, Jr., recognized that many churches in the community were almost totally reliant on migrants for the bulk of their members.[3] And in 1912, he wrote in *The Negro in Pennsylvania*: "In a large city like Philadelphia or Pittsburgh, where men are busy and time is valuable, the incoming migrant from the South would be at a great loss had he not the church to which to go, at first, at least" (pp. 116–17). Black churches had been confronted with a large influx of southern blacks for many years before the First World War, and former Southerners made up large proportions of Philadelphia's congregations. At Mother Bethel, for example, in 1915, almost 56 percent of the congregation had been born in former slave states.[4]

Furthermore, black churches undertook a great deal of work to help the migrants, and their members were usually very concerned to give the newcomers a helping hand. Lack of understanding and unwillingness to change were abundant in Philadelphia's African Methodist churches. But in the final analysis, the proliferation of churches during and after the Great Migration resulted more from the desire of migrants to recreate the religious institutions that had served them well in the South than from the hostility of northern blacks.

Response of African Methodist Leaders to the Migration

One of the difficulties facing a historian studying the response of black churchgoers to the migration is that many of the most vocal black church leaders clearly believed that established blacks were not fully meeting the needs of the migrants. As a result, it is difficult for the historian not to agree. However, close scrutiny soon reveals that many black leaders had in fact set an impossible standard and that established blacks did much more for the migrants than anyone would expect who is aware of how poorly immigrants have often been treated by their new communities.

The high standard of black leaders derived from ideology and, in particular, theology. African Methodists believed that they were similar to their white brothers and sisters, except that they themselves were not hypocritical, while other Christians demonstrably were. After all, had not these other Christians held them in bondage and discriminated against them in the pews? Those who shared this belief, men like Reverdy C. Ransom, T. Thomas Fortune, R. R. Downs, and Richard R. Wright, Jr., felt that the arrival of migrants in northern cities represented a chance for African Americans to show that they had advanced in Christianity beyond white hypocrisy. Downs argued in the *Christian Recorder*, for example, that the A.M.E. Church should reach out to "the oppressed" in accordance with the principles of "human rights [which] gave birth to African Methodism." He continued:

> Eliminate this basic truth-principle, and "Our Church" so styled, has no other claim to a legitimate, institutional, religious existence in the family of Methodist Churches. It must represent such an idea of right principle, or it is nothing; and we are in the eyes of others false in our boasts and proclamations. Therefore, our brethren from the Southland, fleeing from injustice and caste oppression, should receive from us a frank and open institutional reception according to our profession.[5]

Further, the idea of progress was an important part of African Methodist ideology, an idea that was based upon the notion of racial uplift. The existence of large numbers of extremely poor African Americans living in conditions of squalor did not reflect well on the community as a whole, and many black religious leaders felt that a crusade was necessary to "uplift" the impoverished migrants. The disappointment of ministers and other black intellectuals with church members who seemed to show more concern for individual, family, and group prestige than for the newcomers helped to create the myth that black churches failed to respond to the problems arising from the migration.

The irony of this is that the black middle classes, according to this view, were acting in a way that might be expected of members of the white middle class, whose success in the business realm blacks were supposed to emulate. The black leaders were thus asking their followers to perform a difficult, if not impossible, task. Not only were African Americans supposed to pull themselves up by their bootstraps; they were also supposed to pull "the race" up at the same time. While European ethnic groups seemed to benefit from the success of individual European Americans, whether the successful individuals helped members of their group or not, African Americans did not benefit unless those of their race who were successful put aside their own desire for prestige and advancement and helped their brothers and sisters. Since it was the desire for advancement that had motivated them to strive toward material success, it was unrealistic to expect them to act in this altruistic way. This is why E. Franklin Frazier's attack on the "Black Bourgeoisie" was harsh, and also why black religious leaders were bound to be disappointed by the manner in which established blacks responded to black migrants.[6]

Nearly all church leaders believed that northern blacks should reach out to the newcomers and lend them a helping hand. None went so far as Bishop Levi J. Coppin, who, when he had seen African country folk entering cities in the Cape Colony, had felt that they "should really somehow be placed in the care of Christian guardians." However, many agreed with the bishop that "the Church should stand ready to meet them [the newcomers] at the 'gate of the city' and offer them protection and guidance that an unsuspecting plain man from the country needs, when suddenly ushered into modern city life."[7]

T. Thomas Fortune supported the migration as a way for black people to fulfill the scriptural purpose that had brought them from the shores of Africa, to "make them as one with the National Race type."[8] George Wesley Allen, editor of the *Southern Christian Recorder*, saw the hand of providence behind the migration, "breaking down barriers to a long-oppressed and struggling people." Just when opposition to blacks was at its peak, "a door of opportunity was divinely opened in the more favorable industrial sections of the country." The chance to move north was seen as a test of "Negro manhood." "If these emigrants make good in the elements of good citizenship," the editor wrote, "they will disapprove [*sic*] the doctrine of our oppressors, who say the Negro is indolent, shiftless, unreliable, without morals and totally unfitted for citizenship. This will be an irresistible defense for the entire race, North and South, but especially the South."[9]

Given the importance attributed to the northward migration, the intellectuals believed it was imperative that those who were already established in the North welcome the newcomers in their midst. Richard R. Wright went so far as to beg northern blacks to welcome "their brother" from the South.[10] R. R. Downs likewise tried to persuade his readers to be more open to the migrants. "Why should they be met at the city's gates with doubts and suspicion," he questioned, "as though they were enemies to and destructive of civilization?" He pointed to some of the migrants' qualities:

> Skilled men among these people have been from generation to
> generation, in all branches of industries; besides many of them represent
> money and property. They are quite far from being beggars, loafers or
> vagabonds. They may, many of them, come from farms; but we cannot

argue from that that they are unfit and a menace. Many of them owned farms and are the children of farm owners. Perhaps one might note the crudeness of country manners, but it is not because they are vicious or immoral. It is as cruel as it is unkind, even unchristian, to charge all the vagrancy and acts of immorality to the Negro of the South.

"Speaking for our Church," Downs continued, "we cannot but give them otherwise than a reception in accord with our knowledge of their mechanical skill and ability." He believed that the fears that some northern blacks had about the influx of migrants were "the product of a diseased imagination, and our doubts of them evidence our lack of faith in the Negro and our own moral weakness." Downs reminded his readers of Leviticus 19:34: "God says," he wrote, "But the stranger that dwelleth with you shall be unto you as one born among you, and thou shalt love him as thyself; for ye were strangers in the land of Egypt: I am the Lord your God."[11]

Reverdy C. Ransom, editor of the A.M.E. Church *Review* and another supporter of the migration, advanced a manifesto for his denomination "in this epochal hour when new pages of history are being written every day." Ransom warned of "obligations and opportunities which can neither be avoided [n]or ignored." While the corporations and industrial concerns would take care of the economic side of the migration, the churches had to provide moral support for the migrants. "The moral and social aspects involved in the movement of so many thousands into a new and strange environment, remains the work of the Church and kindred organizations," Ransom wrote. "The Church must create new forms of service and new lines of activity to meet the instant demands of a new situation." He recognized that much was being done by individual churches, "but our denomination has not, up to now, attempted to organize the immense resources at its command to conserve the moral and spiritual welfare of the many thousands who increasingly are swarming into the North, East, and Western sections of our country." Ransom considered it quite unworthy of members of the A.M.E. Church to regard the southern blacks as merely "a menace or a problem." For Ransom, as for Wright and Fortune, these newcomers constituted an opportunity.[12]

The editor of the *Southern Recorder* also focused on the need for northern blacks to help their southern brothers and sisters. "It is of the highest importance," George Wesley Allen wrote,

> to every member of the race who possesses any degree of race pride to get busy among these emigrants and help them in every way possible to

get a proper start in their new homes. Some of these people will be found to have correct ideas and will take a right view of things, adapting themselves to their new surroundings, and will make good useful citizens. Others are destitute of many of the prime elements of good citizenship, and are, therefore, not very helpful to any community. It is among this class that special work is necessary, to avoid fatal blunders which will cripple the interest of the whole race.

The writer was encouraged, in particular, by the work being done in Philadelphia by the Interdenominational Ministerial Alliance, which had organized church members to take in lodgers. He hoped that other communities would adopt similar plans "to fortify these immigrants against vice and weakness of every form, and whatever would cause them to prove a failure."[13]

The writings of Wright, Ransom, Fortune, and Allen influenced many northern pastors and clearly impressed Robert J. Williams at Mother Bethel. The leaflets he distributed around the South attempting to persuade Southerners to move north revealed a commitment to the migration similar to that shared by these men. Williams's arguments for coming north resembled those of his colleague Wright. Both men endeavored to contradict those Southerners who were advancing reasons for blacks to remain in the South. For Williams, the best response to these people was "to state the facts as they are":

> All honest people are agreed that the opportunities are better in the
> North today for colored people than they have ever been. The wages
> paid are higher than what they get in the South. The average wage paid
> to colored men in the South is not over $1.00 per day for ten hours work.
> The average wage in the North is over $2.00 per day for eight hours,
> more than double what it is in the South. The cost of food and clothing
> are about the same. House rent is higher in some places, but not double
> what it is in the South. These three items are the principal expenses of
> living. If the earnings are more than double and only one of the three
> principal expenses are higher, you can easily determine for yourself
> whether or not you will make a mistake to come North.

Other "facts" that Williams mentioned were the better schooling, better employment opportunities and political rights for blacks, and the availability of justice "administered according to the law" not "by the color of the skin." While Williams admitted that there was prejudice in cities like Philadelphia, he agreed with Wright that "that prejudice has not to this time broken down the law of justice."

Likewise, Williams shared the view of men like Wright and Ransom that the movement north of thousands of blacks was as significant as the exodus of Israelites out of Egypt. On the envelope in which his leaflets were sent, for example, Williams printed words from Malachi 3:1:

> Behold, I will send my messenger, and he shall prepare the way before me: and the Lord, whom ye seek, shall suddenly come to his temple, even the messenger of the covenant, whom ye delight in: behold, he shall come saith the Lord of hosts.

Williams also alluded to this association by printing an excerpt from Exodus 6:6 alongside the quotation from Malachi. It read: "I am the Lord, and I will bring you out from under the burdens . . . and I will redeem you with a stretched out arm, and with great judgments."[14] And, in the *Recorder*, Williams wrote, "I believe it is the voice of Abraham's God, saying get thee out from among the people and go to the land that I shall afterward show thee."[15] The pastor clearly felt that by encouraging black people to move and by offering them assistance on their arrival in Philadelphia he was performing a service both for his people and for God, just as Moses had done in earlier times. "Come thou with us," Williams wrote, quoting from Numbers 10:29, "and we will do thee good: for the Lord hath spoken good concerning Israel."

The support of African Methodist intellectuals for the migration persuaded many A.M.E. ministers and churchgoers to aid the migrants when they arrived at the gates of the city. As a result, many congregations worked very hard to improve the lot of those who came north and to provide tangible benefits for them.

The Work of Black Churches on Behalf of Migrants

While individual members of the established Philadelphia black community often expressed a great deal of dislike for the migrants, whom they saw as a threat to their positions, black churches on the whole stretched forth a helping hand. The churches were very receptive to the arrival of new members. Throughout the period of heaviest migration, many churches continued to invite new members into their congregations through the religion pages of the *Tribune*, and many reported large increases in membership both during the war and in the early 1920s.[16] There were good reasons for congregations to want more members, not least of which was to increase the prestige of both their pastor and themselves in the community. Churches like Allen A.M.E., Mother Bethel

A.M.E., First African Baptist, Central Baptist, Tindley Temple M.E., and Holy Trinity Baptist, all went through periods of expansion that increased the prominence of their pastors. Even Morris Brown A.M.E., noted for being exclusive, welcomed migrants.

Preston Paul Gaines, pastor of Morris Brown in 1917, noted that several southern people had joined his church. He wrote, "We find them of a high type of character; they are loyal and very responsive to all the demands of the church. I also know them to be industrious. There are many living in my community who are not members of my church, but there is no fault found of them so far."[17] Similar developments were occurring in Baptist churches. Wesley F. Graham of Holy Trinity Baptist reported that "about seventy-five of the friends who have come from the far South in the great exodus movement have joined my church." Graham was also impressed by the quality of the new members. "I find that they are an excellent, pious, industrious class of people, some of them being above the average in intelligence," he wrote. "They make excellent church members, faithful in attendance, liberal in their giving, and very attentive to the preaching of the gospel. Nearly all of them, however, are from rural districts and have been either cotton-growers or truck farmers."[18] There was little cause for members of Holy Trinity to dislike the newcomers because of their southern origin, even if they were from rural districts and therefore less accustomed to city life.

The greatest problem caused by the migration was in housing, both in terms of its availability for the newcomers and its standard; many people were being forced to live in rundown dwellings. Three groups connected with black churches developed in response to this challenge: two organized essentially by white philanthropic and business groups, the other by black churches alone. The most lasting group was the Committee on Negro Migration, which became the central organization for dealing with problems arising out of the migration.

The chairman of this organization as well as of the subcommittee on housing was John Ihlder, whose work on behalf of black migrants in Philadelphia (along with that of the secretary, John T. Emlen) received widespread praise from leaders of the black churches. The committee worked as an umbrella organization bringing together social workers, church officials and leaders, and representatives of industries such as the Franklin Sugar Refining Company and the Pennsylvania Railroad. It received help from the Armstrong Association (the local branch of the Urban League), Travelers Aid (which dealt with new arrivals at the railway stations and secured temporary shelter), the Society for Organizing Charity, and the Philadelphia Housing Association. Some black churches were represented directly by ministers: Wesley F. Graham was chairman of the Committee on Churches, and William A. Harrod of First African Baptist was a member at large.[19]

The committee studied migration extensively, located vacant apartments for migrants, and set up a job center to list openings. It also suggested that temporary structures be erected to house the newcomers and persuaded the Pennsylvania Railroad, for example, to contribute tents and box cars for shelter.[20] In the long term, the committee hoped "that we shall be able to secure a considerable new area for negro occupancy," though in the end this was to be achieved more by white flight than by deliberate planning.[21]

The second white-initiated group arose out of a meeting of the Commission on Work among the Colored People, a Protestant Episcopal organization. Under the leadership of Bishop Rhinelander, a subcommittee was formed to take action for better housing conditions in March 1917.[22] Archdeacon Henry L. Phillips, whose work at the Church of the Crucifixion (an institutional church providing many social welfare programs) had brought much praise from W.E.B. Du Bois twenty years earlier, was a prominent member of this subcommittee. While the subcommittee had an independent beginning, its members soon realized that their most constructive work would be to assist, rather than duplicate, the work of the Committee of Negro Migration.

Black churches meanwhile established the Interdenominational Ministerial Alliance. As early as January 1917, "a great race meeting" of black pastors, including several from the A.M.E. Church, was held at Holy Trinity Baptist Church to consider how best to respond to problems resulting from the migration.[23] The responses developed were manifold. The I.M.A. attempted to alleviate problems facing the migrants at every stage of their move north. It used its connections with southern churches and religious journals to provide information for potential migrants, helped new arrivals find jobs and housing in the city, and attempted to persuade some of those who might be prejudiced against the newcomers to welcome them.

To solve the migrants' problems in Philadelphia itself, the I.M.A. pushed for the enrollment of newcomers in congregations and for aid for them through the churches. The Rev. Tindley of East Calvary was asked to develop a plan for relieving the housing shortage. He suggested that church members take in lodgers; East Calvary led the way, with several hundred members taking migrants into their homes. A.M.E. churches, having recently accommodated several hundred delegates from around the country during the denomination's Centennial Conference at Mother Bethel, also participated in this initiative (it is even possible that some delegates returned as migrants to stay with the people who had housed them during the conference). Tindley's solution was never sufficient, however, not only because some established blacks did not want to accept migrants as members of their households, but also because one of the fundamental problems with housing was overcrowding, which Tindley's plan could only exacerbate.[24]

The I.M.A. also established an information bureau in one of East Calvary's buildings. The bureau was opened "for the purpose of serving the benefit of the large number of people coming from the South and other lands to the city of Philadelphia as well as for the unfortunate among us who have lived here before."[25] It was to be a "bureau of information entirely free of charge to the applicant," but a place also that offered a fairly substantial content of "uplift" and training. An article in the *Christian Recorder*'s migration issue described the programs to be carried out at the building.

> Here we are to direct [people] to places of employment and places where they may find good homes to live in. A daily demonstration of much importance will be given to mothers and house keepers intended to instruct them in these matters so that with small incomes they can keep a clean house or room and prepare good and wholesome food. Sewing circles are to receive and remake or make clothing for those who are too poor to properly clothe their children. Visiting committees are to visit in the sections where such is needed, to impart impetus and information in all the little things needed to make home happy and family comfortable. Tracts also are to be distributed bearing on questions of temperance and morality. All the many sides of life are to be looked after by this social service establishment.

Commitment to such programs belies the impression that churches remained detached from the migrants, though some migrants may have been offended or alienated by the patronizing attitude underlying some of the help offered.

Finally, the I.M.A. sent a letter with useful information for prospective migrants to churches in the South. The letter, which was reprinted in the *Recorder*, provides a complete picture of the process of migration, albeit through the eyes of northern ministers, and reveals that the organization had gathered a great deal of information from working with the new arrivals. Like many such letters, it laid out all the benefits of migrating north, but it also provided useful advice. It told prospective migrants to beware of employment agents; to refrain from selling properties in the South for less than full market value; and to trust their money to no one without proof that he "represents all that he claims to represent." The letter also suggested that heads of household come north alone at first to secure a job and housing before sending for any kin and that prospective migrants not leave an employer without giving notice, pointing out that employers' references were valuable. Some of the advice in the letter was quite specific. "Don't buy straight tickets," the advice on traveling north read. "If you come over 700 miles, or 300 miles and expect to go back, buy a mileage book for $20. Our people have paid the railroads possibly $50,000 more than they should, merely by buying straight tickets and not mileage."[26] The letter reveals the level of commitment that members of the I.M.A. made to the migrants. However, it also reveals a bias on the part of the organization toward migrants with resources who were able to prepare for their trip before leaving.

When the second upsurge in migration occurred in late 1923, the Interdenominational Ministerial Alliance no longer existed. It had disbanded when the rate of migration had returned to its prewar levels. This did not mean, however, that churches no longer cared about the migrants. Instead, the churches coordinated their work with the Committee on Negro Migration. Their contribution to this organization was very effective, as a report of July 9, 1923, issued by this body attests.

> The social problem arising from this influx of strangers not familiar with urban living is being provided for by welfare organizations and the Churches of the denomination to which the majority belong. These churches are seeking out newcomers in their districts and making them welcome, offering advice and assistance where needed, acquainting them with city ways. New arrivals without a local destination are being met at the trains. The Migration Committee is listing their names, their church, and fraternity affiliations and transferring this information to a committee made up of representatives from prominent negro organizations. This committee sends the information to churches and branch lodges with which the migrants would naturally wish to affiliate.[27]

Clearly, the committee felt that it was getting a great deal of assistance from the churches.

Another report of the Committee on Negro Migration singled out

Allen A.M.E. Church as "doing especially important work in looking out for the migrants." The report continued,

> Through the suggestion of Dr. John P. Turner, a member of the Board of Managers of the Armstrong Association, a committee has been formed to welcome the migrants to that church. This committee also makes inquiry into the family condition and has arranged for directing the individuals to institutions and homes. This church has offered its services to the Migration Committee in whatever capacity it may be used.[28]

While Allen was singled out in this way, it was not the only church offering help to the migrants. Churches like Harry P. Anderson's Mother Bethel and Tindley's East Calvary did similar work.

Besides working with the committee, individual churches and denominations also continued to carry out their own plans to alleviate the problem of housing migrants. Ministers of the A.M.E. Church, for example, established the Richard Allen House in 1924, which acted as a halfway house for newcomers. The house was open to all migrants for a short period on their arrival in Philadelphia. Residents were helped to find their friends and relatives, if they had any in the city, and to find permanent housing. The Richard Allen House also provided an employment service.

The *Tribune* believed, however, that churches were doing less than they might to support the migrants. They noted that the A.M.E. initiative "is one of the few efforts of the churches in the large cities to help handle the question of migration."[29] These complaints are shown to be erroneous by the Committee on Negro Migration reports. Perhaps Clarence Whyte summed up the work of the churches most accurately when he noted, in 1923, that "the churches are awake to the seriousness of the problem [of migration] and are doing all that is possible for them to do for the newcomers."[30]

The churches, then, were doing a great deal to aid the migrants. The main limitation on their work derived from their particularism. During times of depression they could very effectively aid people in a general way by establishing soup kitchens and passing out coal to the needy, and they could organize committees to push for better housing. When it came to aiding specific migrants, however, either by bringing them into their homes as lodgers or by welcoming them into their congregations, they either wished to discriminate among newcomers, or they found themselves unable to appeal to them. During the war at least, Methodist congregations gave preferential treatment to people who brought letters of transmittal from their old churches. Letters identified the bearers as persons of reasonable standing in their former congregations and provided rough indicators of respectability.

Moreover, the story of the migration is not frictionless. The fact that so many black intellectuals felt it necessary to appeal to established blacks in the northern cities to be more welcoming to the newcomers suggests a degree of enmity in the minds of some more settled blacks toward the new arrivals.

"Too Vicious to Be Tolerated"

Had the idealism of black church leaders been the only influence on black churchgoers, the story of the migration and the church's role in it might have been truly remarkable, rivaling any moral crusade that has ever occurred. However, other influences were also evident, one of which was the desire of established Philadelphians to retain control of the congregations they had worked so hard to secure. Another was their belief that the arrival of the migrants was leading to a deterioration of living standards for members of the black community and an increase in white racism. Yet another, as we have seen at Mother Bethel, was the desire for political power and prestige on the part of individual ministers wishing to use the influx of migrants to their own benefit. Such influences would lead to more prejudicial attitudes toward the Southerners and a withdrawal of the hand of greeting by many blacks.

Paradoxically, the separation of the African American community from surrounding white communities exacerbated the tensions arising from social and cultural differences existing among sections of the black community, making it more difficult for African Americans to develop the racial solidarity that was often witnessed within other ethnic groups. Both old and new black residents of Philadelphia were forced to gain prestige and security from within a community that was beleaguered by poor housing conditions and limited city services. Understandably, therefore, the older residents often felt resentment toward the newcomers and blamed them unfairly both for increased white prejudice against all blacks and for the deterioration of living standards in the black community.

As might be expected, the more established black Philadelphians did not always heed the advice of men like Wright and Ransom. According to Ralph H. Jones, Charles Albert Tindley's biographer and a man who was baptized in 1906 in Tindley's church, some members of East Calvary regarded the newcomers as "dumb, ignorant, poorly clothed southerners."[31] Forrester Washington, head of the Armstrong Association, summed up the prevailing opinions in 1917 thus: "Both the native colored and white people of our community have a feeling that the Southern man is more criminal than the northern which creates a very unpleasant attitude towards the newcomers."[32] Carter G. Woodson used the harshest terms to describe such hostile sentiments: "They [the migrants] are not wanted by the whites and are treated with contempt by the native blacks of the northern cities, who consider their brethren from the South too criminal and too vicious to be tolerated."[33] Clearly, these sentiments were very real among the established Philadelphians, and they cannot be glossed over or dismissed lightly.

In her 1921 study of the migrants, Sadie T. Mossell explained the hostility of established blacks toward the newcomers in the following way:

> The city had long possessed a relatively small population of Negroes of culture, education and some financial means. They had always enjoyed the same social and educational facilities as the whites and courteous treatment from them. But, with the increase in population by a group of generally uneducated and untrained persons, these privileges were withdrawn . . . the old colored citizens of Philadelphia resented this, [and] placed the blame at the migrant's door and stood aloof from him.[34]

Mossell's assessment of the privileges of the black community prior to the migration was perhaps a little exaggerated, possibly tinged by the romanticism of a youth protected from the harshest forms of social prejudice. Nevertheless, white prejudice did increase after the influx of Southerners. Schools, restaurants, hotels, lunch counters, dime store counters, and some theaters began to bar black people.[35] Philadelphia began to introduce practices normally associated with the South. Members of the black elite, not too surprisingly, were upset by these developments, and they may also have feared that "lynch law" would come north along with the migrants.

Mossell, a member of Union A.M.E. Church, considered the church the most important institution for improving the standard of living of newcomers and thought it in the interest of the community as a whole to aid them. For until these people were uplifted, the community as a whole would be shunned by Philadelphia's white society.[36] But while some established Philadelphians shared Mossell's desire to uplift the migrants, many others wished to maintain their distance or, when that was not possible, to shun them.

Even Major Richard R. Wright, Sr., father of the editor of the *Christian Recorder*, who had many influential friends and financial security, faced considerable prejudice from established black Philadelphians when he arrived in the city. With the help of his son and other ministers in the A.M.E. Church, the former president of a Georgia black college founded the Citizens and Southern Bank. One afternoon, as he sat watching the carpenters begin the building that would house the bank, an "upper crust" lady approached him. She scowled at him and asked him where he was from. To this, the major responded, "I'm from Georgia." The conversation that ensued revealed the animosity of some established Philadelphians toward the migrants:

> "Why don't you go back where you came from? Coming up here ruining us; making believe you going to open a bank."
> "I have eight children, Madame. My wife is coming next month."
> "My! My! Why don't you go back and stay. All those children. You can't make a living up here. A bank in this old store?"
> "Yes, Madame, this bank will be the Citizens and Southern Bank. You see, in the first place, it is the Citizens Bank. You are a citizen of Philadelphia, I know."
> "Yes, indeed. Both father and mother born right here in Philadelphia."
> "Where did your grandfather come from, Madame?"
> "Philadelphia."
> "Well, may I ask where your great grandfather come from?"
> "From Virginia."
> "Well, this bank—The Citizens and Southern Bank will cater to the citizens first, you see. They come first. Then it will include all of us Southerners next."[37]

The woman clearly expressed her detestation of the newcomers, and had he been less sharp-witted and less able to turn the woman's prejudices against her, the major would no doubt have harbored a grudge against the woman. After such an experience, migrants who did not have connections among the Philadelphia elite would have tried to avoid interaction with established blacks altogether. Instead, Wright saw the situation as an opportunity to highlight, in a light-hearted manner, the hypocrisy of those who were unwilling to welcome the newest arrivals from the South.

When Wright's bank was finally established, it was often ridiculed because it was closely associated in many people's minds with the migrants. Many former Southerners, especially those from Georgia, bought stock in the bank partly out of respect for the major. As a result of this association, according to Richard Wright, Jr., "Some of Philadelphia's Negro-American leaders, including one newspaper, tried to make a joke of the bank starting so humbly and having so many preachers on its board of directors, and opening and closing its board meetings with prayer." He continued, "Someone asked my father why he opened the bank with prayer. He said quickly, 'I thank God for everything. But I pray for the bank because I want God to keep the smart Negro-Americans from stealing the money from the dumb ones.'"[38]

Hostilities between established Philadelphians and the new arrivals, though they undoubtedly existed, have most likely been exaggerated, or misunderstood. First, acts of hostility were more noteworthy than acts of friendship, just as incidents of crime receive more attention than those in which the law is obeyed. And as with crime, it can be assumed that acts of hostility were the exception, not the norm. Second, antimigrant sentiment may have been the language through which class antagonisms were expressed. It is difficult to believe that many African Americans who bought shares at the Citizens and Southern Bank would have expressed a dislike for any members of the Wright family. People who brought resources with them into the community were most likely welcomed, just as Wright was by African Methodist leaders. By contrast, those who came north without resources most likely received the full brunt of the invective of some members of the elite.

Because the African American community was largely of southern origin, friction between newcomers and more established blacks, whenever it occurred, represented either a denial of southern origin or heritage among the latter (as in the instance of the "upper crust" lady) or a conflict between different types of migrants. For example, Wesley F. Graham, the popular minister of Trinity Baptist Church who assisted many of the new arrivals, distinguished between "respectable" and "mean negroes." "While we do not believe there will be any trouble in this city," he wrote, "there are many mean negroes, we know, who go about armed with razors and pistols, and they should be dealt with according to the law. We ourselves stand ready to assist in this."[39]

Color also divided Philadelphia's African American communities. Color bias among blacks is seldom given the attention it deserves, partly because it is difficult to deal with discrimination on the basis of skin pigmentation within a community of people who, collectively, are discriminated against because of the color of their skin. Nevertheless, differentiation along the lines of color was important between 1890 and 1940. It is quite noticeable, for example, in photographs of leading men and women within A.M.E. churches (trustees, ushers, and so on), that most of them would be considered light skinned.[40] Whether light skin was representative of the congregations from which these leaders emerged, or whether it characterized people who tended to become leaders, is open for interpretation. In either case, some form of discrimination was present.

The presence among the migrant population of many darker-skinned African Americans most likely led to some friction in the city's black churches. Such friction never made its way into newspapers like the *Tribune* or the *Independent*, however, as leaders of the community would not want to focus directly on such prejudice existing within the community. Instead, the prejudice was couched in terms of class and sectionalism, with the new arrivals being criticized as "greenhorns" and "Southerners." That friction did exist can be seen in the schism at First African Baptist Church. Here the leading members of the church, self-styled as "toasties," reserved the most prominent pews for themselves, and darker-skinned members were relegated to the back of the auditorium and the balcony. By 1921, the latter had had enough of this indignity and, following Richard Allen's path over two hundred years earlier, left the church en masse.[41]

While intraracial conflicts tended to revolve around things like rural versus urban background and class and color distinctions, they were articulated through a sectionalist rhetoric. A *Tribune* editorial entitled "The Exodus" dwelt at length on the complaints made against the new arrivals. "A great hue and cry has been going up on the part of our citizens over the awful problem forced upon us by the incoming wave of colored men and their families from the South," the editor wrote. "We complain that these people misbehave, are not cleanly, are loud of speech, are addicted to drink and good time." This blanket criticism of the migrants was in fact based on the different origins of the newcomers. "Their environment has been different," the author noted, "and they have been moved from small cities into the great urban center of Philadelphia." Migrants from urban environments, who had learned some of the restraints of urban industrial life, were exempt from such criticism.

The *Tribune* editor believed that if the "weaker brother" was properly welcomed he would soon adjust to urban life and "help our race to a higher standing in the community." The assumption that many of the new arrivals were inferior was explicit. "It is our duty," he wrote, "to take up these people, show them mainly by example how quiet, orderly and sober and cleanly we are and thus inspire them with new ambition to reach the high plane upon which we dwell."[42] Such negative assessments of many of the migrants were fairly general even among those who wished to help them. Quite possibly, therefore, the migrants themselves were alienated both by those who wished to shun them and by those who wished to aid them.

Ministerial leadership counteracted the tendency of established blacks to vilify the newcomers as a group. During the 1920s, ministers were usually highly respected members of the black community. It is unlikely that black churchgoers ignored pronouncements from the pulpits urging support for the migrants. Further, as members of the professional class, the ministers had many contacts among the elite of the community. R. R. Wright, Jr., was not just editor of the *Christian Recorder*; he was also a friend and associate (through the Citizens and Southern Bank) of many of the community's leading individuals like Walter C. Beckett, the funeral director, and Raymond Pace Alexander, the prominent lawyer (whose parents had moved north from Richmond at the beginning of the century). Beckett's records are full of requests for money for various charity undertakings. It can be assumed that he responded liberally because he was frequently thanked for financial assistance and invited to benefit functions given by organizations for people who had made, or were expected to make, contributions.[43]

Enmity toward the newcomers, either thought or expressed, was not so strong that it undermined the positive work of the congregations. Of course, it should not be taken lightly. Isolated instances of prejudice were enough to make those who experienced them (or those who were informed about them) feel unwelcome. As institutions, however, black churches were not wholly responsible for making the migrants feel unwelcome.

What may have been more damaging to racial unity than outright hostility was the Progressive sentiment that the poorer newcomers needed "uplifting." This attitude reflected a vision of northern urban superiority and southern rural inferiority that the newcomers were often unwilling to endorse. Confronted by the opinion that they would have to be reformed before being given full membership in the religious and secular institutions of the community, the new arrivals turned their backs on these institutions and created their own. In some ways, then, it was the high standards held by the intellectual elite that caused some of the problems. The crusade of uplift demanded by the likes of Downs, Wright, and Ransom might have been appealing because it reaffirmed the established Philadelphian's sense of superiority.[44]

Causes of Proliferation of Black Churches

If migrants are considered as having some degree of agency in the process of adjustment to northern urban life, then it is unlikely that the proliferation of churches was merely the result of the hostility of established Philadelphians or the failure of established churches to meet the needs of the new arrivals. When differences within the migrant population are fully appreciated, the expectation that all southern migrants would feel comfortable, provided they were welcomed, in any of the established churches, is untenable. While language barriers did not exist between established and migrant blacks (as they did between different Catholic ethnic groups), class and cultural differences based on geographical origin were often sufficient to create divisions as great as those among people from different countries. Thus to expect all southern migrants to feel comfortable in all established churches is akin to expecting Italians to feel comfortable in already established Irish congregations.[45]

While it is very hard to prove conclusively, evidence suggests that churches proliferated because migrants who moved north from rural districts desired to commune among people with whom they could feel "at home" and to recreate the smaller, closer-knit congregations that they were used to in the South. A southern black man or woman on arrival in Philadelphia would be very hesitant about joining a church. He or she would hunt around for a place that "had the home-like welcome."[46] This would have been a specific kind of church for each newcomer. A person who had been a member of a large Methodist church in the South might have felt comfortable joining a large church like Mother Bethel or East Calvary Church, but one who was used to a small congregation where everyone knew everyone else would have looked for such a church. Instead of joining a church that already existed, some people met with friends and relatives to form their own church.

The reports of the Committee on Negro Migration during 1923

reveal a tendency on the part of some new arrivals in Philadelphia to avoid joining existing churches (see Table 10.1). Between July and August membership among migrants fell from 54.5 percent to 24.9 percent, and it remained low in September. It is unlikely that the churches altered their behavior toward the newcomers markedly in the space of a couple of months. The explanation for the change lies in the changing origins of the migrants themselves. The investigation schedules published in July showed that after June "larger numbers of migrants came from small towns and rural sections."[47] These were exactly the people who would have wished to commune in smaller groups than the large city churches. Most likely, many of those who had been church members in the South were still searching for a church in which they would feel comfortable.[48]

The connection between rural origins of migrants and low levels of church membership can also be detected in the study of migrants com-

Table 10.1. Distribution of Migrants among the Denominations, 1923

Affiliation	May	June	July*	Aug.	Sept.
Baptist	149	278	77	51	39
Methodist	47	158	18	16	19
A.M.E.	—	146	8	15	19
A.M.E. Zion	—	0	0	0	0
M.E.	—	12	8	1	0
C.M.E.[†]	—	0	2	0	0
Episcopal	7	13	2	6	5
Presbyterian	5	0	0	6	0
7th Day Adventist	0	0	3	0	0
United Christian	0	9	0	0	0
Holiness	0	1	0	0	0
Protestant	0	13	0	0	0
Members	208	472	110	79	63
Nonmembers	144	249	92	238	119
Total	352	721	202	317	182
% members	59.1	65.5	54.5	24.9	34.6

*July figures represent adults only. Figures for the other months include children.
[†]C.M.E., Colored Methodist Episcopal.
Source: Negro Migration Committee reports, May to September, 1923; Negro Migrant Study (UATU), Urb. 3, Series II, Box 1, folder 2.

pleted in 1924 by William D. Fuller. Historian Fredric Miller argues in his study based on Fuller's worksheets that there was a distinct connection between place of origin and church membership in the North and that black people from the larger cities (those with populations above fifty thousand) were more inclined to join a church once they arrived at their northern destination.[49] At the time, Fuller reasoned that the low level of church affiliation among migrants in Philadelphia was primarily due "to ignorance of such organizations within the city." This seems hard to believe given the visibility of black churches and the efforts they were making to help migrants. Ignorance may perhaps explain the drop in the rate at which migrants joined fraternal societies in Philadelphia. Some southern organizations did not have branches in the city, and in contrast to churches, members were selected by the orders, rather than the other way round. However, although it was harder for migrants to get information about the orders, the rate at which they joined fraternal orders declined less precipitously than the rate at which they joined churches.[50] The second reason Fuller gave for the decline in church membership is more compelling. He noted that when the migrant was asked why he did not belong to a church in the North, he responded in part "that he would not know any of the congregation."[51]

The migrants' desire to commune with people they knew, or in churches that resembled their southern houses of worship, helps to explain the relative decline of the A.M.E. Church in Philadelphia compared to the Baptist Church.[52] While a few friends could easily come together to establish a new Baptist church (as was the case for the many storefront churches that remained within the Baptist fold), the episcopal structure of the denomination made it more difficult to form an A.M.E. church. A new congregation was required to secure the support of the episcopal conference that it wished to join, and the choice of minister for the church would be dictated by the bishop of the district. These two requirements led many former African Methodists to opt for affiliation with either the Baptist denomination or even with the newer Holiness and Spiritualist denominations.[53] Consequently, African Methodist congregations were not heavily represented among the most common new storefront churches. In 1932, when Benjamin Mays and Joseph Nicholson undertook their research on northern urban black churches, at least 45 percent of all Baptist churches were located in storefronts. By contrast, only 19 percent of A.M.E. congregations worshiped in such places.[54]

Perhaps the most telling example of migrants from the same area communing together on arrival in Philadelphia can be seen in the establishment of two Baptist churches, Morris Chapel and Greenwood. Established in West Philadelphia in 1921, Morris Chapel was formed around a congregation of twenty-six people. Twenty of them came from Greenwood, South Carolina, where they had been members of a church named Morris Chapel. For the first couple of months, the group merely conducted a Sunday school in a storefront, as they had no pastor to lead them. They then persuaded the Rev. A. B. Jordan to organize them. He was also a native of Greenwood and was pastor of another church in Philadelphia, the Greenwood Baptist Church. Needless to say, a large proportion of the members of this church were also natives of the South Carolina town.

Jordan pastored both churches for a few years until Morris Chapel found another minister. The two churches did not combine, most probably because combining would have created a larger congregation than most of the members had been used to in the South.[55] However, even when the two churches had different pastors, they remained close. When one of them moved to North Philadelphia, the other soon followed.[56]

Mays and Nicholson found several other churches in Philadelphia that had been established as a result of a family or a small group of friends moving to the city and wishing to worship together. During and after the Great Migration, small churches, often storefronts, proliferated. While in 1897 there were only 55 churches and missions, by 1932 there were 205.[57] Of these, 115 (56 percent) were in storefronts, houses, halls, or theaters. To the outsider, the impression was that black Philadelphians were overchurched. But these churches were important to the migrants who would not join the larger churches and who needed some kind of social support system to help them adjust to urban life.

The cause for this proliferation of churches was not the antagonism of established blacks toward new arrivals. Indeed, Mays and Nicholson noted that very few churches actually excluded migrants. "Most [churches]," they wrote, "were democratic in the desire for new members." The problem arose because many migrants did not feel at home in a city church. Mays and Nicholson placed the blame for this squarely on the shoulders of the existing churches, reproaching them for not being "prepared for the emergency caused by migration." But, as noted earlier, churches prior to the Great Migration had always been looked upon as places to which newcomers could go for support.

If the more established church members erred, it is more likely to have been because of their overemphasis on the "problem" of the migration than because they actively excluded migrants from their congregations. Of course, there were very real needs (for housing, for example) that suddenly had to be met owing to the large increase in migrants in Philadelphia. But the "problem" in the minds of many established black Philadelphians took on a more cultural dimension. What is meant here can best be explained by quoting Mays and Nicholson: "The Negro urban church has been placed in a position to become an important factor in the adjustment of the rural Negro to the social, civic, religious and economic conditions of the city, all of which differ widely from those in rural areas." They complained that resident Christians did not always have the "requisite sympathy, imagination, and resourcefulness to make [newcomers] feel at home and to introduce them gradually to new ways of life and thought."[58] The assumption here is that the cultural baggage, including forms of worship, that the migrants brought with them from the South was inferior to, and needed to be replaced by, the normative practices of the urban North.

The irony then may be that black migrants would have wished to commune among themselves because the established northern churches were overly conscious of the need to help them adjust. While they themselves wished to recreate aspects of the South with which they had been happy, northerners wished them to conform to their own "superior" practices. What some Northerners may have overlooked (and what historians accustomed to seeing the North as preferable to the South have been slow to recognize) is that not all migrants had wanted to leave the South; not all of them found the southern rural life oppressive; and certainly not all of them believed life in the North was superior. Instead of embracing northern religious practices, many newcomers formed their own churches. When they did join the large established churches, they often continued to associate with people having similar backgrounds to themselves. At Mother Bethel, for instance, the result was the formation of Georgia and South Carolina Clubs to sustain connections among Southerners.[59]

The need to commune with people of similar experiences to oneself may have been as strong among migrant blacks as it was among European immigrant groups. Southern migrants formed new congregations not especially because of the failings of the older ones but because they wished to share their religious services with people of similar origins, just as Italians wished to stay together. The spiritual failings of established churches should not be held responsible, therefore, for the proliferation of churches, the development of the new storefront migrant communions, and the so-called cults.

Certainly, prejudice was evident in the attitudes of many members of Philadelphia's established black churches toward the new arrivals, though this prejudice tended to be directed especially toward those who might be considered refugees arriving in the city relatively impoverished. But the importance of such prejudice should not be overstated. Many migrants wished to commune in small groups among themselves anyway and could not have been tempted to join the large African Methodist churches whether or not the members were welcoming. Further, such prejudice was only one part of an ideology that also included a theology stressing the hypocrisy of being unwelcoming toward other Christians and a Progressive political philosophy urging the need to "uplift" "backward" peoples.

CHAPTER 11

Conclusion

The nomination in 1991 of Clarence Thomas for U.S. Supreme Court Justice was greeted with, among other things, surprise: surprise that President George Bush was able to find a black conservative to replace retiring (black) liberal Justice Thurgood Marshall; surprise that the nominee would receive support from many black Americans (among whom, African Methodist ministers were visible); and surprise that the African American community is not the monolithic bloc it is often perceived to be. Thomas's views on social welfare and affirmative action policies upset the routine and glib equation of "black," (and its ancillary associations of crime, drugs, welfare) and "liberal" (with its soft-on-crime, soft-on-the-lazy, and the other implications) in popular culture (especially television). Endorsement of Thomas and his position by other black professionals compounded the puzzlement and anxiety generated by the "discovery" of black middle-class people with textbook conservative views.

With the second set of hearings, convened after Professor Anita Hill's accusations against Thomas became public, equilibrium was regained. The disorder introduced by the "discovery" of social and political diversity in the community of American blacks was swept away by the sexual nature of the allegations and the sensationalism of the uncut, uncensored hearings, which, as many observers noted, trumpeted (and at some points seemed to reaffirm) other aspects of the discourse on black culture: rampaging black male sexuality and emasculating black women.

It is easy to pin the blame for such stereotyping on the "media" and so to dismiss it as insignificant. However, attitudes and assumptions about deviations of "black culture" from an equally mythologized mainstream American culture also inform scholarly and policy-oriented representations of African Americans in American society and history. In the interlinking scholarly and academic arenas, social problems associated with America's inner cities are linked with black Americans, who are disproportionately represented in these areas. At the same time, patterns of social deviance ranging from violence against people and property to substance abuse to high rates of birth out of wedlock are attributed to the "pathology" of black culture, with little pause for consideration of the politics behind definitions of deviance.

The failure to recognize diversity among black communities is, in part, a consequence of the kinds of work that have been produced as part of African American history since the 1950s. This body of literature has not adequately recognized the ways in which racism in American society has increased, rather than diminished, social divisions within African American communities. Perhaps impressed by appearances of solidarity in the civil rights and other protest movements, and distracted by concepts such as "the black community," "the Black Church," and "Black Power," which developed in connection with these movements, historians have tended to view the ghetto, in particular, as monolithic. This understanding has led to the notion of a "paradox of the ghetto," which suggests that as racial prejudice has increased in the cities the potential for the development of a unified black movement and redress of grievances has also increased.[1]

The paradox that I have described here is very different. Rather than unity developing in the face of racial oppression, as one might expect given the old Marxian formula of immiserization leading to revolution (though Marx was well aware of ethnic divisions within the working class), the process of ghettoization has led to social stratification. By focusing on a black religious denomination's response to the Great Migration in a particular city, this book has endeavored to illustrate this process at work. The central concern of this study has been to highlight diversity within African American communities. As such, concepts like the monolithic ghetto, the "black church," and a uniform group of "black Southerners" have all been contested: Ghettos, I have argued, have been and remain divided along class, gender, and color lines; African Methodists are not the same as black Episcopalians and Baptists because their ideas were shaped by white Methodists as well as by the reservoir of African religious traditions that survived American slavery;

and, African American migrants have been a diverse population, made up not just of what some would consider the forward-looking, progressive elements of southern society but also of men and women who were forced to leave the South as refugees from social, political and economic oppression. It is in this direction, toward the discovery of internally divided communities, that historians must travel if African American history (and indeed American history generally) is to be "deromanticized."[2]

African Methodists are a unique group of people, with a particular brand of Protestantism that has drawn many of its influences from white Christianity. Their philosophy of "uplift" represents particular class and gender visions and was at its most influential in Philadelphia when a strong master–servant relationship between white and black Philadelphians existed, when "separate spheres" ideology was prevalent, and when most African Americans seemed to fit within the same economic and social group. As ghettoization continued and blacks became more segregated from surrounding ethnic communities and more internally stratified economically, the influence of African Methodism declined and its constituency began to shrink. Black communities now became more divided, with emergent black professional elites, an unstable middling class of workers in industrial occupations, and an increasingly denigrated lower class based in service occupations who were unable to follow prescribed roles for womanhood and manhood.

African Methodists came to see migration, which was often understood as the motor of improved social position, as one of the causes of their decline. Since they were the dominant black denomination in the city, any change was likely to be viewed negatively. But added to this, the tradition of migration continuing from the nineteenth century did not seem positive in the eyes of many leading African Methodists. While the migration population was diverse prior to the First World War, the better-prepared individuals and families (labeled "migrants" in this work) who arrived in the city before 1916 were generally from areas of Maryland and Virginia that had not been penetrated by African Methodists. Consequently, few members of this group entered the A.M.E. Church. Instead, they gravitated toward the Baptist Church and accounted for the emergence of large Baptist congregations in the city. Those people in this early migration who would have been classified as "refugees," predominantly single women moving into service occupations, were seldom welcomed into African Methodist churches. All the social problems that social commentators associated with "the race"—illiteracy, prostitution, and vice generally—were attributed to the disproportionate number of such women in African American communities.[3] African American migration at this time, then, seemed akin to Irish immigration (also characterized in terms of ethnic or racial proclivities rather than in terms of the consequences of poverty), a reflection of the group's marginality—only worse, because of intense racial discrimination. There was nothing about migration that African Methodists could celebrate.

This changed with the "Great Migration" as many more African Methodists began to come north from South Carolina, Georgia, and Florida, and as the availability of industrial jobs attracted a larger number of men and whole families. The central image in this migration was not the single black female arriving at Philadelphia's docks in need of social services to find work in somebody else's home. Rather, its central image was the married man arriving by train at Broad Street Station, getting work in a factory, and bringing his wife and children north to live with him. As a result of such changes and the vision of many of the denomination's leaders, who saw the political benefits to be gained from an expanding black community in the city, African Methodists did take the lead in promoting the "Exodus" from the South.

Before long, however, the vicissitudes of the labor market and the racial prejudice of employers and union workers alike took the luster off this migration. Exclusion, depression, and factory relocation to the suburbs by the Second World War brought back the migration characterizations of marginality and social pathology. In the meantime, African Methodist churches had been outnumbered by Baptist and Holiness churches, and many of their most successful members had joined more prestigious Episcopal and Presbyterian congregations.

Divisions within the ghettos existed prior to the civil rights laws of the 1950s and 1960s, which paved the way for limited black mobility into the suburbs. Some middle-class African Americans took the same path followed by other middle-class Americans in "escaping from the ghetto." Divisions within ghettos became divisions in relation to the ghettos; the women of Brewster Place were separated from the suburban families of Linden Hills.[4] In Philadelphia, "the city of homes," black middle-class enclaves could emerge within the city limits. Some prosperous African Americans like the Alexanders—Raymond Pace and Sadie Tanner Mossell—attemptd to integrate the Mount Airy section of Philadelphia. But for the rest of black Philadelphia, neighborhood divisions began to demarcate certain sections of the city as middle-class black communities and others as belonging to the lowest class, or "underclass." West Philadelphia, for example, which white Philadelphians and student sojourners see as a heavily armed and patrolled university colony surrounded by the ever-impinging drug-infested ghetto, is in fact many communities. As early as the 1930s, black Philadelphians living in West Philadelphia referred to parts of this section as "top" and "bottom." Those living closer to the western edge of the city, Cobbs Creek, where the infamous Move bombing occurred, lived in the more prosperous, "respectable" area—the "top."[5] People living in the "bottom," below 52nd Street, often stayed out of the "top" and believed with good reason that their neighbors looked down on them. Similar divisions emerged in North and South Philadelphia.[6]

Such divisions are a staple of most scholars' immigration models. Immigrants arrive in an American city, lose their traditional habits, and adopt American values and culture, and then move to the suburbs. Clearly the validity of this "American Dream" (how long does the period of adjustment take? do all groups follow this path? and so on) is open to question, but the myth still animates people. But when African Americans conform to this immigration model their experience is made problematic. While other ethnic groups have seemed to benefit from the prosperity of some of their members, regardless of what these individuals did with their money, successful black men and women have been berated by the likes of E. Franklin Frazier for not reaching down into the ghetto to aid their brothers and sisters. Implicit within this notion is the suggestion that other groups have pulled themselves and their kin up without the assistance of social programs; why, then, can't African Americans? As we have seen throughout this book, however, African Methodists did exactly what they believed they ought to do in order to "uplift the race" but to no avail. The barriers to advancement are such that black banks, theaters, groceries, and other businesses can be established in abundance with widespread church and community support, but if money does not come from outside the community in the form of jobs and investment, any downswing in the economy brings these ventures crashing down. If, instead of positing a uniform black community and ascribing blame to its more successful members for the failings of the group, we detect diverse groups of people all discriminated against by racism, then responsibility for improving the living conditions of poor people is not passed on to the victims themselves but is left squarely with a society that is unwilling to pay taxes for universal health care,

decent transportation systems, available and affordable housing, job opportunities, and other social necessities. For even if black capitalism
could be as successful as its greatest supporters dream, would not an
"underclass" still exist in America?

The awareness of divisions, the recognition that African Methodists shared ideas with white Methodists and that some new arrivals in the
city were "migrants" while others were "refugees," must not lead us to
believe that some African Americans (Episcopalians, African Methodists,
migrants generally) have been assimilable into the mainstream while
others (Baptists, members of storefront churches, and "refugees") have,
indeed, shared a "culture of poverty."[7] What we should begin to recognize, instead, is that the discourse on the "culture of poverty"—the
determination of "mainstream" society to write off people who seem
unwilling to participate in the "American experiment"—has been a constant in American history since colonization.

This is merely America's "orientalism,"[8] the imposition on the
"Other" of unchanging attributes that forever account for its inability to
rise to the level of "ethnic" Americans. It is this anvil of oppression that
needs to be transformed, not the people whose sparks burn out in the
ghettos.

Notes

Chapter 1: Introduction

1. Richard R. Wright, Jr., *Two Cents: What the Negro Gives His Church* (Nashville: A.M.E. Sunday School Union, 1940), pp. 4–5.

2. Hans A. Baer, *The Black Spiritual Movement: A Religious Response to Racism* (Knoxville: University of Tennessee Press, 1984), p. v. Ghettoization studies have all argued for the centrality of the church in the black community; see Kenneth L. Kusmer, *A Ghetto Takes Shape: Black Cleveland, 1870–1930* (Urbana: University of Illinois Press, 1976), p. 92. The same is true for studies of the Great Migration; see James R. Grossman, *Land of Hope: Chicago, Black Southerners and the Great Migration* (Chicago: University of Chicago Press, 1989) p. 92. However, no clear analysis of the extent or limit of the churches' influence on either migration or the ghetto has emerged from this literature. Since Albert J. Raboteau's *Slave Religion: The "Invisible Institution" in the Antebellum South* (New York: Oxford University Press, 1978), social historians have been paying greater attention to churches. See, for example, Clarence E. Walker, *A Rock in a Weary Land: The African Methodist Episcopal Church during the Civil War and Reconstruction* (Baton Rouge: Louisiana State University Press, 1982), and Evelyn Brooks Higginbotham, *Righteous Discontent: The Women's Movement in the Black Baptist Church, 1880–1920* (Cambridge: Mass.: Harvard University Press, 1993).

3. For the purposes of this study, the term African Methodist includes African Methodist Episcopal, African Methodist Episcopal Zion, Colored Methodist Episcopal, and Union African Methodist Episcopal denominations, as well as black congregations in the Methodist Episcopal Church. Generally, the focus is on the A.M.E. Church. However, because differences among the denominations usually revolved around their political structures rather than theological, ideological, and social differences, inclusion of other denominations is legitimate. Although affiliated to a largely white denomination, Tindley Temple M.E.

Church was sufficiently independent (especially during Tindley's pastorate) that describing it as African Methodist seems appropriate.

4. W.E.B. Du Bois, *The Souls of Black Folk* (New York: Bantam Books, 1989), p. 145.

5. Jeane B. Williams, "We Gather Together to Ask the Lord's Blessing," *Christian Recorder*, Mar. 24, 1986; Walker, *A Rock in a Weary Land*, pp. 4–29.

6. Julie Winch, *Philadelphia's Black Elite: Activism, Accommodation, and the Struggle for Autonomy, 1787–1848* (Philadelphia: Temple University Press, 1988) pp. 9–15.

7. Such fears were justified by Denmark Vesey's preachings in the denomination's Charleston congregation prior to his conspiring to lead a slave uprising; William W. Freehling, *Prelude to Civil War: The Nullification Controversy in South Carolina, 1816–1836* (New York: Harper, 1966), p. 55.

8. Richard R. Wright, Jr., ed., *The Centennial Encyclopaedia of the A.M.E. Church* (Philadelphia: A.M.E. Book Concern, 1916), p. 284. Further particulars of this development can be found in David H. Bradley, *A History of the A.M.E. Zion Church* (Nashville: Parthenon Press, 1956); and Christopher Rush, "Rise of the African Methodist Episcopal Zion Church," in Milton C. Sernett, ed., *Afro-American Religious History: A Documentary Witness* (Durham: Duke University Press, 1986), pp. 150–59.

9. In 1897, the A.M.E. Church had fourteen churches in the Philadelphia area with a total of 3,210 members. At this time there were only three A.M.E. Zion churches. W.E.B. Du Bois, *The Philadelphia Negro: A Social Study* (Philadelphia: University of Pennsylvania, 1899), pp. 209, 211.

10. Grace Union A.M.E. was located at 15th and Lombard and another independent Methodist church, St. Matthew Methodist Protestant (perhaps the predecessor to St. Matthew's A.M.E. Church), was located in West Philadelphia at 58th and Vine Streets. The Colored Methodist Episcopal Church had six congregations in the city and around twelve hundred members. Ibid., p. 213.

11. I am grateful to Rev. Jeane B. Williams for this information; see also Edward L. Wheeler, *Uplifting the Race: The Black Minister in the New South, 1865–1902* (New York: University Press of America, 1986), p. 13.

12. Du Bois, *Philadelphia Negro*, p. 204.

13. George W. Clinton, "The Mission of Methodism to the Backward Races," *A.M.E. Church Review* (henceforth *Review*) 28 (Jan. 1912): 671.

14. This dichotomy between accommodation and equality resembles that between accommodation and resistance found in African American historiography generally. See Manning Marable, *How Capitalism Underdeveloped Black America* (Boston: South End, 1983) p. 26. As C. Eric Lincoln and Lawrence H. Mamiya have pointed out, black churches (the "mediating institutions") have incorporated these two poles into their ideological and theological makeup; *The Black Church in the African American Experience* (Durham: Duke University Press, 1990), pp. 14–15. During the period of this study they did so through the philosophy of "uplift."

15. "Uplift" conforms to a notion of "hegemony" that recognizes the influence of the nonelites in shaping or making their worlds. See Raymond Williams, *Marxism and Literature* (Oxford: Oxford University Press, 1977); Ernesto Leclau

and Chantal Mouffe, *Hegemony and Socialist Strategy: Towards a Radical Democratic Politics* (London: Verso, 1985); and E. P. Thompson, "The Transforming Power of the Cross," in *The Making of the English Working Class* (New York: Vintage Books, 1966), pp. 350–400.

16. Wheeler, *Uplifting the Race*, p. xvi. Wheeler maintains that focusing on the concept of *uplift* provides a more complex, dialectical picture of the work of black ministers. He writes: "Accommodation, which of course had a submissive tone, also had a subversive quality. On the one hand, uplift meant accommodation and surrender to the concepts, principles, and ideals of the dominant society. On the other, uplift was a denial of what white society meant by accommodation for it spoke of a possibility to move beyond the limits prescribed by the dominant society," p. xvii.

17. Elliot Rudwick, *W.E.B. Du Bois: Propagandist of the Negro Protest* (New York: Atheneum, 1978); August Meier, *Negro Thought in America, 1880–1915* (Ann Arbor: University of Michigan Press, 1966).

18. James Porter, "African Methodism as a Factor in the Progress of Our Race," *Review* 7 (Jan. 1891): 320.

19. See Spencer Crew, *Field to Factory: Afro-American Migration, 1915–1940* (Washington, D.C.: Smithsonian Institute, 1989).

20. Joe William Trotter, Jr., *Black Milwaukee: The Making of an Industrial Proletariat* (Urbana: University of Illinois Press, 1985) pp. 264–82; Trotter, ed., *The Great Migration in Historical Perspective: New Dimensions of Race, Class and Gender* (Bloomington: Indiana University Press, 1991); see also Robert Gregg, "Group Portrait with Lady," review of Trotter's *The Great Migration*, in *Reviews in American History* 20 (3 Sept. 1992): 354–59.

21. St. Clair Drake and Horace R. Cayton, *Black Metropolis: A Study of Negro Life in a Northern City* (New York: Harper & Row, 1962); Gilbert Osofsky, *Harlem: The Making of a Ghetto, Negro New York, 1890–1930* (New York: Harper & Row, 1966), and "The Enduring Ghetto," *Journal of American History* 55 (1968): 243–55; Allan H. Spear, *Black Chicago: The Making of the Negro Ghetto, 1890–1920* (Chicago: University of Chicago Press, 1967); David M. Katzman, *Before the Ghetto: Black Detroit in the Nineteenth Century* (Urbana: University of Illinois Press, 1973); Kusmer, *A Ghetto Takes Shape*; James L. Borchert, *Alley Life in Washington: Family, Community, Religion, and Folklife in the City, 1850–1970* (Urbana: University of Illinois Press, 1980); and Theodore Hershberg, ed., *Philadelphia: Work, Space, Family, and Group Experience in the 19th Century* (New York: Oxford University Press, 1981).

22. Trotter, *Black Milwaukee*, p. 275.

23. Ibid. This criticism is unfair in the case of Kenneth Kusmer, whose brilliant analysis of the differences among black elites is clearly what is needed for the study of the African American community generally; it should be extended to cover other divisions in the community—those between men and women, skilled and unskilled workers, and primary and secondary industry workers: Kusmer, *A Ghetto Takes Shape*, pp. 91–112.

24. Ibid., p. 274.

25. Such divisions are highlighted for an earlier period in Winch, *Philadelphia's Black Elite*, passim.

26. Matthew H. Jones, interviewed Feb. 12, 1988.

27. Trotter, *Black Milwaukee*, p. 276.

28. Trotter, *Great Migration*. In this work, which intends to open the doors to new scholarship, only token reference is made to religion and churches.

29. Thompson's *Making of the English Working Class* and Herbert Gutman's *Work, Culture and Society in Industrializing America* (New York: Vintage Books, 1976) are cited approvingly by Trotter and most other proletarianization historians; *Black Milwaukee*, p. 276; *Great Migration*, pp. 98, 122. Gutman's use of Thompson, on whom most historians draw, turns him into a modernization theorist, with immigrants resisting proletarianization through their traditional cultures, which focus on "moral economy." Once the period of transformation is completed, resistance ends. The "field-to-factory" vision of African Americanists is in accordance with such modernization notions. The importance of religion in the making of the migrants' world might have been gleaned from another strand of Thompsonianism, Eugene Genovese's *Roll, Jordan Roll: The World the Slaves Made* (New York: Vintage, 1974).

30. Such a perspective has been provided by Theodore Hershberg et al., in a classic analysis of ghettoization, "A Tale of Three Cities: Blacks, Immigrants, and Opportunity in Philadelphia, 1850–1880, 1930, 1970," in Hershberg, ed., *Philadelphia*, pp. 461–91.

31. E. Franklin Frazier, *The Negro Church in America* (New York: Schocken Books, 1966). Frazier's analysis of black churches in northern cities is largely based on the work of Benjamin E. Mays and Joseph W. Nicholson in *The Negro's Church* (New York: Arno Press, 1933).

32. Frazier, *Negro Church*, pp. 47–67.

33. Ibid., pp. 51, 48, 53. The last argument was based on Arthur Huff Fauset, *Black Gods of the Metropolis: Negro Religious Cults in the Urban North* (Philadelphia: University of Pennsylvania Press, 1971), first published in 1944.

34. Frazier, *Negro Church*, p. 86.

35. However, Frazier saw through the argument advanced during the 1930s that blacks were overchurched. He recognized that the question was "irrelevant" because churches played an important role in blacks' "associational" lives that was not matched by white churches. Ibid., p. 55. See Mays and Nicholson, *The Negro's Church*, chapter 16.

36. James H. Cone, *Black Theology and Black Power* (New York: Seabury Press, 1969), p. 31. See also Cone, *A Black Theology of Liberation* (New York: Lippincott, 1970), and Jean Luis Segundo, S.J., *The Liberation of Theology* (Maryknoll, N.Y.: Orbis Books, 1985), pp. 25–38.

37. Cone, *Black Theology*, pp. 32, 36.

38. Ibid., pp. 121 (see also 105), 123. Concurring with Cone about theology before the ghetto, C. Eric Lincoln has suggested a division between "Negro" and "Black" theology, between that adhered to by black churches prior to the development of the ghetto and that of black churches since this development; Lincoln, ed., *The Black Experience in Religion* (New York: Doubleday, 1975). Cone's assumption was that the ghetto would produce both unity among black people and a theology articulating this unity. This assumption is, as the foregoing

analysis of ghettoization has shown, ungrounded. Further, he treats "Negro Theology" in a reductionist fashion, as an inferior theology adhered to by people who were duped by their oppressors into complacency and contentment. It would inevitably give way to a liberation theology once blacks became segregated from the larger white society into their ghettos. However, while accommodation was an important part of theology prior to the development of the ghetto, so also was protest; see Wheeler, *Uplifting the Race*, p. xvii.

39. Gayraud Wilmore agrees with this view, suggesting that church leaders after emancipation were not involved in the "freedom movement." He argues that ministers were "too imitative of the white clergy in their politics and given to moralizing and peacemaking"; *Black Religion and Black Radicalism* (Garden City, N.Y.: Doubleday, 1972), p. 132.

40. Peter J. Paris, *The Social Teachings of the Black Churches* (Philadelphia: Fortress Press, 1985), p. 127, develops an alternative to Black Theology, which he calls "the black Christian tradition." He writes, "The fundamental principle of the black Christian tradition is depicted most adequately in the biblical doctrine of the parenthood of God and the kinship of all peoples" (p. 10). See also David Wood Wills's critique of Cone in "Aspects of Social Thought in the A.M.E. Church, 1884–1910" (Ph.D. diss., Harvard University, 1975), pp. 47–49.

41. Delores S. Williams, "The Black Woman's God" (paper delivered at the University of Pennsylvania's President's Forum: "Colorlines: The Enduring Significance of Race," Feb. 14, 1987). Williams, one of the leading black women theologians, has founded this perspective on a tradition of biblical appropriation that uses the trials and tribulations of the biblical character Hagar as its focus. This tradition is, according to Williams, "at the core of the black women's understanding of God's relation to their tasks as nurturers." Left alone in the wilderness with her son, Ishmael, and without wealth—flock, servants, or even shelter—Hagar unsurprisingly has appealed to many black women, including writers like Anna J. Cooper and Paulene Elizabeth Hopkins.

42. The term *Great Migration* appeared soon after the World War I migration northward commenced. Given that considerable population movement among blacks occurred before the war and that post-1940 migrations would dwarf all their predecessors, the "greatness" of the 1916 to 1930 migration requires some scrutiny. The designation probably derived as much from the nature of the migration's participants (a higher proportion of men and family units migrated at this time) and from the fact that this migration coincided with the opening of work in industry to African Americans as from the actual number of migrants moving at any one time. Thus, the designation tells us a great deal about the attitudes toward African American migration among contemporaries and historians alike. See Gregg, "Group Portrait With Lady," p. 357.

43. Frederic Miller, "A Black Migration to Philadelphia," *Pennsylvania Magazine of History and Biography* 108 (3 July 1984): 316.

44. See, for example, Carter G. Woodson, *A Century of Negro Migration* (Washington, D.C.: The Association for the Study of Negro Life and History, 1918), pp. 167–80; Emmett J. Scott, *Negro Migration during the War* (New York:

Oxford University Press, 1920), pp. 13–25; and Kusmer, *A Ghetto Takes Shape*, pp. 157–60.

45. This does not mean that "pull" factors dominated among the reasons for migrants leaving home. Many people were being pushed to migrate, but it was the "pull" factors that brought them to Philadelphia instead of a southern city, for example. Motivation for leaving home is discussed at length in Chapter 8.

46. The propaganda of newspapers like the Chicago *Defender* was clearly important in this process. This newspaper vilified the South and described the North as "the Promised Land." It also attacked so-called "good niggers" who tried to persuade blacks to remain in the South. See Richard B. Sherman, ed., *The Negro and the City* (Englewood Cliffs, N.J.: Prentice-Hall, 1970), pp. 6–13. African Methodist journals such as the *Christian Recorder* and the *A.M.E. Church Review* also favored migration.

47. Gilson Willets, *Workers of the Nation* (New York: Collier and Son, 1903), p. 714. The author is extremely racist, and suggests that blacks' desire to move to the city because they love "a life of indolent pleasure, and this [they] can find in the cities." Nevertheless, his description of the movement to the cities of thousands of black workers is correct.

48. The role of lynching in the process of migration has been disputed. Individuals sometimes mentioned the threat of lynching as one reason for leaving the South. However, Charles S. Johnson noted that the migrants did not come from the counties in which the highest number of lynchings occurred. Charles S. Johnson, "How Much is the Migration a Flight from Persecution?" *Opportunity*, Sept. 1923, p. 274. In fact, it appears that lynching was used in different, sometimes conflicting ways by southern whites. There were accounts, at least in the northern press, of poorer whites threatening black farmers with lynching at harvest time as a way of appropriating their land. At the same time, white landowners who needed a workforce and who opposed the migration, may have used lynching as a way of intimidating blacks to remain in the South. See William Fuller, "The Negro Migrant in Philadelphia," in Negro Migrant Study Collection, Urban Archives, Temple University, Urb. 31, Box 1, folder 1, pp. 13–14.

49. Miller, "A Black Migration to Philadelphia," p. 317.

50. Trotter, *Great Migration*, p. 42.

51. This description was established in the 1930s in the work of Louise V. Kennedy, *The Negro Peasant Turns Cityward* (New York: Columbia University Press, 1930), and Clyde Vernon Kiser, *Sea Island to City: A Study of St. Helena Islanders in Harlem and Other Urban Centers* (New York: Columbia University Press, 1932). For more recent versions, see Neil Fligstein, *Going North* (New York: Academic Press, 1981); Daniel Johnson and Rex Campbell, *Black Migration in America* (Durham: Duke University Press, 1981); Allen B. Ballard, *One More Day's Journey: The Making of Black Philadelphia* (Philadelphia: Institute for the Study of Human Issues, 1984); Peter Gottlieb, *Making Their Own Way: Southern Blacks' Migration to Pittsburgh, 1916–1930* (Urbana: University of Illinois Press, 1987); and Grossman, *Land of Hope*.

52. Crew, *Field to Factory*.

53. Carole Marks, *Farewell—We're Good and Gone: The Great Black Migration* (Bloomington: Indiana University Press, 1989), pp. 3, 33. For the response of a member of the "old school" to Marks, see Peter Gottlieb's review in *Journal of American History* 77, no. 2 (Sept. 1990): 708–9.

54. Ballard, *One More Day's Journey*, p. 186; and "The Journey," in Irene Ursula Burnham, ed., *Let This Be Your Home: The African-American Migration to Philadelphia* (Philadelphia: Afro-American Historical and Cultural Museum, 1991).

55. Grossman, *Land of Hope*, pp. 9, 37.

56. Marks, *Farewell*, p. 3.

57. Gottlieb, "Rethinking the Great Migration," in Trotter, *Great Migration*, p. 77. Gottlieb's analysis fits with Nicholas Lemann's thesis in *The Promised Land: The Great Black Migration and How It Changed America* (New York: Knopf, 1991).

58. Evelyn Brooks Higginbottom, "African-American Women's History and the Metalanguage of Race," *Signs: Journal of Women in Culture and Society* 17 (Winter 1992): 251–74.

Chapter 2: "Drowned by a Torrent of Migration"

1. The difference between "modern" black ghettos and the ethnic ghettos that preceded them is made clear thoughout Olivier Zunz's *The Changing Face of Inequality: Urbanization, Industrial Development, and Immigrants in Detroit, 1880–1920* (Chicago: University of Illinois Press, 1982).

2. Richard R. Wright, Jr., *The Negro in Pennsylvania* (Philadelphia: A.M.E. Book Concern, 1912), p. 66.

3. Du Bois, *Philadelphia Negro*, pp. 58–62; Wright, *Negro in Pennsylvania*, p. 69. See also, Roger Lane, *The Roots of Black Violence* (Cambridge: Harvard University Press, 1986), pp. 20–21.

4. Wright, *Negro in Pennsylvania*, p. 69.

5. Ibid., p. 76.

6. The term is Zunz's, used to describe the black community in Detroit; *Changing Face of Inequality*, p. 378.

7. In this respect, Philadelphia appears to differ greatly from Detroit as described by Olivier Zunz, who has written, "What is remarkable when we move back in time to examine conditions before the ghetto was formed is that northerners were so unprepared to receive southerners and that the Black community had none of the means of white immigrant communities to incorporate newcomers into its ranks." *Changing Face of Inequality*, p. 378. Philadelphia's black institutions before the war appear to have been very well prepared to receive Southerners.

8. Richard R. Wright, Jr., *The 1908 Philadelphia Colored Directory* (Philadelphia: Philadelphia Colored Directory Co., 1908), p. 51.

9. Sadie T. Mossell, "The Standard of Living among One Hundred Negro Migrant Families in Philadelphia," *Annals of the American Academy* 98 (1921): 174.

10. Ibid., p. 177.

11. Using as their justification the dubious results of new intelligence tests imported from France, members of the Philadelphia School Board began to establish industrial schooling for blacks and to segregate, where possible, schools and, where impossible, classrooms. See Vincent P. Franklin, *The Education of Black Philadelphia: The Social Educational History of a Minority Community, 1900–1950* (Philadelphia: University of Pennsylvania Press, 1979), pp. 44–50.

12. *Philadelphia Tribune* (henceforth *Tribune*) 36, no. 44 (Feb. 21, 1920).

13. Mossell, "Standard of Living," p. 217.

14. Population statistics are calculated from published census data: *Eleventh U.S. Census* (1890); *Twelfth U.S. Census* (1900); and *Fourteenth U.S. Census* (1920).

15. Ibid. and *Sixteenth U.S. Census* (1940). The rest of the city's black population was located either in Germantown or dotted around the white communities; these people usually worked as servants in white households.

16. Mossell, "Standard of Living," p. 178.

17. *Tribune* 32, no. 3 (Dec. 4, 1915); *Public Ledger*, Jan. 28, 1918.

18. Mossell, "Standard of Living," p. 177. Zunz has argued that the "malaise of 'old Detroiter' against newcomers" was in fact the result of a pervasive social problem, namely "the basic inability of most blacks to expand their community to make room for the newcomers." *Changing Face of Inequality*, p. 380. This holds true for Philadelphia, though before the war blacks had been able to accommodate newcomers.

19. *Tribune* 37, no. 11 (Jan. 29, 1921).

20. Wright, *Negro in Pennsylvania*, pp. 64–65. During the period of this study, Mother Bethel A.M.E. Church was not officially recognized by the A.M.E. denomination as its mother church. Nevertheless, "Bethel" and "Mother Bethel" will be used interchangeably here to identify this church.

21. *Twelfth U.S. Census* (1900); *Fourteenth U.S. Census* (1920); *Sixteenth U.S. Census* (1940).

22. Ibid; *Fifteenth U.S. Census* (1930).

23. In 1920, for instance, the Twenty-fourth, Thirty-fourth, and Forty-fourth Wards, situated above Market Street, had 13, 5, and 8 percent black population. The black population increased in these wards in the 1920s, so that by 1930 the Twenty-fourth Ward was 24 percent black, the Thirty-fourth was 16 percent black, and the Forty-fourth was 26 percent black. By way of comparison, the black population south of Market Street in 1930 made up only 7 percent of the total population of this area. Ibid.

24. Carter G. Woodson, *A Century of Negro Migration* (Washington, D.C.: Association for the Study of Negro Life and History, 1918), pp. 190–92.

25. Hershberg, *Philadelphia*, p. 488.

26. Negro Migrant Study, Urban Archives, Temple University (UATU), Urb 31, Box 1, Folder 2.

27. Mossell, "Standard of Living," p.177.

28. This was probably achieved as it is today, by not openly advertising available houses in some neighborhoods.

29. Woodson, *Century of Negro Migration*, p. 187.

30. Mossell, "Standard of Living," p. 175.

31. 1924 Migrant Study worksheets, Negro Migrant Study (UATU).

32. *Tribune* 40, no. 1 (1923): 2. Whyte was principal of Durham-Pollock School and a member of the Committee on Negro Migration.

33. Woodson, *Century of Negro Migration*, pp. 187–89.

34. Emmett J. Scott, *Negro Migration during the War* (New York: Oxford University Press, 1920), p. 136.

35. *Tribune* 40, no. 1 (1923): 2.

36. The exception to this rule of increasing susceptibility to disease concerns polio. Contrary to belief current at the time, migrants coming from rural areas and people living in congested areas were more likely to have built up immunity to polio than those living in wealthier and more hygienic areas. Nevertheless, immigrants and black migrants were held responsible for the polio epidemic in 1916, and fear of and prejudice against the newest arrivals in northern cities were thereby increased. See Naomi Rogers, "Screen the Baby, Swat the Fly: Polio in the Northeastern United States, 1916" (Ph.D., diss., University of Pennsylvania, 1986), pp. 17–18.

37. Woodson, *Century of Negro Migration*, p. 189.

38. Whyte, *Tribune* 40, no. 1 1923): 2.

39. *Tribune* 34, no. 46 (Oct. 12, 1918), for example. During the influenza epidemic most black churches canceled services for fear of spreading the virus even wider. During the worst period public gatherings were prohibited. "Fight the Ravages of the White Plague among New York's Negro Population," *Opportunity*, Jan. 1923, pp. 23–24; Roscoe C. Brown, "The Work of the U.S. Public Health Service with Negroes," *Opportunity*, Feb. 1923, p. 12; Eugene Kinkle Jones, "The Negro's Struggle for Health," *Opportunity*, June 1923, pp. 4–6; V. D. Johnson, "A New Estimate of Negro Health," *Opportunity*, Sept. 1923, p. 271.

40. *Public Ledger*, Jan. 26, 1917. In 1921, houses in the black community usually rented for between $170 and $220 annually, and blacks generally had to commit 10 to 20 percent of their family incomes to rent; Mossell, "Standard of Living," p. 23.

41. Philadelphia Presbytery, *Brothers in Christ: A Survey and Report on the Church and the Negro* (Philadelphia: The Presbytery, 1946), p. 10.

42. *Sixteenth U.S. Census* (1940).

43. Philadelphia Presbytery, *Brothers in Christ*, p. 10.

44. Wright, *1908 Philadelphia Colored Directory*, pp. 57–61; *Philadelphia Independent* (henceforth *Independent*), June 2, 1935, p. 3.

45. Walter Licht, *Getting Work: Philadelphia, 1840–1950* (Cambridge: Harvard University Press, 1992), pp. 46, 126. Ralph H. Jones, *Charles Albert Tindley, Prince of Preachers* (Nashville: Abingdon Press, 1982), pp. 80–82. For a more complete discussion of working opportunities and conditions for Philadelphia's migrants, see Charles Hardy III, "Race and Opportunity: Black Philadelphia during the Era of the Great Migration, 1916–1930" (Ph.D. diss., Temple University, 1989).

46. Licht, *Getting Work*, pp. 45; Hershberg, *Philadelphia*, pp. 461–91; and, for a similar perspective on developments in Pittsburgh, Gottlieb, *Making Their Own Way*, pp. 89–112.

47. Interview with Rev. Matthew H. Jones. With his mechanical ability, Jones was later able to set up his own garage, out of which taxicabs worked.

48. Richard B. Sherman, ed., *The Negro and the City* (Englewood Cliffs, N.J.: Prentice-Hall, 1970), p. 48.

49. Licht, *Getting Work*, p. 125.

50. *Independent*, June 2, 1935,

51. Ibid., Sept. 15, 1935.

52. Jacqueline Jones, *Labor of Love, Labor of Sorrow: Black Woman, Work and the Family, from Slavery to the Present* (New York: Vintage Books, 1986), p. 164.

53. Mary Church Terrell, "A Few Possibilities of the National Association of Colored Women," A.M.E. Church *Review* 13 (Oct. 1896): 222.

54. Terrell, "Duty of the National Association for Colored Women to the Race," *Review* 16 (Jan. 1900): 348.

55. Darlene Clark Hine, "Black Migration to the Urban Midwest: The Gender Dimension," in Trotter, *Great Migration*, pp. 127–46. This essay represents one of the first attempts to view migration from the perspective of women and gender.

56. Professional and Business Women's Supplement, *Tribune* 29 (June 29, 1912). See also Wright, *1908 Philadelphia Colored Directory*.

57. In 1911, the article reported, 900 were met and 593 were aided. Four of the migrants came from the West Indies, 311 from Maryland, and 239 from Virginia; ibid.

58. Terrell, "A Few Possibilities," p. 222.

59. Frances E.W. Harper, *Iola Leroy, or Shadows Uplifted* (New York: AMS Press, 1971), pp. 205–12.

60. *Independent*, June 2, 1935, p. 3. Even John Wanamaker, who was renowned for his funding of black educational endeavors and whose righthand man, Robert Ogden, was a member of the Board of Trustees at the black institute at Hampton, Virginia, avoided employing blacks. In 1908, Wanamaker was confronted by a black delegation begging him to do so, but his response was that blacks should establish their own department store; Solomon Porter Hood, "The Negro's Latest and Greatest Move," *Review* 25 (July 1908): 19–24. By the 1920s, Rev. Tindley managed to persuade Wanamaker to start employing members of the Tindley Temple congregation, but one suspects this was only as porters, wrappers, custodians, stock workers, and other nonsales positions; Jones, *Charles Albert Tindley*, pp. 98–103. Wanamaker feared, perhaps rightly given the racial climate, that his customers, predominantly white middle-class women, would object to being served by black saleswomen; Susan Porter Benson, *Counter Cultures: Saleswomen, Managers, and Customers in American Department Stores, 1890–1940* (Urbana: University of Illinois Press, 1986); and Sherman, *Negro and the City*, p. 48.

61. Jones, *Labor of Love, Labor of Sorrow*, pp. 160–90.

62. Wright, *1908 Colored Directory*, passim, and *Negro in Pennsylvania*, passim.

63. Kusmer, *A Ghetto Takes Shape*, pp. 91–112.

64. Of course, the number of ministers in 1935 is probably underestimated because of the difficulty of counting many preachers who ran small storefront churches, though many of these men (and women) may not have been considered members of the professional class anyway.

65. William Julius Wilson, *The Declining Significance of Race* (Chicago: University of Chicago Press, 1978), p. 144.

66. Kusmer, *A Ghetto Takes Shape*, p. 274.

67. Mossell, "Standard of Living," p. 217.

Chapter 3: Evangelism and Social Service

1. African American churches include those churches generally included within the concept "the Black Church"—those churches belonging to the older denominations, Episcopal, Methodist, Presbyterian, Catholic, and Baptist. This concept is a sociological abstraction used, according to I. R. Mukenge, because the churches "have common elements in their history, doctrines and organization and therefore are referred to as an analytical unit"; *The Black Church in Urban America* (New York: Universities Press of America, 1983), p. 6. See also Richard I. McKinney, "The Black Church: Its Development and Present Impact," *Harvard Theological Review* 64, no. 4 (Oct. 1971): 425–81. While there is some validity to this argument, I argue that the singular "Black Church" overlooks important denominational differences and tends to diminish the complexity and variation within African American churches. As is the case with ghettoization, a common history of racial oppression does not lead to unity.

2. Emma Lapsansky, "Since They Got Those Separate Churches," *American Quarterly* 32 (Spring 1980): 58.

3. Hershberg, *Philadelphia*, p. 378. Churchgoers had a higher standard of living than nonchurchgoers: they had larger families (since they had a lower rate of infant mortality), more two-parent-headed households, and lower residential density levels; in addition, they were disproportionately wealthy. It is difficult to know whether their wealth resulted from the benefits of membership or because the churches generally attracted more prosperous people. Hershberg does not show what churches did to secure their members advantageous living conditions.

4. Du Bois, *Philadelphia Negro*, pp. 197–221.

5. Mays and Nicholson, *The Negro's Church*, pp. 299–300.

6. First African Baptist was noted for its wealthy congregation. According to Samuel Bacote in *Who's Who among Colored Baptists of the U.S.* (New York: Arno Press, 1980; 1913), "[First African Baptist] is composed principally of professional people, whose combined wealth is nearly a million dollars" (p. 41).

7. The church members included those with family names like Tanner, Moor, Brown, Telegrone, Mears, Orrs, Thomas, Middleton, Nichols, Frys, Henrys, Parke, Dade, and Butler, which Coppin assumed most of his readers would recognize. Levi J. Coppin, *Unwritten History* (New York: Negro Universities Press, 1968), pp. 219–20.

8. *Tribune* 31, no. 10 (Jan. 30, 1915): 2.

9. *Independent*, Apr. 14, 1935, p. 6.

10. Fauset, *Black Gods of the Metropolis*, p. 7.

11. *Tribune* 31, no. 10 (Jan. 30, 1915): 2.

12. "The Philadelphia Tribune 75th Anniversary Year Book" (pamphlet, 1959), p. 25.

13. Fauset, *Black Gods of the Metropolis*, pp. 97, 100. Ira de Augustine Reid, "Let Us Prey!" *Opportunity* 4 (Sept. 1926): 274–78.

14. Fauset, *Black Gods of the Metropolis*, p. 10; see also Du Bois, *Philadelphia Negro*, p. 208, and Mays and Nicholson, *The Negro's Church*, p. 215.

15. Hermann Schmalenbach, "The Sociological Category of Communion," in Talcott Parsons, ed., *Theories of Society: Foundations of Modern Sociological Theory* (New York: Free Press, 1961), pp. 331–47.

16. Mossell, "Standard of Living," pp. 31, 23, 43.

17. This happened at Berks Street Baptist Church, for instance, where 90 percent of the congregation was out of work in 1933. The church defaulted on its interest payments and was padlocked by the sheriff; *Tribune* 49, no. 9 (Jan. 19, 1933). Other churches with similar difficulties were Mt. Zion A.M.E., *Tribune* 43, no. 8 (Jan. 22, 1927); and Ebenezer Baptist, *Tribune* 49, no. 47 (Oct. 12, 1933).

18. Coppin, *Unwritten History*, pp. 245–46.

19. As Hightower T. Kealing noted in an editorial in an 1898 issue of the A.M.E. Church *Review*, "The uncertain persistence of character in any section of a great city leads to the question whether we are not on the verge of a return to simpler and cheaper church structures: for it is uselessly extravagant to erect mammoth and expensive piles to be deserted in a few years, or sold at a sacrifice; not to mention the weightier consideration that the very grandeur of our great churches so abashes the poor and humble folk that they will not enter them and their studied and constant absence from worship in these churches unconsciously begets, by the law of habit and association, an aristocracy in the church of God." Editorial, "Migratory Churches," *Review* 15 (Oct. 1898): 669. The warnings of Kealing were never heeded by other African Methodists.

20. *Christian Recorder*, Aug. 13, 1891.

21. *Christian Recorder*, July 9, 1891.

22. Wright, *Centennial Encyclopaedia*, pp. 303–4.

23. *Recorder*, Oct. 29, 1891.

24. Henry McNeil Turner, "Bishop's Annual Report," *Recorder*, May 21, 1891.

25. Coppin, *Unwritten History*, p. 259.

26. Ward A.M.E., *Tribune* 28, no. 11 (Jan. 27, 1912). Ruby C. Boyd, *On This Rock* (Philadelphia: Innovate Publishing, 1976), includes a picture of the ceremony at which Mother Bethel's mortgage was burned.

27. Walter C. Beckett Collection (UATU), Urb 19, Box 4, Folder 177.

28. St. Matthews A.M.E. Church Bulletin, Walter C. Beckett Collection (UATU), Urb 19, Box 4, Folder 162. See also Wesley A.M.E. Zion, Jan. 29, 1947, letter describing debt liquidation campaign, ibid., Urb 19, Box 4, Folder 190. Revivals and rallies used specifically for money-raising purposes were common in churches of other denominations also. See "The New Era Budget Drive" and

"The New Era Every Member Canvass" held by William Lloyd Imes at Lombard Central Presbyterian Church in 1921 and 1922; Lombard Central, Minutes of Session (Presbyterian Historical Society, PHS), Mar. 15, 1922, and Record of Meetings (PHS), Dec. 7, 1921.

29. Walter C. Beckett Collection (UATU), Urb 19, Box 4, Folder 177.

30. William A. Creditt, *Tribune* 31, no. 20 (Apr. 10, 1915): 2.

31. Ibid. Billy Sunday was famous for saying, among other things, "Put the ball over the plate for Christ."

32. Joseph R. Washington's description of the "jackleg" preacher found in the Holiness and Pentecostal churches might fit some of these evangelists; Washington, "The Black Holiness and Pentecostal Sects" in Lincoln, *Black Experience in Religion*, pp. 210–11.

33. Mays and Nicholson, *The Negro's Church*, p. 91.

34. *Tribune* 31, no. 25 (May 15, 1915): 1.

35. This and the following stories about Herman Rucker are from *Tribune* 43, no. 22 (June 16, 1927); no. 8 (Jan. 22, 1927); no. 10 (Feb. 5, 1927); no. 22 (April 30, 1927); no. 12 (Feb. 19, 1927), no. 20 (June 16, 1927).

36. Jones, *Charles Albert Tindley*, pp. 131, 138.

37. James Weldon Johnson, quoted in Seth M. Scheiner, "The Negro Church," in William G. Shade and Roy C. Herrenkohl, eds., *Seven on Black: Reflections on the Negro Experience in America* (Philadelphia: Lippincott, 1969), p. 106.

38. Wright, *Two Cents*, pp. 6–10.

39. Wright, *Negro in Pennsylvania*, p. 119.

40. Matthew Anderson, *Presbyterianism: Its Relation to the Negro* (Philadelphia: John McGill White, 1897), p. 36. See also pamphlets held at Presbyterian Historical Society.

41. Du Bois, *Philadelphia Negro*, p. 216.

42. Wright, *Negro in Pennsylvania*, p. 83.

43. *Tribune* 31, no. 49 (Oct. 30, 1915). The church also purchased a building through its Minute Men's Association "especially for [unspecified] work among men, and through its Charity Aid Society, purchased a property for a home for aged persons." Wright, *Negro in Pennsylvania*, p. 118.

44. Richard R. Wright, Jr., *Eighty-Seven Years behind the Black Curtain* (Philadelphia: A.M.E. Book Concern, 1965), p. 191.

45. When Citizens and Southern was first established in 1920, Wright, Sr., invitated W. C. Beckett, the successful black undertaker, to attend the opening ceremony. Beckett received another letter from Wright, dated July 28, 1924, and finally opened an account in 1928. He became a director at the bank in 1930. Beckett was also a director of the Rosha Building and Loan Association, which also had many pastors and prominent church members on its board. Walter C. Beckett Collection (UATU), Urb 19, Box 1, Folder 36; Urb 19, Box 4, Folder 199; Urb 19, Box 4, Folder 158. Raymond Pace Alexander, the prominent lawyer and Baptist (his wife was an African Methodist), was also involved in both organizations.

46. For example, a meeting was held in September 1930. Joining the directors were Marshall L. Shepard, W. F. Graham, C. W. Stewart, Charles S.

Spivey, William A. Harrod, H. P. Jones, and Robert J. Landston. The majority of these ministers were Baptists, showing that Wright made connections outside the A.M.E. denomination. Letter of Sept. 13, 1930, ibid., Urb 19, Box 4, Folder 199.

47. Wright, *Eighty-Seven Years*, p. 194.

48. Bishop Rhinelander of the Protestant Episcopal Church established a subcommittee to work on the problem of migration. Former minister of the Church of the Crucifixion, Henry L. Phillips, was a prominent member of this group. Letter of Nov. 1, 1917, the Diocese of Pennsylvania to Mr. Ihlder, Negro Migrant Study, Housing Association of the Delaware Valley, *Delaware Housing Association Collection* (HADV) (UATU), Urb. 3, Box 2, folder 121.

49. Du Bois, *Philadelphia Negro*, p. 217.

50. Henry L. Phillips, *A Historical Discourse at the Semi-Centennial Celebration, May 16, 1897* (Philadelphia: Church of the Crucifixion, 1897), p. 18.

51. Mossell, "Standard of Living," p. 176.

52. *Tribune* 40, no. 29 (June 14, 1924).

53. Central Presbyterian Church, Minutes of the Joint Board Meeting (PHS).

54. Elizabeth Clark-Lewis, "'This Work Had a End': African-American Domestic Workers in Washington, D.C., 1910–1940," in Carol Groneman and Mary Beth Norton, eds., *"To Toil the Livelong Day": America's Women at Work, 1780–1980* (Ithaca: Cornell University Press, 1987), pp. 202, 209.

55. Ella May Storey, interviewed by Susan Borenstein, Nov. 30, 1985.

56. Wright, *Eighty-Seven Years*, p. 164.

57. *Tribune* 49, no. 1 (Nov. 24, 1932); 50, no. 24 (May 4, 1933).

58. Wright, *Eighty-Seven Years*, p. 164.

59. For a full description of the riots and the murder of Bullock by Patrolman Roy Ramsey, see Vincent P. Franklin, "Philadelphia Race Riot," *Pennsylvania Magazine of History and Biography* 99 (1972): 339–42.

60. *Ibid.*, p. 344; *Tribune* 34, no. 39 (Aug. 17, 1918): 1; no. 45 (Sept. 28, 1918): 1.

61. *Tribune* 34, no. 39 (Aug. 17, 1918); no. 41 (Aug. 31, 1918); no. 46 (Oct. 5, 1918). At Pinn Memorial, Richard R. Wright, Jr., was the guest speaker.

62. Franklin, "Philadelphia Race Riot," pp. 344–45.

63. "Philadelphia Tribune's 75th Anniversary Year Book," p. 25. Christopher Perry, founder of the *Tribune*, was also a charter member of the Citizens Republican Club. African Methodist connections with the Republican party were strong in all northern cities; see Reverdy C. Ransom, *The Pilgrimage of Harriet Ransom's Son* (Wilberforce, Ohio: Wilberforce University, 1935), pp. 215–18; Wright, *Eighty-Seven Years*, p. 164.

64. "Philadelphia Tribune's 75th Anniversary Year Book," p. 22. E. Washington Rhodes's ability to solicit support from Philadelphia's elites is seen in the formation of the Co-operating Committee to increase black contributions to the United Campaign Fund Drive of 1932. Such African Methodists as R. R. Wright, Sr., Rev. Harry P. Anderson, and Walter C. Beckett were leading members of this committee; ibid., pp. 18–19.

65. Wright, *Negro in Pennsylvania*, p. 112.

Chapter 4: Uplifting "Backward Peoples"

1. For a full discussion of the influence of Bishop Payne's work on A.M.E. theology, see Wills, "Aspects of Social Thought in the A.M.E. Church."

2. The major figures and texts of the Social Gospel movement were: Washington Gladden, *Applied Christianity* (New York: Arno Press, 1976; 1886); William Dwight Porter Bliss, editor of *The Dawn*, the monthly magazine of the Christian Socialist Society; Charles Monroe Shelden, *In His Steps: What Would Jesus Do?* (Chicago: Advance Pub. Co., 1897); and Walter Rauschenbusch, *Christianity and the Social Crisis* (New York: Macmillan, 1908), *Christianizing the Social Order* (New York: Macmillan, 1912). In general, Social Gospel thinkers were more concerned with channeling church resources toward dealing with increasing class conflict rather than with tampering with liturgical practices to reflect the aspirations of the oppressed. See C. Howard Hopkins, *The Rise of the Social Gospel in American Protestantism, 1865–1915* (New Haven: Yale University Press, 1967), pp. 121–327.

3. See Willen A. Visser't Hooft, *The Background of the Social Gospel in America* (St. Louis: Bethany Press, 1963), pp. 30–44, which discusses the importance of Methodism to the development of the Social Gospel. In contrast to Calvinism, which places great emphasis on the will of God for the salvation of the individual, Methodism places more emphasis on the individual's role in his or her own salvation. While this humanistic impulse necessarily places greater emphasis on the individual in society, it does not necessarily lead to the alignment of Christianity with the cause of the oppressed (as in a liberation theology).

4. In the middle of a sermon Tindley would burst into song, and the audience would join in. This was known as a "songfest." Horace Clarence Boyer, "Charles Albert Tindley: Progenitor of Black-American Gospel Music," *Black Perspectives in Music* 11 (Fall 1983): 109.

5. Paris, *Social Teachings of the Black Churches*, p. 82.

6. This was true in spite of the fact that Richard R. Wright, Jr., wrote: "While founded by a religious denomination [the *Review*] has never sought to be denominational. It has always been, and is now, a vehicle of expression for the best thought of the highest scholarship of the race in every department of human knowledge. *Centennial Encyclopaedia*, p. 355.

7. Coppin, *Unwritten History*, p. 253.

8. Ibid., p. 256. Coppin wrote of taking over as editor of the *Review* from Bishop Tanner: "I was fortunate enough to keep the old friends of the Review and to make new ones. I could always depend upon my old friends T. Thomas Fortune and T. McCants Stuart to come to my rescue, as I could also Judge Straker" (p. 254).

9. Blacks accepted white theological views, as James H. Cone suggests, but they did not merely accept the eschatalogical "white lie" that they would be rewarded in the afterlife for their burdens in this world. African Methodists were very much concerned with the physical world and with the "uplift" of African Americans within that world. Paris, *Social Teachings of the Black Church*, p. 40; "Organic Union—Symposium," *Review* 9 (Jan. 1893): 224–40. Reverdy C. Ran-

som, for example, wrote: "The founders of the A.M.E. Church were satisfied with the doctrine and polity of the M.E. Church. What they strove for was to worship God on the basis of absolute equality of all men at the altars of religion," *Preface to the History of the A.M.E. Church* (Nashville: AME Sunday School Union, 1950), p. 52.

10. Bishop Benjamin T. Tanner, "Bethel's One Hundred Nineteenth Anniversary," *Review* 25 (Oct. 1908): 75.

11. Wheeler, *Uplifting the Race*, p. 12. Wheeler has summarized African Methodist theology both accurately and succinctly: "AMEs were Arminian in their understanding of the freedom of the human will, and they affirmed the ability of the sinner to either accept or reject the salvation offered in Jesus. Like other Methodists, AME preachers also taught that saved persons could lose their salvation by faithlessness. As a result, they emphasized Christian holiness. African Methodists were encouraged to cultivate a desire and longing for complete sanctification in this life. The AME Church believed that perfection was attainable in this life, and that 'glorification' occurred after death." It was distinct from the Baptist faith, which was essentially Calvinist, in placing more emphasis on good deeds. Baptism alone was insufficient to save a Methodist, who always had to strive to avoid "backsliding." In all its essentials, therefore, African Methodism resembled Methodism.

12. J. T. Jenifer, "Why I Am an African Methodist," *Review* 7 (Jan. 1891): 277–91.

13. Solomon Porter Hood, writing in 1893 while he was pastor of Morris Brown A.M.E. Church in Philadelphia, went even further. His article, "Liturgy in the Methodist Church," restated Methodist fundamentals in order to remind African Methodists about the path that John Wesley had laid out for them. "Methodism in doctrine and form," he wrote, "must be that which John Wesley taught." *Review* 10 (Jan. 1894): 343–48. Another *Review* article that shows the similarity between African Methodism and mainstream Methodism is T. G. Stewart's "The Third Witness," *Review* 7 (Jan. 1891): 261–63.

14. Paris, *Social Teachings of the Black Churches*, p. 45.

15. Ibid., pp. 75–77.

16. A. C. Garner, "True and False in Revival Methods of the Race," *Review* 19 (Apr. 1903): 489.

17. William H. Ferris, "A Historical and Psychological Account of the Genesis and Development of the Negro's Religion," *Review* 20 (Apr. 1904): 344, 351.

18. The concept of race employed by both black and white intellectuals at this time derived from nineteenth-century scientific theories which, as K. Anthony Appiah shows in *In My Father's House: Africa in the Philosophy of Culture* (New York: Oxford, 1992), were without foundation.

19. Of the *Review* authors, only J. T. Jenifer, who had been secretary of the Commission on Organic Union with the A.M.E. Zion Church in 1890, actually celebrated division. "It is more effective," he wrote, "when a number of persons engaged to do a part of the same work, yet entertaining different opinions as to the best means of doing it, [are] separate and distinct in order that there may be perfect freedom and individuality." "Why I Am an African Methodist," p. 278.

20. Wills, "Aspects of Social Thought in the A.M.E. Church," p. 34.

21. Porter, "African Methodism as a Factor in the Progress of the Race," p. 321.

22. The "symposium" on organic union between the A.M.E. and A.M.E. Zion Churches revealed the attitude of African Methodists to any kind of unification with other denominations. The authors supported unification on principle but believed that it was unfeasible. John Patterson Sampson's opposition to it was typical. "The present generation knows nothing about the causes which impelled the separation," he wrote, "yet we have two great structures, built up on separate lines from the base, requiring reconstruction throughout the entire organism." Thus, he concluded, "I regard the proposition on the part of many as vain, visionary and extravagant." "Organic Union—Symposium," *Review* 9 (Jan. 1893): 223–40. Unification was unfeasible owing to the difficulty in merging two or more independent bureaucracies. Slight differences in practices between denominations became major issues as the churchmen discussed unification, and individuals gained within their own denominations prestige and power that they might lose if unification occurred.

23. See John T.S. White, "The Sermon as a Work of Art," *Review* 20 (Apr. 1904): 354–55; John C. Brock, "Music—Its Origin and Development," 16 (July 1899): 133; Francis A. Stewart, "The Gospel in Song," 17 (Apr. 1901): 349–50; F.T.M. Webster, "Singing as Well as Praying," 20 (Apr. 1904): 374–75. Lawrence W. Levine, *Black Culture and Black Consciousness: Afro-American Folk Thought from Slavery to Freedom* (New York: Oxford University Press, 1978), pp. 30–55.

24. See John Durham, "The AME Church as Seen from Without," *Review* 7 (July, 1890): 90–91; R. R. Downs, "An Educated Ministry," 9 (Apr. 1893): 316–17; and W. H. Thomas, "The Religious Characteristics of the Negro," 9 (Apr. 1893): 390; J.T.S. White, "The Place of Emotionalism in the Sermon," 29 (Oct. 1912): 186–87.

25. Downs, "An Educated Ministry," p. 316.

26. Examples of articles discussing A.M.E. educational institutions are: James A. Handy, "A Complete Education," *Review* 7 (July 1890): 71–78; William D. Johnson, "The Educational Work of the A.M.E. Church," 8 (Apr. 1892): 391–98; and John M. Henderson, "Our Educational Work," 10 (Oct. 1893): 294–300.

27. Edward A. Clark, "Sunday Manners," *Review* 29 (Apr. 1913): 336.

28. Porter, "Afro-American Methodism as a Factor in the Progress of the Race," p. 318.

29. Gaines, "The True and the False in the Revival Methods of the Race," *Review* 19 (Oct. 1902): 496.

30. Wills, "Aspects of Social Thought in the A.M.E. Church," p. 27. See also Bishop Daniel Payne's *Recollections of Seventy Years* (New York: Arno Press, 1968), pp. 253–57.

31. Scott B. Jones, "What Is the Best Method of Conducting Revivals in the A.M.E. Church?" *Review* 8 (Oct. 1891): 221.

32. Garner, "True and False in Revival Methods of the Race," pp. 491–93.

33. Harper, *Iola Leroy*, pp. 47, 239.

34. Katherine D. Tillman, ed., *Quotations from Negro Authors* (Fort Scott, Kans.: Tucker Print Shop, 1921), pp. 5, 8 (Anna M. Henderson), 5 (M. F. Pitts), 12–13 (Tillman), 9 (Burroughs).

35. Tillman, *Aunt Betsy's Thanksgiving* (Philadelphia: A.M.E. Book Concern, n.d.), p. 2; see also *The Spirit of Allen: A Pageant of African Methodism* (Philadelphia: A.M.E. Book Concern, 1922).

36. Harper, *Iola Leroy*, p. 168.

37. Hopkins, *Rise of the Social Gospel*, pp. 121–327; see also Robert T. Handy, ed., *The Social Gospel in America, 1870–1920* (New York: Oxford University Press, 1966); and Ronald C. White, Jr., and C. Howard Hopkins, eds., *The Social Gospel: Religion and Reform in Changing America* (Philadelphia: Temple University Press, 1976). A.M.E. and A.M.E. Zion Church leaders played an active role in the Federal Council of Churches of Christ in America, which held its meeting of 1908 in Philadelphia. See Coppin, "The Federal Council of the Churches of Christ in America," *Review* 25 (Jan. 1909): 227–30, and Kealing, "The Great Federal Council Meeting in Philadelphia," ibid., pp. 231–37.

38. The adherence of black religious leaders to Social Gospel beliefs and the influence of this movement among African Americans generally have not been appreciated fully by historians. The most important work on black thought during the period, August Meier's *Negro Thought in America, 1880–1915* (Ann Arbor: University of Michigan Press, 1966) makes no mention of the Social Gospel. This is surprising as the author recognizes the importance of the church in the Afro-American community (p. 15). In effect, Meier's work is a study of black *secular* thought and thinkers during the period.

39. Walter B. Weare, "The Idea of Progress in Afro-American Thought, 1890–1915," in *The Quest for Social Justice: The Morris Franklin Lectures, 1970–1980*, ed. Ralph M. Aderman (Madison: University of Wisconsin Press, 1983).

40. C.O.H. Thomas, "Politics, Ministers and Religion," *Review* 11 (Oct. 1894): 283, 276, 278, 280. J. W. Smith, it is true, was of the opposite opinion— that "no clergyman could preach politics without damaging religion, [and] a clergyman, as such, ought never to appear on a political platform." He argued that "if he could drop the 'reverend' and become plain 'mister' it might be different, but his office clings to him with his white cravat." "Ministers and Politics," *Review* 11 (July 1894): 182. However, Smith's was clearly the minority opinion among *Review* authors.

41. J. W. Norris, "A Plea for the Negro," *Review* 9 (July 1892): 28–29.

42. G. Herbert Renfro, "Is the Afro-American League a Failure?" *Review* 9 (July 1892): 16.

43. J. B. Stansberry, "The State of the Country," *Review* 7 (July 1890): 86.

44. S. F. Williams, "Education of the Negro," *Review* 7 (July 1890): 67, 69.

45. James A. Handy, "A Complete Education," *Review* 7 (July 1890): 74–75.

46. Du Bois, *Souls of Black Folk*. Numerous editorials dealt with business issues, and in 1908 a business department was established in the *Review*. Examples of articles on business initiatives are: James Storum, "Building Associations: Their Efficiency as Money-Saving and Home-Winning Institutions," *Review* 7

(Oct. 1890): 146–51; T. Thomas Fortune, "The Free Coinage of Silver," 10 (July 1893): 101–12; Booker T. Washington, "Taking Advantages of our Disadvantages," 10 (Apr. 1894): 478–82; John A. Johnson, "Financial Factors," 11 (July 1894): 148–59; "The National Negro Business League," 22 (July 1905): 24–33.

47. Reverdy C. Ransom, "The Negro and Socialism," *Review* 13 (Oct. 1896): 196–97.

48. George W. Forbes, "The Socialism Was Not Dr. Ransom's but That of the Present Day," *Review* 30 (Jan. 1914): 240–45.

49. H.C.C. Astwood, "Social Economy," *Review* 16 (Apr. 1900): 435–37.

50. Dennis C. Dickerson, "The Black Church in Industrializing Western Pennsylvania, 1870–1950," *Western Pennsylvania Historical Magazine* (Apr. 1981), pp. 329–44, shows the clear connection between white businesses and black churches in Pittsburgh. The same connection existed in Philadelphia, though on a smaller scale. John Wanamaker and Robert C. Ogden helped Matthew Anderson build up Berean Presbyterian and supported Anderson's financial initiatives. Wanamaker also helped Charles Tindley at East Calvary.

51. "The Exodus," *Tribune* 33, no. 26 (May 19, 1917).

52. Ransom, *Preface*, p. 161. Ransom continued, "We think that most of the ministers and church officers of this day [1950] are trying to repair the mistakes made by their fathers in providing a welcome to the strangers within their gates." If black Baptist and African Methodist services resemble each other today, therefore, it may be because African Methodists have belatedly moved away from "ritualism and formalism." Even so, African Methodist services are still generally acknowledged to be more conservative and reserved than those of Baptist churches.

53. Matthew H. Jones, interview, Feb. 12, 1988.

Chapter 5: "Pulpit Extension"

1. George A. Singleton, *The Romance of African Methodism: A Study of the A.M.E. Church* (New York: Exposition Press, 1952), p. 141.

2. Levi J. Coppin, *The Key to Scriptural Interpretation: Or, Expository Notes on Obscure Passages* (Philadelphia: A.M.E. Publishing House, 1895), dedication to Dr. Edward T. Bartlett. See also Coppin, *Unwritten History*, p. 251; and Wright, *Centennial Encyclopaedia*, pp. 74–75.

3. Coppin, "Place of Religious Press in Modern Life," *Review* 28 (Jan. 1912): 649. Coppin represented what Richard R. Wright, Jr. described as the "minister as editor," using his editorial page as his pulpit, which he entered "only after prayer and meditation." Wright, "The Minister as Editor," *Review* 29 (Apr. 1913): 344.

4. Coppin, "Religious Press in Modern Life," p. 649.

5. Coppin, *The Relation of Baptized Children to the Church* (Philadelphia: A.M.E. Publications Department, 1890), pp. 62–78; quoted in Tanner, "Our Latest Works," *Review* 7 (Oct. 1890): 133.

6. Coppin, *Scriptural Interpretation*, pp. 3–4.

7. Mark 10:25–31; see also Matthew 19:30, 20:1–16.

8. Sernett, *Afro-American Religious History*, p. 92.

9. Genovese, "The Gospel in the Quarters," in *Roll, Jordan, Roll*, pp. 232–55, especially p. 129.

10. Coppin, *Scriptural Interpretation*, pp. 14–21.

11. Coppin, *Unwritten History*, pp. 254–55.

12. Coppin, "Editorial: The Russian and the Negro," *Review* 7 (July 1890): 104–6.

13. "Editorial," *Review* 10 (July 1893): 198.

14. Coppin, "Soul Culture in Song," *Review* 29 (July 1912): 40–47. Coppin, however, did not advocate the singing of spirituals in church services.

15. *The A.M.E. Hymn and Tune Book* (Philadelphia: A.M.E. Book Concern, 1902). Coppin composed the music for "Our Father's Church" (words by the future Bishop Tanner), "My Infant Lord, to Thee I Gladly Bring," and "The Friends of Christian Education Call" (words by Bishop Payne); he wrote the words for "The A.M.E. Church Rallying Song" and both words and music for "Onward! Onward! Onward Christian Soldiers" (pp. 369, 373–75). Coppin's wife, Fanny Jackson, also contributed to the hymnal (p. 383).

16. Coppin, "Soul Music in Song," p. 42.

17. Charles Hart Sheen, "The 'Bard of Methodism' and English Hymnology," *Review* 30 (Apr. 1914) 301–3.

18. Levi J. Coppin, *Observations of People and Things in South Africa, 1900–1904* (Philadelphia: A.M.E. Book Concern, 1905), p. 133.

19. Coppin's association with Bishop W. J. Gaines brought about the election of H. T. Kealing as editor of the *Review*. Gaines had revealed that William Preston, a Missourian candidate for the episcopacy in 1896, had abandoned his wife. In retaliation, Preston's southern supporters proceeded both to vote down Coppin's candidacy for bishop (several candidates could be elected in one year) and to vote against renewing his editorship, stuffing the ballot box with votes in favor of the Texan candidate. At least this is Ransom's interpretation of the events. Ransom, *Pilgrimage*, p. 75.

20. Wills, "Aspects of Social Thought," pp. 75, 39.

21. Ransom, *Pilgrimage*, pp. 226–28.

22. Mother Bethel, Minutes of the Preachers' Association, microfilm, Historical Society of Pennsylvania (HSP), roll 9.

23. Ransom, *Preface*, p. 178. Ransom continued, "We have not yet, in an official way re-examined the doctrine and polity we inherited from the Methodist Episcopal Church, but the time is at hand when our thinkers, our religious seers, our reformers and prophets shall re-examine these things in the light of the present political, religious, moral, social and economic conditions prevailing in our country and throughout the world" (p. 179).

24. Ransom's ideas and life can be found in his writings: *The Pilgrimage of Harriet Ransom's Son*, *Preface to the History of the A.M.E. Church*, *The Spirit of Freedom and Justice* (Nashville: A.M.E. Sunday School Union, 1926), *Year Book of the Negro Churches* (Wilberforce, Ohio: Wilberforce University, 1935–36), *The Negro: The Hope and Despair* (Wilberforce, Ohio: Wilberforce University, 1935), and *How Should the Christian State Deal With the Negro Problem*, an address deliv-

ered to the National Reform Convention in the Park Street Congregational Church, Boston, Oct. 3, 1905.

25. Wright, "The Minister as Editor," pp. 343–44.

26. For Abbott's contribution to the migration, see Grossman, *Land of Hope*, pp. 74–91.

27. Richard R. Wright, Jr., *The Encyclopaedia of African Methodism* (Philadelphia: A.M.E. Book Concern, 1947), pp. 311–12. Wright's thesis at the University of Pennsylvania was published in 1912 by the A.M.E. Book Concern under the title, *The Negro in Pennsylvania*.

28. Ransom was the most vocal advocate of the institutional movement within the denomination. Using Jane Addams as his inspiration and Hull House as his prototype, in 1900 he established the Institutional Church and Social Settlement in Chicago, a church that would provide social services for its members and the surrounding community. See Ransom, *Pilgrimage*, pp. 103–18.

29. Wright, *Eighty-Seven Years*, pp. 148–49.

30. Wright, *Encyclopaedia* (1947), p. 312; "Social Work and the Influence of the Negro Church," *Annals of the Academy of Politics and Social Science* (July–Dec. 1907); "Self-Help in Negro Education" (pamphlet, Cheyney, Pa.: Committee of Twelve for the Advancement of Interests of the Negro Race, 1909); see also "The Negro Problem: Being Extracts from Two Lectures" (pamphlet, Philadelphia: A.M.E. Book Concern, 1911).

31. Wright, *The Outline of the Teaching of Jesus: Or the Fundamentals of Christian Doctrine* (Philadelphia: A.M.E. Book Concern, 1911), pp. 3–4, 39–40, 82, 92.

32. Wright, *Eighty-Seven Years*, p. 125; Blossie Coble interview, Aug. 12, 1989.

33. Throughout both encyclopedias biographies always mention level of educational attainment. A preacher's ability to arouse an emotional response is almost never referred to. Rev. Jean Williams has pointed out to me that Wright omitted many ministers who, had their approach to church worship been different, might have been included.

34. Wright, *Eighty-Seven Years*, p. 192; *Encyclopaedia* (1947), p. 311.

35. Wright, quoted in *Review* 34 (July 1917): 21–22.

36. Wright, *Eighty-Seven Years*, p. 314.

37. Wright, *Review* 33 (Jan. 1917): 133.

Chapter 6: Service and Prestige

1. *Gender* here is used in the way it is defined by Joan Wallach Scott in *Gender and the Politics of History* (New York: Columbia University Press, 1988): "The term 'gender' suggests that relations between the sexes are a primary aspect of social organization (rather than following from, say, economic or demographic pressures); that the terms male and female identities are in large part culturally determined (not produced by individuals or collectivities entirely on their own); and that the differences between the sexes constitute and are constituted by hierarchical social structures" (p. 25).

2. This is not to suggest that women did not wish also to gain prestige from church membership (clearly, success in service endeavors would bring prestige with it). The important point is that women usually attained prestige through service or through their husband's position in the church. Men gained prestige by holding positions of power.

3. Katherine Davis Tillman, "Women as Helpers of the Ministers in the Spiritual and Social Activities of the Church," *Review* 29 (Apr. 1913): 342.

4. H. T. Kealing, "Women in Society," *Review* 20 (July 1903): 127. See also Sarah E. Tanner, "The Mite Society," *Review* 12 (Jan. 1896): 378–82.

5. Mrs. M. Guile, "The Ideal Minister's Wife," *Review* 30 (Apr. 1914): 304. The word *helpmeet* was often used instead of *helpmate*. According to the Oxford English Dictionary, this word derived from a misunderstanding of Genesis 2:18–20, reading "help meet" as one word.

6. James H.A. Johnson, "Woman's Exalted Position," *Review* 8 (Apr. 1892): 402–5.

7. M. E. Lee, "The Home-Maker," *Review* 8 (July 1891): 63–64. Roger Lane, *William Dorsey's Philadelphia and Ours* (New York: Oxford University Press, 1991), p. 188.

8. Hannah Jones, "Women as Educators," *Review* 9 (Apr. 1893): 322.

9. Mary Church Terrell, "A Few Possibilities of the National Association of Colored Women," *Review* 13 (Oct. 1896): 220.

10. Terrell, "Duty of the National Association of Colored Women to the Race," *Review* 16 (Jan. 1900): 352.

11. Selena C. Gaines Dickerson, "The Responsibilities and Duties of the Women of the Twentieth Century," *Review* 32 (Oct. 1915): 110. See also Mary V. Bass, "Home Missions," *Review* 14 (Apr. 1898): 450.

12. Tillman, "Afro-American Women and Their Work," *Review* 11 (Apr. 1895): 477–99.

13. Tillman, "The National Association of Colored Women's Clubs," *Review* 31 (Oct. 1914): 174; Dickerson, "Responsibilities and Duties," pp. 108–11.

14. Fannie Barrier Williams, "The Awakening of Women," *Review* 13 (Apr. 1897): 392–98.

15. A. J. Cooper, in *A Voice from the South* (New York: Negro Universities Press, 1969), entitled one of her chapters "Womanhood: A Vital Element in the Regeneration and Progress of the Race."

16. Terrell, "Duty of the National Association of Colored Women to the Race," p. 347.

17. Jacqueline Jones, *Labor of Love*, pp. 152–91.

18. Paula Giddings, *When and Where I Enter: The Impact of Black Women on Race and Sex in America* (New York: Bantam, 1984). Caroll Smith-Rosenberg, *Disorderly Conduct* (New York: Oxford University Press, 1985), pp. 167–81.

19. During its first seven years, the organization met more than 7,000 black women and girls as they disembarked from ships that had brought them north. In 1911 alone, 900 new arrivals were met at the docks and 593 were aided. Of these, 311 came from Maryland and 239 from Virginia. Professional and Business Women's Supplement, *Tribune*, June 29, 1912, p. 4.

20. C. H. Johnson, "How the Laymen May Best Cooperate with the Minister for Spiritual and Social Ends," *Review* 29 (Apr. 1913): 361–62.

21. Harper, *Iola Leroy*, p. 253.

22. Tillman, "Women as Helpers of Ministers," p. 342.

23. Alice M. Dunbar, "What Has the Church to Offer the Men of Today?" *Review* 30 (July 1913): 5–10.

24. St. Matthews A.M.E. Church bulletin, Walter C. Beckett Collection (UATU), Urb 19, Box 4, Folder 162. Beckett advertised in publications of all black denominations, for example, the *Messenger*, ibid., Folder 160.

25. Members of orders did not always join those associated with their church. Beckett, a member of Union A.M.E. Church, preferred to join a group based closer to his residence in Germantown. Ibid., Folder 159.

26. S. H. Coleman, "Free-Masonry as a Secret Society Defended," *Review* 14 (Jan. 1898): 327.

27. William H. Heard, a member of the Masons, Odd Fellows, True Reformers, and Good Templars, addressed meetings of the Odd Fellows at "Mother" Bethel in 1890, *Christian Recorder* 28, no. 45 (Oct. 30, 1890). He also set aside a day in a dedications exercise as a Pythians' day, 28, no. 47 (Nov. 13, 1890). Robert J. Williams established his own group of Masons at the same church soon after his arrival in 1916. Ruby Chappelle Boyd, ed., *On This Rock: The Mother Church of African Methodism* (Philadelphia: Innovate Printing Co., 1976), p. 65.

28. The Order of Elks grew in importance among African Americans during the 1920s and tended to have a more secular base than the orders considered here. It also had a wider membership than these orders, which tended to recruit members from the more successful people within the congregations. Its leadership, however, was predominantly middle class, and it functioned within the community very much like the other orders. In E. Franklin Frazier's words, "the Order of the Elks is a means to power and income for middle-class Negroes, and there is an intense struggle for the offices in the organization." *Black Bourgeoisie* (New York: Free Press, 1965), p. 82.

29. W. F. Teister, "The Idea of Freemasonry," *Review* 12 (1895): 407, 414. Similarly, Coleman argued, "The principles of the institution do certainly teach us our social and religious duties. We are instructed to be good men and true, and strictly to obey the moral law; to be peaceable citizens, and conform to the civil law of the land in which we live; to cultivate the social virtues, promote the general welfare, to avoid all quarrels, and hold in veneration our ancient patrons." "Free-Masonry," p. 336.

30. Teister, "Idea of Free Masonry," pp. 414, 413.

31. Coleman, "Free-Masonry," pp. 330, 337.

32. Frazier, *Black Bourgeoisie*, p. 81.

33. He also became an Odd Fellow.

34. Matthew H. Jones, interviewed Feb. 12, 1988.

35. "Fraternalism," *Tribune* 33, no. 26 (May 19, 1917).

36. "The Exodus," ibid.

37. Tillman, "Afro-American Women and Their Work," p. 488.

38. Jacqueline Jones, *Labor of Love*, p. 6; quoted in Evelyn Brooks-Higginbotham, "Beyond the Sound of Silence: Afro-American Women in History," *Gender and History* 1 (Spring 1989): 12.

39. Henry McNeil Turner, quoted in Jualynne Dodson, "Nineteenth-Century A.M.E. Preaching Women," in Hilah F. Thomas and Rosemary Skinner Keller, eds., *Women in New Worlds* (Nashville: Abingdon Press, 1981), p. 282.

40. Dodson, "Nineteenth-Century A.M.E. Preaching Women," pp. 283–84.

41. Minutes of the Preachers Association, Dec. 13, 1897 (Mother Bethel Microfilm, HSP, roll 9).

42. T. G. Steward in *Recorder*, Jan. 29, 1891.

43. William H. Heard, *From Slavery to the Bishopric* (Philadelphia: A.M.E. Book Concern, 1924), p. 75.

44. Lane, *William Dorsey's Philadelphia and Ours*, pp. 143, 264.

45. H. T. Kealing, "Editorial: Fanny Jackson-Coppin," *Review* 29 (Apr. 1913): 379; Fanny J. Coppin, *Reminiscences of School Life, and Hints on Teaching* (Philadelphia: A.M.E. Book Concern, 1913).

46. Tillman, "Women as Helpers of Ministers," p. 341.

47. Wright, *Encyclopaedia* (1947), p. 231. Dickey Prowell was a southern migrant. She probably joined Mother Bethel on arrival in Philadelphia and became one of Reverend Williams's supporters at the church.

48. Ibid., p. 182.

49. Today, according to Caroline Stickney Beck, at churches like Mother Bethel A.M.E., "the separation of a male sphere and a female sphere is recognized and accepted by most of the members. The men hold the major offices and the women raise most of the money." "Our Own Vine and Fig Tree: The Persistence of an Historic Afro-American Community" (Ph.D. diss., Bryn Mawr College, 1981), p. 191.

50. Order of the Eastern Star, *History of the Deborah Grand Chapter, 1909–1981* (Philadelphia, 1981), and conversation with two current members of the order.

51. James H.A. Johnson wrote (in clearly a self-serving fashion since he wished to dissuade women from acting politically): "A true woman, like Dorcas or Amanda Smith, thinks she is as great in the pew as man is in the pulpit; and hence she strives to satisfy the Lord and not the bubbling ambition of her soul." It is understandable that such attitudes were internalized by some women especially as an implied criticism of men was inherent in them. "Woman's Exalted Position," *Review* 8 (Apr. 1892): 404. See also M. E. Lee's description of Mrs. Tanner, the bishop's wife, in "The Home-Maker," *Review* 8 (July 1891): 64.

52. R. L. Chappelle, "Women as Helpers of the Ministers in the Spiritual and Social Activities of the Church," *Review* 29 (Apr. 1913): 339–40.

53. Tillman, "Women as Helpers of the Ministers," pp. 341–42. The "feminine forces" Tillman referred to were evangelists, deaconesses, stewardesses, missionary workers, Sunday school teachers, and trustee helpers.

54. Tillman, "Afro-American Women and Their Work," pp. 485–86.

55. Wright, *Centennial Encyclopaedia*, pp. 320, 324.

56. *Recorder*, Apr. 17, 1890.

57. Wright, *Centennial Encyclopaedia*, pp. 332–33.

58. Mary F. Handy, "The Minister's Wife," *Review* 29 (Apr. 1913): 337.

59. Mary Handy had similar requirements: "A woman of Christian character, thoroughly consecrated to the ministry, modest, painstaking though plain as
to dress." Ibid.

60. Mrs. M. E. Guile, "The Ideal Minister's Wife," *Review* 30 (Apr. 1914):
p. 304–5.

61. Mother Bethel, Minutes of the Corporation, Oct. 8, 1917, microfilm,
HSP, roll 7.

Chapter 7: "Flaming Torches"

1. Because the pastor's wife helped the church function smoothly, an un-
married minister was at a serious disadvantage. He was usually encouraged to
marry as soon as possible, and should a married pastor become a widower, he
would often be encouraged to remarry for the sake of his ministry. Wright, *Centennial Encyclopaedia*, p. 317.

2. Ransom, *Pilgrimage*, pp. 261–74.

3. W. Spencer Carpenter, "The Minister as a Big Brother," *Review* 29
(Oct. 1912): 110–11.

4. Biographical information has been gathered from the 1916 and 1947
encyclopedias of the A.M.E. Church (Wright, *Centennial Encyclopaedia* and *Encyclopaedia* [1947]) about sixty-four ministers of Philadelphia born between 1830
and 1901. This information has an elitist bias because only the more successful
ministers were included in the denomination's encyclopedias. Nevertheless, because Philadelphia was the center of African Methodism and the First Episcopal
District was one of the most prestigious, a large proportion of A.M.E. ministers
who served in the city before 1940 had entries in one of the two encyclopedias. Sixty-three (or 53 percent) of the one hundred nineteen ministers who are
known to have served in Philadelphia between 1890 and 1940 were recorded in
one of the two encyclopedias. The group cannot be considered entirely representative of A.M.E. ministers in Philadelphia, let alone nationwide. However, some
pieces of information (e.g., place of origin) should fairly represent the city's ministers, while others (e.g., education) suggest what was required for a minister to
succeed in perhaps the most difficult ministerial market.

5. Wright, *Centennial Encyclopaedia*, p. 243.

6. Twelve ministers (19 percent) had been undergraduates at Wilberforce.

7. The average ages at which individuals reached the positions of deacon
and elder were 27 and 29.6, respectively. Fifteen, or 23 percent, of the ministers
were recorded as having been presiding elders at one time or another.

8. Wright, who heavily emphasized education, might have omitted from
the two encyclopedias several people who were prominent in the church in the
city because they lacked formal education.

9. Wright, *Eighty-Seven Years*, p. 125.

10. Mays and Nicholson, *The Negro's Church*, p. 91.

11. Matthew H. Jones, interview, Feb. 12, 1988.

12. Wright, *Centennial Encyclopaedia*, p. 317.

13. Jones interview.

14. The percentage of married ministers is not especially high. It is likely that several of the fifteen who did not mention their marital status were also married. The average number of children per family (where children were mentioned) was 4.13. This is well below the average of nine siblings that the ministers had grown up with. Both figures, however, are perhaps suspect. Many ministers were still of child-rearing age when the number of their children was recorded. Nevertheless, the number of children per family did perhaps diminish from one generation to the next.

15. Wright, *Centennial Encyclopedia*, p. 317.

16. J. W. Walker, "What Are the Characteristics of a Great Preacher?" *Review* 25 (July 1908): 3–5. See also P. A. Nichols, "How to Be a Successful Preacher and Pastor," *Review* 29 (Oct. 1912): 190–94, which reiterates Walker's essential points. Another author quoted a poem by Cowper, *Review* 25 (July 1908): 1.

17. Nichols, "How to Be a Successful Preacher and Pastor," p. 194.

18. Although in 1930, according to Mays and Nicholson, the average minister's pay was roughly comparable to that of the average black person in other professions; *Negro's Church*, p. 57.

19. C. H. Stepteau, "The Minister as a Business Man for the Church," *Review* 29 (Apr. 1913): 42. See also the articles by John T. Jenifer and D. M. Baxter, ibid., pp. 326–32.

20. A. L. Gaines, "The Minister in Relation to Church Entertainments and Social Diversion," *Review* 29 (Apr. 1913): 334.

21. *Tribune* 31, no. 24 (May 8, 1915): 4.

22. William A. Creditt, *Tribune* 31, no. 20 (Apr. 17, 1915): 2.

23. J.T.S. White, "Problems Which Confront the Pulpit Today," *Review* 29 (Oct. 1912): 186.

24. Charles Spencer Smith, *History of the A.M.E. Church* (Philadelphia: A.M.E. Book Concern, 1922), p. 320.

25. Du Bois, *Philadelphia Negro*, pp. 211–12.

26. Carpenter, "Minister as Big Brother," pp. 108–9.

27. Henry McNeil Turner, *Recorder*, June 26, 1890.

28. William H. Heard, *Independent*, May 12, 1935, p. 4. The bishop had made several attempts to move ministers about against their wishes and those of their congregations. In 1933, Mt. Zion threatened to withdraw from the connection because the bishop refused to reinstate Rev. Slade as their pastor. The members favored Slade by a vote of 194 to 13. Slade's popularity was such that he had been able to reduce the church's debt from $30,000 to $16,000, even though the church was known for financial woes. *Tribune* 50, no. 39 (Aug. 17, 1933).

29. Further, the standard deviation between 1930 and 1949 was more than double what it had been previously, signifying a lot of variance from this mean.

What this suggests is that a large number of pastorates were lasting a lot longer than 5.5 years, while a large number were ending well before the third term.

    30. Ransom, *Preface*, p. 162.

Chapter 8: Many "Promised Lands"

    1. Grossman, *Land of Hope*, passim.

    2. The term *refugee* is used by Allen Ballard in *One More Day's Journey*, pp. 184, 186–87. James Grossman describes his subjects as either "black Southerners," with all the uniformity that this term can imply, or "migrants" who were well prepared for their journey north; *Land of Hope*, pp. 4–9, 66–97, and especially, 102. Grossman downplays the significance of those migrants who left "recklessly" and concentrates on "information networks" and "scouts" or "pioneers." Carole Marks uses the term "mudsills" in *Farewell, We're Good and Gone*. Marks creates a composite picture of the migration participant: "He is a black male between the ages of 25 and 34, he is the resident of a medium-sized southern city, he has worked between five and ten years at one or two industrial enterprises, he is usually an unskilled laborer, and he often is married with children. The reasons he gives for moving north, are all positive—to better his economic circumstances, to improve educational opportunities for his children, and to obtain greater freedom of movement. In short, he is a man drawn from 'favored and vigorous elements of the general population'" (p. 35). Marks describes this "representative migrant" as male in spite of her complaint that historians have ignored the role and participation of women in the migration. Once women and children are included in the migration population the possibility of creating a uniform migrant, and the value in doing so, evaporates. Combining these three authors' one-dimensional portraits provides further evidence for diversity and for the existence of what I call here a migration continuum.

    3. Fannie's attendance at school was unusual; most sixteen-year-olds were working. Her attendance at school while her mother worked is interesting in light of Elizabeth H. Pleck's contention that black women's unswerving faith in education often led a mother to decide to do paid work rather than remove an older child from school. Pleck, "A Mother's Wages," in Pleck and Nancy F. Cott, eds., *A Heritage of Her Own* (New York: Simon & Shuster, 1979), pp. 378–79. See Brooks Higginbotham, "Beyond the Sound of Silence: Afro-American Women in History," p. 31, n. 25.

    4. William D. Fuller, "The Negro Migrant in Philadelphia," in Negro Migrant Study (UATU), Urb. 31, Box 1, folders 1–2, pp. 28–29.

    5. This finding was supported by the Negro Migration Committee Survey of 1923, Negro Migrant Study (UATU), Urb. 31, Box 1, folders 1–2.

    6. Fredric Miller, "A Black Migration to Philadelphia: A 1924 Profile," *Pennsylvania Magazine of History and Biography* 107 (July 3, 1984). Miller concludes that the sample is not skewed significantly. Only young, single migrants who came north were seriously underrepresented owing to their transience; Miller, ibid., pp. 319–20, 326–29.

7. This is not the only division apparent within the migration population. Sex, age, and class differences also warrant further study.

8. Darlene Clark Hine, "Black Migration to the Urban Midwest: The Gender Dimension, 1915–45," in Trotter, *Great Migration*, pp. 133, 138.

9. Positive reasons included responses like: "better chances in North," "to make more money," "travel," "experience north," "just a notion," and "for a change." These seem to reflect an attitude of looking beyond the local situation to other possibilities. Negative reasons were more self-explanatory: "boll weevil," "bad conditions in South," and "no work in South."

10. See Grossman, *Land of Hope*, for a discussion of the propaganda inspired by Booker T. Washington and his supporters to persuade black farmers to remain on the land; pp. 38–65.

11. Negro Migration Committee Reports, March through July 1923 (UATU).

12. Eta, .24; significance, .02; standard deviation, 10.8 for the rural and 6.7 for the urban group.

13. Eta, .39; significance, .00.

14. The mean number of children of rural families increased from 1.7 for household heads under twenty-five to 3.7 for heads aged thirty and over. For urban household heads, the figures were 0.8 and 1.4 respectively (Eta, .31; significance, .01).

15. Eta, .29; significance, .00.

16. For urban families, the weekly income per family member was more than $8.30, while for rural families it was $6.70. This difference was achieved with the same proportion of women (roughly 54 percent) staying outside the paid work force.

17. According to the worksheets, the interviewers asked whether the new arrivals were church members. It is very unlikely, however, that any of them had actually become members in the short time they had been in the city. "Member" most likely means "attends on a regular basis."

18. Church affiliation did not vary by time of arrival. The same proportion of those arriving in late 1922 was linked to a church as of those arriving in late 1923.

19. The differences among migrants may have been clearer still in terms of membership in the secret orders. These organizations were nothing if not "differentiating," and only a minority of the migrant population was members of these organizations. A report of the Philadelphia Negro Migration Committee in 1923 indicated that while 90 percent of the migrants were church members in the South, only about 35 percent belonged to fraternities having welfare and benefit features. Of these, about 60 percent belonged to what are described as "fraternities of high order"—the Odd Fellows, Knights of Pythias, and Masons. The Good Samaritans, Knights of King Solomon, Supreme Circle, Sons & Daughters of Pearce, and many others made up the less well-known and lower-class low orders. Philadelphia Negro Migration Committee, July 9, 1923 (UATU).

20. Grossman, *Land of Hope*, pp. 111–12.

21. Monroe Work, "Research with Respect to Cooperation between Urban and Rural Communities," *Opportunity* (Feb. 1923), pp. 7–8.

22. Long lists of complaints were made by recent arrivals about water facilities, inadequate lighting, and lack of decent sanitary provisions, as well as overcrowding in the Philadelphia Housing Association's 1924 Migrant Survey; see the original worksheets in the Negro Migrant Study (UATU) Urb. 31, Box 1, folders 1–2.

23. Ibid. Nicholas Lemann, in *The Promised Land: The Great Black Migration and How It Changed America* (New York: Knopf, 1991), pp. 28–32, has argued that migrants brought a sharecropping culture to the urban north that was unable to sustain stable families. This "culture of poverty" thesis would have been contested by Monroe Work. Work's comment here strikes to the heart of one of the most critical failings of migration (and immigration) historiography, namely its failure to analyze the gender implications of migration; see Hine, "Black Migration to the Urban West."

24. Joe William Trotter, Jr., *Coal, Class and Color: Blacks in Southern West Virginia, 1915–32* (Urbana: University of Illinois Press, 1990), and Earl Lewis, *In Their Own Interests: Race, Class and Power in Twentieth Century Norfolk* (Berkeley: University of California Press, 1991), highlight the importance of nonnorthern migrations.

25. They were encouraged to do so by the A.M.E. church organ, the *Christian Recorder*: "Don't come without a letter of introduction from your pastor. This will mean a great deal to you;" "Letter from the Ministers of Philadelphia, Penna.," *Recorder* 65 (May 31, 1917): p. 4, in *Housing Association of Delaware Valley* (HADV) office files, 1917–1920, Urban Archives, Urb. 3, Box 2, folder 122 Henceforth this issue will be referred to as *Recorder* (migration issue).

26. The representativeness of these letter-bearers is uncertain. The emphasis placed upon letters of transmittal by the A.M.E. Church during the war years, and the large number of letters remaining at Mother Bethel, suggest that the letter-bearers may be a representative sample of newcomers to that church. Many people did join the church without letters, however.

27. Three or fewer migrants came from each of the following: Alabama, California, Connecticut, Delaware, Iowa, Michigan, New Jersey, New York, North Carolina, Pennsylvania, Texas, Virginia, and Washington, D.C.

28. Grossman, *Land of Hope*, pp. 100–101.

29. The 1924 study of Philadelphia migrants shows a similar shift from the upper to the lower South as a source of migrants; Miller, "A Black Migration to Philadelphia," p. 322. Cheaper transportation was made available during the war to help attract laborers into northern cities.

30. *Fourteenth U.S. Census*, vol. 3.

31. Ibid., vol. 6, p. 917.

32. Ibid., p. 920.

33. This possibly accounts for the fact that many members of Mother Bethel now consider the church to be a "South Carolina church." Beck, "Our Own Vine and Fig Tree," p. 218. This might at first seem surprising, since more people came to Bethel from Florida and Georgia. While there is a Georgia Club

at the church, it has neither the influence nor the membership of the South Carolina Club. The reason perhaps lies in the origin and motivation of the migrants from the various states. Tending to be more urban than their South Carolina counterparts, migrants from Florida and Georgia may have used both Philadelphia and Bethel as stepping stones to better opportunities elsewhere. The South Carolina migrants, who had been less willing to move from their rural homes in the first place, perhaps tended to stay put once they arrived in Philadelphia.

34. The letters typically say: "We take pleasure in recommending her to any church she desires to come under the watchcare of or join. She leaves with our prayers and good wishes." Allen Ballard, *One More Day's Journey: The Story of a Family and a People* (New York: McGraw-Hill Book Co., 1984), p. 177.

35. Singleton was also a member of the Masons, Odd Fellows, and Knights of Pythias, as well as of the Republican Party, so he may have had connections with people in the north through these national organizations. Wright, *Centennial Encyclopaedia*, p. 204.

36. Wright, *Encyclopaedia* (1947), pp. 310–11.

37. See Robert Gregg, "Sparks from the Anvil of Oppression: Philadelphia's African Methodists and the Great Migration, 1890–1930" (Ph.D. diss., University of Pennsylvania, 1989), appendix L.

38. Wright, *Encyclopaedia* (1947), p. 204.

39. Mary Debardeleben, "Causes of Migration, As Stated by a Southern White Woman," *Recorder* (migration issue). See also Rev. G. W. Williams, "An Open Letter to the Bishops of the A.M.E. Church," *Recorder* (migration issue), p. 2, in which the author requests the transfer of "a few good pastors from the South" to places in the North "where they can get to these people and save them to our Church."

40. In 1947, St. Phillips still had a congregation of well over one thousand members. Wright, *Encyclopaedia* (1947), p. 389.

41. Helen Cinnamond, in *Housing Association Collection* (HAC), UATU, Urb. 3, Box 2, folder 20.

42. Southern blacks who responded to Richard R. Wright, Jr.'s, questionnaire generally answered the question about "the effect on the Negroes who do not leave" by answering that it would lead to an improvement in their situation. *Recorder* (migration issue).

43. *Recorder* (migration issue), p. 2. See also articles by Rev. W. G. Alexander of Savannah and Dr. R. B. Brooks on the same page.

44. Debardeleben, *Recorder* (migration issue), pp. 1, 5.

45. HAC, UATU, Urb. 3, Box 2, folder 20.

46. In 1924, the Housing Association suggested that the most recent migrants were "of a better grade" than their wartime predecessors; Miller, "Black Migration," p. 325. It is difficult to know whether this description and that of Cinnamond are accurate or whether they result from the more recent migrants' attempt to appear better-off in order to avoid the negative assessment made of their predecessors. It is likely, however, that among the migrants at all times were both poorer and richer members but that with time information about what

was needed to migrate and what could be expected in the North increased, so that the later migrants were better able to marshall their limited resources.

47. Wright, *Centennial Encyclopaedia*, p. 33. Baxter was treasurer of the Masonic Benefit Association and director of the Jacksonville Masonic Temple.

48. Wright, *Encyclopaedia* (1947), p. 564.

49. *HADV*, Office Files, UATU, Urb. 3, Box 2, folder 121.

50. Ballard, *One More Day's Journey*, pp. 184, 186–87.

51. Charles A. Hardy III, "Goin' North: Tales of the Great Migration," *Philadelphia Daily News*, Feb. 4, 1985.

52. Margaret Laing, letter to Philadelphia Housing Association, HADV, Urb. 3, Box 21, folder 121.

53. *Fourteenth U.S. Census*, vol. 6.

54. Ballard, *One More Day's Journey*, p. 165.

55. Freehling, *Prelude to Civil War*, p. 55.

56. Clarence E. Walker, *A Rock in a Weary Land* (Baton Rouge: Louisiana University Press, 1982), pp. 72–74.

57. Wright, *Centennial Encyclopaedia*, p. 33.

58. Ballard, *One More Day's Journey*, pp. 173, 174, 179.

Chapter 9: The Earnest Pastor's Heated Term

1. The occasion for the meeting was that Williams had borrowed money from the A.M.E. Connection and never repaid it; *Tribune* 36, no. 23 (Apr. 24, 1920). The Order of Freemasons, in which Williams was a leading figure, regarded failure to repay a loan as almost a cardinal sin. The pastor's failure in this regard may have lost him considerable support in his congregation. Some members even claimed that they had seen Williams and his supporters carrying guns.

2. It was unusual, at this time, to name a church after a living bishop. It goes without saying that Williams gained politically from establishing a church with this name.

3. Wright, *Centennial Encyclopaedia*, pp. 249–50.

4. His reputation was not seriously diminished, and indeed may have been enhanced, by his support of liquor licenses for various Chester taverns, even though drinking was still considered anathema by African Methodists; *Tribune* 36, no. 23 (Apr. 24, 1920).

5. Since Philadelphia was the center of African Methodism, a great deal of prestige was attached to being a pastor of one of the city's A.M.E. churches. As noted earlier, Philadelphia ministers therefore tended to be a more elite group than those elsewhere, and they were a well-educated group on the whole.

6. Rev. William A. Creditt's article in "In the Pulpit and the Pew," on Evangelist Wilbank, known as the "Black Billy Sunday," indicates that black preachers shared the traditional preaching styles of the white churches. This style was taught in the black theological seminaries that had been set up by whites after the Civil War to refine the Christianity of the freed men and women. As pastor of First African Baptist Church, Creditt was in a position to know what

practices were usual in Philadelphia churches. *Tribune* 31, no. 20 (Apr. 10, 1915): 2.

7. *Tribune* 32, no. 49 (Oct. 28, 1916).

8. I am indebted to Allen Ballard for this information.

9. Mother Bethel, Minutes of the Corporation, 1898, microfilm, HSP, roll 7.

10. Ibid., 1910; Beck, "Our Own Vine and Fig Tree," p. 172. No newspaper reports on what has been called the "so-called split" of 1910 have been found, and mention of it in the minutes of the corporation is not specific. It is uncertain, therefore, how many broke away from the church and how much impact the split had on Bethel. It does show, however, that there were considerable tensions within the congregation and that members were not united behind the cause of clearing the church debt. In 1908, just before the split, the church reported 1,148 members; Wright, *1908 Colored Directory*, p. 22.

11. Wright, *Centennial Encyclopaedia*, p. 86.

12. Williams's motivation extended beyond financial considerations. The South seemed to be often on his mind, and he retained strong connections with family and friends who remained in Maryland. In 1916, he returned to Berlin for ceremonies marking the establishment of an A.M.E. church in that town. Prominent among the members of this church was Williams's cousin, Peter Tindley. *Christian Recorder* 64 (June 8, 1916): 1.

13. Mother Bethel A.M.E., Information Bureau Leaflet. Original leaflets are held at Mother Bethel; copies are in the author's possession.

14. Beck, "Our Own Vine and Fig Tree," pp. 96, 41. Du Bois described Bethel as a black working-class church; *Philadelphia Negro*, pp. 203–4.

15. *Tribune* 33, no. 17 (Mar. 17, 1917); during the Centennial Convention of the A.M.E. Church, held in 1916 at Mother Bethel, the congregation had had to organize to accommodate a large number of delegates from other cities in the homes of members. It is possible that Bethel used a similar method to house the migrants, just as East Calvary M.E. Church did, though the migrants, who might have to stay for a long time and who were not honored guests, may not have received quite the same welcome as the delegates. See list of lodgers under "Reserve Homes" in Mother Bethel, microfilm, HSP, roll 9.

16. Mother Bethel, Information Bureau leaflet.

17. *Tribune* 33, no. 19 (Mar. 31, 1917); 32, no. 42 (Sept. 9, 1916).

18. The report of Williams's service at Wesley A.M.E. Zion Church, where he was invited to preach, reads: "There was a shout in the camp!" $103.90 was collected that Sunday. *Tribune* 32, no. 48 (Oct. 21, 1916).

19. *Tribune* 32, no. 49 (Oct. 28, 1916) and 33, no. 3 (Dec. 9, 1916).

20. "Earnest Pastor Works during Heated Term: To Increase the Membership of His Church and Is Eminently Successful. Over One Hundred Saved," *Tribune* 32, no. 49 (Oct. 28, 1916). It is ironic that the *Tribune* should have used the word "Heated" in the headline. It probably refers to Williams's style of preaching and the fervor it aroused in the congregation, and yet it is also appropriate as a description of the conflict that was to develop later.

21. *Tribune* 33, no. 25 (May 12, 1917).

22. During Williams's early period at Bethel, the number of new members joining the congregation was usually recorded in the church news section of the *Tribune*, entitled "In the Pulpit and the Pew."

23. *Tribune* 33, no. 2 (Dec. 2, 1916).

24. *Tribune* 32, no. 49 (Oct. 28, 1916).

25. *Tribune* 33, no. 9 (Jan. 20, 1917).

26. *Tribune* 33, no. 25 (May 12, 1917).

27. Boyd, *On this Rock*, p. 65.

28. Richard R. Wright, Jr., was president of the association, but this was before he became a pastor in Philadelphia; Franklin, "The Philadelphia Race Riot," pp. 344–45.

29. Mother Bethel, Minutes of the Corporation, Oct. 8, 1917. Traditionally, Methodists tested sincerity by subjecting newcomers to a six-month trial to determine whether they evidenced a desire for salvation; see C. M. Tanner, *A Manual of the A.M.E. Church, Being a Course of Twelve Lectures for Probationers and Members* (Philadelphia: A.M.E. Book Concern, 1900), and J. T. Jenifer, "Why I Am an African Methodist," *Review* 7 (1890): 282.

30. According to one member of the church, "[Williams] would tell his members the trustees didn't like them because they were from the South." Beck, "Our Own Vine and Fig Tree," p. 224.

31. When Bethel was founded in 1794, members of the congregation wished to establish their independence from the white Methodist denomination. They achieved this by incorporating the church, setting up the corporation to control all church matters. Even after the African Methodist Episcopal Church was founded in 1816, members of Bethel sought to retain independence from the black episcopacy. Consequently, they made sure that the pastor of Bethel, who was appointed by the bishop of the Philadelphia Conference, was not allowed to become a trustee. This made Bethel an exception in the connection, for at most other A.M.E. churches the pastor was allowed to preside over the board. Many members feared that a bishop might try to use one of his appointed pastors to force the congregation to make changes that they were unwilling to accept. By keeping a clear division of power, and by keeping financial matters in the hands of the trustees, the congregation felt reasonably secure; ibid., p. 170.

32. Mother Bethel, Minutes of the Corporation.

33. The system of election prior to 1910 enabled Powell to maintain his position without fear of opposition. The ballot was prepared by a nominating committee rather than by nominating from the floor. This undemocratic procedure was overthrown when Isaac Moseley, one of Edwards's supporters, resigned in protest. This enabled Edwards to get nominated in 1912, suggesting that plans to depose Powell were longstanding. Mother Bethel, Minutes of the Corporation, Apr. 11, 1910, p. 169.

34. The *Centennial Encyclopaedia* includes group photographs of Bethel's trustees, stewards, and historical commissioners, illustrating the prestige that could be gained from being members of these bodies, pp. 346–47.

35. Mother Bethel, Minutes of the Corporation, Oct. 8, 1917, Apr. 12, 1920.

36. Mother Bethel, Sunday School Board Records of Attendance, microfilm, HSP, roll 9.

37. Williams's scheme was subsequently reported in the *Tribune* 36, no. 23 (Apr. 24, 1920).

38. The nominees were: C. A. Briscoe for president, S. R. Coupts for secretary, R. G. Brown for treasurer, and William Roberts, William D. Daley, and John Cason for trustees. Unfortunately, any letters of transmittal that these men may have brought with them have not survived, so their places of origin cannot be determined. None of them was listed in the 1916 membership roll.

39. H. T. Kealing, "Editorial: Connection Incorporation for the A.M.E. Church," *Review* 16 (1899): 269.

40. Williams's claim to the bishopric would have been a strong one: He had been a presiding elder, a position "of power, strength and forcibleness in the Methodist Church." (A. S. Jackson, "The Presiding Elder System," *Review* 10 [1893]: 301; he had the support of Bishop Tyree after naming a church for him; and Mother Bethel Church had supplied numerous bishops in the past (of the nine pastors preceding Williams, three had become bishops: C. T. Shaffer, Levi J. Coppin, and W. H. Heard). Although the reform of Bethel would have made him many enemies, many bishops would have been grateful to him. For information about the election of bishops, see Ransom, *Pilgrimage*, pp. 261–74.

41. Beck, "Our Own Vine and Fig Tree," p. 101; of the letter-bearers from the South, however, sixty-two were women and fifty-seven were men—not a large majority of women.

42. Wright, *Centennial Encyclopaedia*, p. 304.

43. Only when the constitution and bylaws of the corporation were changed in 1953 were women included as members of the corporation; Boyd, *On this Rock*, p. 69.

44. In 1908, Richard R. Wright, Jr., described the area around 6th and Lombard as a largely "Negro-Jewish district"; *1908 Colored Directory*, p. 48. By 1920, more blacks had left the area and more immigrants had settled there; *Fourteenth U.S. Census* (1920). For information about the construction of the church and its significance, see *Recorder* 28 (Oct. 30, 1890), 28 (May 8, 1890), and in particular 28 (Nov. 27, 1890); also William H. Heard, *From Slavery to the Bishopric*, pp. 76–77.

45. M. W. Thornton, "Richard Allen's Descendents," *Review* 24 (1907): 253; and H. T. Kealing, "Allen's Crypt," *Review* 17 (1900): 392.

46. Beck, "Our Own Vine and Fig Tree," p. 123; Levi J. Coppin, "Rev. C. T. Shaffer, D.D.," *Review* 7 (1890): 203.

47. Rev. William M. Thornton, for example, wrote: "How well the church has respected and preserved these relics of its christening, how precious are they in their possession, and how carefully are they guarded! No price could purchase their removal; as long as African Methodism survives, these momentoes will ever hold their place of inestimable worth"; "Richard Allen's Descendents," p. 253.

48. Williams had been indiscreet in planning this meeting. His agent, William H. Thompson, had sent out a notice four days before, on March 25, to a number of the conspirators. It read, "You are requested to attend a special men's

conference with the Pastor Rev. R. J. Williams of Bethel at my office, S.W. corner of 17th & South Streets, Monday evening March 29th, 1920 at 7:30 p.m."
The notice obviously fell into the wrong hands. It is also interesting to note,
given Williams's support among female members of Bethel, that women were
not included in the planning stages of the coup. *Tribune* 36, no. 23 (Apr. 24,
1920).

49. Minutes of the Corporation, Apr. 12, 1920. The Information Bureau
leaflet, distributed around the South, names Hart as chairman. Thompson's name
appears in the corporation minutes on numerous occasions prior to Apr. 12, 1920.
As an attorney, he was a prominent member of Bethel.

50. *Tribune* 36, no. 23 (Apr. 24, 1920).

51. Mother Bethel, Minutes of the Corporation, Apr. 12, 1920. The meeting is also reported in *Tribune* 36, no. 23 (Apr. 24, 1920).

52. The preamble to this resolution in the corporation minutes reads: "For
some months past, and up to the present time the said church has been sub-
jected to humiliation, ridicule and has also been made ashamed by the acts of its
pastor . . . and as this church is, and has been, and prays that it shall ever be, the
shining light of African Methodism it desires to rid itself of anything that would
tend toward spoiling its high standard."

53. Frank C. Cummings, ed., *The First Episcopal District's Historical Review
of 200 Years of African Methodism* (Philadelphia: A.M.E. Church, 1987), p. 212. I
am grateful to Rev. Jeane Williams for this source.

54. *Tribune* 36, no. 46 (Oct. 2, 1920); 36, no. 47 (Oct. 9, 1920); and 37, no.
28 (May 28, 1921).

55. Cummings, *200 Years of African Methodism*, p. 212.

56. *Tribune* 36, no. 36 (Aug. 7, 1920). Anderson could appeal to established
members of Bethel because he was a Pennsylvanian by birth and had been educated at Wilberforce University and Drew (New Jersey) Theological Seminary.
He had also been head of the Knights of Pythias in New Jersey and had been
successful in several churches in that state. He showed concern for the migrants,
however, possibly because he had experienced adversity in his own life. He had
supported his mother and sister on a small farm in Salisbury, Pennsylvania while
working at a brickyard and had paid for his education at Wilberforce by doing
dining-car service during vacations; *Centennial Encyclopaedia*, p. 24.

57. For instance, Anderson opened the Richard Allen House, a home for
southern migrants, in 1923; *Tribune* 40, no. 36 (Aug. 2, 1924).

58. Only two members of the board of trustees lost their seats before 1924;
Mother Bethel, Minutes of the Board of Trustees.

59. Older members of Mother Bethel described this exodus, cited in Beck,
"Our Own Vine and Fig Tree," p. 100.

60. *Tribune* 32, no. 8 (Jan. 15, 1915).

61. *Negro World* 9, no. 12 (Nov. 6, 1920), quoted in Randell K. Burkett,
Black Redemption: Churchmen Speak for the Garvey Movement (Philadelphia: Temple
University Press, 1978), p. 55.

62. *Tribune* 36, no. 38 (Aug. 7, 1920).

63. *Tribune* 37, no. 11 (Jan. 29, 1921).

64. *Tribune* 37, no. 35 (July 17, 1921).

65. Burkett, *Garveyism as a Religious Movement: The Institutionalization of a Black Civil Religion* (Metuchen, N.J.: Scarecrow Press, 1978), p. 51.

Chapter 10: "Let This Be Your Home"

1. Olivier Zunz, for example, writes: "What is remarkable when we move back in time to examine conditions before the ghetto was formed is that northerners were so unprepared to receive southerners and that the Black community had none of the means of white immigrant communities to incorporate newcomers into its ranks;" *Changing Face of Inequality*, p. 378. See also Mays and Nicholson, *The Negro's Church*, p. 97; Frazier, *Negro Church*, pp. 47–67; Ida Rousseau Mukenge, *Black Church in Urban America*, p. 59.

2. For example, Union A.M.E. Church bulletin (Dec. 1930), in Walter C. Beckett Collection (UATU), Urb 19, Box 4, folder 177. See also the "In the Pulpit and the Pew" section of the *Tribune* throughout the period. Richard R. Wright, Jr., editor of the *Recorder*, urged African Methodists, "Get these Negroes in your churches; make them welcome"; "Should Negroes Come North" (Aug. 31, 1916). Most churches seemed to follow his directive.

3. Wright, "Social Work and the Influence of the Negro Church," in *Academy of Political and Social Science*, July–December, 1907, p. 89.

4. Mother Bethel, Book of Membership Rolls, 1916, microfilm, HSP, roll 9. To get this estimate of southern-born members, a portion of this congregation has been linked to the 1910 census. Nearly 60 percent of Pennsylvania's urban blacks had been born outside the state, *Thirteenth U.S. Census*, vol. 3.

5. R. R. Downs, "How We Should Deal with Our People Who Are Migrating from the South," *Christian Recorder* (migration issue), p. 2.

6. Frazier, *Black Bourgeoisie*, passim.

7. Coppin, *Observations of Persons and Things*, p. 133.

8. Fortune, *Review* 34 (July, 1917): 129.

9. Allen, *Southern Christian Recorder*, excerpted in *ibid.*, p. 131.

10. Wright, *Eighty-Seven Years*, p. 314.

11. Downs, "How We Should Deal with Our People Who Are Migrating from the South," p. 2.

12. Ransom, *Review* 34 (July 1917): 33–34.

13. Allen, in *ibid.*, p. 132.

14. Mother Bethel, Information Bureau leaflet.

15. "'Mother Bethel,' Philadelphia," *Christian Recorder* (migration issue), p. 8; also quoted in Ballard, *One More Day's Journey*, p. 186.

16. *Tribune* 32, 33 (1917). Migration Committee Report, July 1, 1923, p. 1, in Negro Migrant Study (UATU), Urb. 3, Series II, Box 1, folder 2.

17. P. P. Gaines quoted in "New-Comers Are Loyal," *Recorder* (migration issue), p. 3.

18. Graham quoted in "New-Comers Are Loyal," in ibid., p. 3.

19. Mossell, "Standard of Living," p. 176. See report of Committee on Negro Migration dated July 9, 1917, Negro Migrant Study, folder 2.

20. Scott, *Negro Migration during the War*, pp. 134–35; Franklin, "Philadelphia Race Riot," p. 337.

21. Committee on Negro Migration Report, July 9, 1917, Negro Migrant Study, folder 2.

22. Letter from the Diocese of Pennsylvania, Nov. 1, 1917, Negro Migrant Study, folder 2. See also Report of Committee on Negro Migration, July 19, 1917, ibid.

23. At the meeting, John W. Lee of the Presbyterian Church and William A. Harrod of First African Baptist Church were elected chairman and secretary respectively; "Pastors Plan a Great Race Meeting," *Tribune* 33, no. 9 (Jan. 20, 1917); Mossell, "Standard of Living," p. 8. Many African Methodist pastors were involved in this alliance, and two prominent A.M.E. ministers were on the committee, Richard R. Wright, Jr., as secretary (after Harrod) and I. H. Ringgold as a member. As presiding elder of the Philadelphia District, Ringgold served as representative for all Philadelphia's A.M.E. pastors.

24. Jones, *Charles Albert Tindley*, p. 81. Blacks had higher rates of crowded lodging than other immigrant groups; Licht, *Getting Work*, p. 251.

25. This building had been used for church services before the congregation bought its new church on Broad Street. It was unusual for a church to retain an old building rather than to sell it to help pay for the new church.

26. "Letter from the Ministers of Philadelphia, Penna.," *Christian Recorder* (migration issue), p. 4. Apparently, also, black men wearing red caps were sent to the train station to greet incoming trains that might bring migrants.

27. Negro Migrant Study, Urb. 3, Box 1, folder 2.

28. Report of July 1, 1923; Negro Migrant Study, ibid., folder 1.

29. "Editorial," *Tribune* 40, no. 36 (Aug. 2, 1924).

30. Clarence Whyte, "The Great Exodus," in *Tribune* 40, no. 1 (Dec. 1, 1923): 2.

31. Jones, *Charles Albert Tindley*, p. 81.

32. Ballard, *One More Day's Journey*, p. 187.

33. Woodson, *A Century of Negro Migration*, pp. 186–87.

34. Mossell, "Standard of Living," p. 177.

35. Horatio Viscount Nelson, "Race and Class Consciousness of Philadelphia Negroes with Special Emphasis on the Years between 1927–1940," (Ph.D. diss., University of Pennsylvania, 1969), p. 10; Franklin, *Education of Black Philadelphia*, pp. 44–50.

36. Mossell, "Standard of Living," p. 216.

37. Elizabeth Ross Haynes, *Black Boy of Atlanta* (Boston: House of Edinboro, 1952), pp. 181–82.

38. Wright, *Eighty-Seven Years*, p. 192. The description of migrants as "the dumb ones," perhaps unwittingly reveals the patronizing attitude of more elite blacks (regardless of northern or southern origin) toward poorer blacks.

39. *Evening Bulletin*, July 30, 1917.

40. See Wright, *Centennial Encyclopaedia*, photographs throughout, particularly of Allen A.M.E. Church and Mother Bethel.

41. John Brantley Wilder, *The Toasties* (Philadelphia: 1989), pp. 1–3.

42. "The Exodus," *Tribune* 33, no. 26 (May 19, 1917).

43. Walter C. Beckett Collection (UATU). See, for example, letter inviting Beckett to celebration in honor of R. R. Wright, Jr. (Urb. 19, Box 4, folder 190) and letter from *Recorder* to Beckett regarding a Florida disaster (Urb. 19, Box 1, folder 35).

44. Similar tendencies were noted in Chicago's black community by Grossman, *Land of Hope*, pp. 150–60.

45. Zunz, *The Changing Face of Inequality*, and John Bodnar, *The Transplanted: A History of Immigrants in Urban America* (Bloomington: Indiana University Press, 1985), pp. 144–68, show that churches played an important role in helping immigrants adjust to their new American urban environments. However, while different ethnic groups might share the same church auditoriums, immigrants from one group seldom joined churches of another immigrant group.

46. Many churches advertised themselves in this way, Union A.M.E. and Mother Bethel A.M.E. in particular. Mother Bethel, Information Bureau leaflets, and church bulletin, in Walter C. Beckett Collection (UTAU), Urb. 19, Box 4, folder 177.

47. Unfortunately, the original investigation schedules are no longer extant. The increase in the proportion of rural migrants is partially confirmed, however, by the increased proportion of migrants coming from the lower South as opposed to the upper South. In May and June, Virginia (one of the most urbanized southern states) was the origin of the largest and second largest number of migrants, respectively. Later, Georgia and South Carolina dominated as the origin of migrants. Gregg, "Sparks from the Anvil of Oppression," p. 481.

48. Negro Migration Committee report for July 1923, folder 2, p. 3. The author used the increased proportion of rural migrants to explain the decline in fraternity membership, but the argument holds for church membership also.

49. Thirteen of 38 household heads from large cities (34 percent) had remained church members. Of those who came from smaller communities, the figures were 23 of 103 (22 percent). Twenty-six of 33 household heads from places in the South with between two thousand five hundred and ten thousand inhabitants had belonged to churches in the South but did not do so in Philadelphia. Miller, "Black Migration," p. 347.

50. Thirty-three percent of the 52 individuals who had been members of the orders in the South were still members in the North, compared to 31 percent for church members.

51. Fuller, "Negro Migrant in Philadelphia," pp. 68–69.

52. At the turn of the century, A.M.E. churches were as numerous in Philadelphia as Baptist churches. By 1932, however, there were 112 Baptist churches while only 26 churches were affiliated with the A.M.E. Connection. Du Bois, *Philadelphia Negro*, pp. 209, 214, and Mays and Nicholson, *The Negro's Church*, p. 219.

53. The episcopal structure was most effective in supporting missionary work in areas where no churches of the denomination were located. All the financial resources of a large national organization could be brought to bear on the work in places like South Carolina after the Civil War, or South Africa during the

first decade of the twentieth century. For establishing new churches in areas that were believed to have enough A.M.E. churches already, however, the episcopal structure was very ineffective. Often, African Methodists would have preferred migrants to join already existing churches (some of which were financially beleaguered) than to create completely new congregations.

54. Mays and Nicholson, *The Negro's Church*, p. 219.

55. Frazier, *Negro Church in America*, p. 53.

56. Mays and Nicholson, *The Negro's Church*, p. 35; *Tribune* 49, no. 10 (Jan. 26, 1933).

57. Mays and Nicholson, *The Negro's Church*, pp. 34, 219; Du Bois, *Philadelphia Negro*, p. 200.

58. Mays and Nicholson, *The Negro's Church*, pp. 87, 102, 97.

59. Beck, "Our Own Vine and Fig Tree," p. 227.

Chapter 11: Conclusion

1. Kusmer, *A Ghetto Takes Shape*, p. 275.

2. The term comes from Clarence E. Walker, in *Deromanticizing Black History: Critical Essays and Reappraisals* (Knoxville: Tennessee University Press, 1991), though he uses it to other ends.

3. Trotter, *Great Migration*, p. 2.

4. Gloria Naylor's celebrated novels, *The Women of Brewster Place* (New York: Penguin, 1982) and *Linden Hills* (New York: Ticknor and Fields, 1985), focus on the class and gender divisions within and between black communities; Barbara Christian, "Gloria Naylor's Geography: Community, Class, and Patriarchy in 'The Women of Brewster Place' and 'Linden Hills,'" in Henry Louis Gates, Jr., ed., *Reading Black, Reading Feminist: A Critical Anthology* (New York: Meridian, 1990), pp. 348–73.

5. The Move incident of 1985 highlights the stratified character of the ghetto. Mayor Wilson Goode, in many ways a victim of circumstances, was prompted to action by the protests of working-class black homeowners against what they considered the antisocial behavior of Move supporters on Osage Avenue. The police and fire departments, of course, had a completely different agenda of their own.

6. Interviewees who have resided for a time in West Philadelphia invariably refer to "top" and "bottom"; oral histories undertaken by Donna DeVore for the exhibits, "Let This Be Your Home: Philadelphia's African-American Migration," and "Healing the Body and the Mind: Black Sports in Philadelphia." Tapes held by the Afro-American Historical and Cultural Museum, Philadelphia.

7. An excellent review of the most recent literature and its shortcomings is Micaela Di Leonardo, "Boyz on the Hood," in *The Nation*, Aug. 17/24, 1992. See also "The Assault on Equality: Race, Rights and the New Orthodoxy," special edition of the *Nation*, guest edited by Adolph Reed, Jr., and Julian Bond, Dec. 9, 1991.

8. Edward Said, *Orientalism* (New York: Random House, 1978).

Index

African Methodist churches, 2–3,
223n.3; and business initiatives, 83,
240n.46; and capitalism, 83–85,
241n.50; evangelism in, 45, 50, 52–
57, 65–66, 140–41; financial difficulties of, 50–57; gender and, 105–
27, 243n.1; and "Great Migration,"
94, 96, 98–99, 103–4, 193–205,
241n.52; and industrial education,
83; men in, 105–7, 111–18, 244n.2;
and movie houses, 139–40; pastors
in, 129–44, 177; and philosophy of
uplift, 3–6, 87, 219; rallies in, 53–
54; relative decline of, 5, 16; revivals in, 53–54, 76–77, 120; and
social service, 45–50, 57–63; theology of, 3–6, 69–79, 85–86, 88–91,
95–97, 98, 101–2, 237–38n.9, 238–
nn.11,13; and unification among denominations of, 74–75, 238n.19,
239n.22; women in, 105–11, 118–
27, 244n.2. See also, A.M.E. Church;
A.M.E. Zion Church; M.E. Church;
and individual churches of these denominations
African Methodist Episcopal (A.M.E.)
Church: churches of, in Philadelphia, 224n.9; classes in, 52; education of ministers in, 253n.5;
establishing new congregations in,
213; establishment of, 2, 6; in Florida, 167; and fraternal orders, 136–
37; gender in, 107–27; in Georgia,
162–63; and incorporation, 182–83,
185; joining congregations in,
255n.29; letters of transmittal in,
173, 251n.25; minister-editors in,
87–105; pastors in, 132–37, 140,
247nn.4,6,7, 248n.14; relative decline of, 5, 16, 213; in Reconstruc-

tion, 3, 160; in South Carolina, 171;
and southern migrants, 195, 197,
202, 204, 219; and temperance,
109–10; theology of, 238n.11; and
"uplift," 5. See also African Methodist churches and individual churches
of the denomination
A.M.E. Church Review, 71–73; connection of, with denomination, 72;
editors of, 87–98; establishment of,
71, 112, 140, 167, 237n.8; and gender roles, 107; and incorporation,
185; and migration, 197; and ministerial crisis, 137–38; women writers
in, 77; mentioned, 112, 140, 167,
237n.8
African Methodist Episcopal Zion
(A.M.E. Zion) Church: churches of,
in Philadelphia, 224n.9; establishment of, 2–3, 6; in Reconstruction,
3; in South, 160; and southern migrants, 190–91; unity with Methodists, 75, 238n.19, 239n.22; mentioned, 223n.3, 233n.1, 240n.37. See
also individual churches of the denomination
Afro-American League, 81–82
Alabama, 160, 189, 251n.27
Alexander, Raymond Pace, 41, 210,
220, 235n.45
Alexander, Sadie T. See Mossell,
Sadie Tanner
Allen, George Wesley, 196–98
Allen, (Bishop) Richard, 2, 69, 98,
181, 186, 187, 209
Allen A.M.E. Church: Rev. Carpenter's tenure, 121, 130; response to
migration of, 199–200, 203–4;
women in, 120–21
Allen University, 83

Anderson, (Rev.) Harry P., 135, 188–89, 204, 236n.64, 257nn.56,57
Anderson, (Rev.) Matthew, 58, 241n.50
Armstrong Association (Urban League), 33, 48, 59, 101, 166, 200, 204, 206
Askew, (Rev.) Tony Jackson, 56
Associated Charities (Savannah), 166
Astwood, (Rev.) H.C.C., 84–85
Atlanta, Ga., 13
Augusta, Ga., 99

Bailey, George, 172
Baker, Harriet A., 119
Ballard, Allen, 169, 171–72, 249n.2
Baltimore, Md., 13, 24
Baptist Church: establishing new congregations in, 213–14; and Gospel music, 70; membership in, 157; and migration, 65, 214; pastors in, 188; position in African American communities, 49; and southern migrants, 219; spread of, 260n.52. *See also individual churches of the denomination*
Baxter, (Rev.) Daniel Minort, 166–67
Beck, Caroline Stickney, 246n.49
Beckett, (Rev.) Jabez Campbell, 53, 63, 120, 134
Beckett, Walter C., 53–54, 114, 210, 235n.45, 236n.64, 245n.24
Becton, G. Wilson, 56–57
Bell, Mayme F., 181
Bellamy, Edward, 83
Berean Building and Loan Association, 58
Berean Institute, 58
Berean Presbyterian Church, 46, 58, 241n.50
Berks Street Baptist Church, 234n.17
Bethel A.M.E. Church ("Mother"): Centennial Conference (1916) at, 202; and C.P.A., 64; clubs at, 215, 251n.33; ethnic community surrounding, 28; financial burden of, 52–53; formation of, 2; and Freemasons, 137, 245n.27; and I.M.A., 59; and incorporation, 184–85, 255n.31; and letters of transmittal, 147, 159–60; location of, 28; pres-

tige of, 256n.47; rallies at, 53–54; social composition of congregation of, 46–47; and southern migrants, 114, 132, 143, 159–73, 178–82, 190–92, 193–94, 199–200, 204, 215; and split of 1910, 254n.10; and tuberculosis campaign, 61; women at, 121, 185, 256–57n.48; Williams's pastorate at, 175–89; and W.P.M.M., 124
Bethel A.M.E. Church (Augusta, Ga.), 99
Bethel A.M.E. Church (New York), 97
Black Power, 11, 218
Black Theology, 11–12, 70, 88, 226n.38, 237n.9
Bolden, Edward, 41
Bolding, (Rev.) B. J., 190
Borchert, James, 7
Brent, (Rev.) George, 90–91
Brinscombe, B. W. (migrant), 162
Briscoe, C. A., 256n.38
Broad Street Station, 220
Brooks, (Rev.) W. Sampson, 53, 59
Brown, Edward Cooper, 40
Brown, R. G., 256n.38
Brown and Stevens Bank, 40
Buckley, (Rev.) A. M., 97
Building and Loan Associations, 51, 58, 113
Bullock, Riley, 63, 64
Burroughs, Nannie H., 79
Business initiatives, 39, 83, 103; churches and, 58–59, 113–14; and migrants, 23, 114
Butler, (Rev.) F. H., 63
Butler, (Rev.) William H.H., 135

Caldwell, (Bishop) J. S., 63
Cape Colony. *See* South Africa
Carpenter, (Rev.) W. Spencer: background of, 134, 135; and friction within congregations, 141–42; and pastors' problems, 130–31; mentioned, 121, 138
Casselle, Walter W.H., 41
Catholic Church, 15, 49, 70, 211, 233n.1
Cayton, Horace, 7
Central Baptist Church, 200

Central Presbyterian Church, 46, 58, 61, 234n.28

Chappelle, R. L., 121–22

Cherry Building and Loan, 58

Chester, Pa., 134, 175, 177, 253n.4

Chicago, Ill., 10, 13, 99–100, 260n.44

Childs, Hughsey (migrant), 169

Christian Recorder: and church finances, 52; and letters of transmittal, 251n.25; and migration, 98–103, 195, 199, 202–3; role of, 71, 98; and W.P.P.M., 123–24; mentioned, 69, 108, 120, 163

Christian Science, 97

Church of St. John the Divine (P.E.), 24

Church of the Crucifixion (P.E.), 46, 58, 60, 201, 236n.48

Cinnamond, Helen, 166

Citizens and Southern Bank, 59, 235n.45

Civil War, 3, 69, 88, 120, 253n.6, 260n.53

Clark, Edward A., 75–76

Class divisions, 7–8, 40–43, 46–50, 217–22, 261nn.4,5,6. *See also* Ghettoization; Occupations

Cleveland, Ohio, 7, 40

Clinton, (Bishop) George W., 3, 69

Cobbs Creek, 221

Coleman, S. H., 116, 245nn.29,31

Color (differentiation), 208–9, 218

Colored Methodist Episcopal Church, 2–3

Colored Protective Association (C.P.A.), 48, 63–64, 182

Commission on Work among Colored People, 59, 201

Committee on Negro Migration, 200–201, 203–4, 211–12

Cone, James, 11–12, 226n.38, 237n.9

Cooper, Anna J., 227n.41, 244n.15

Cooper, (Rev.) Henry Harrison, Jr., 134

Cooper, (Rev.) Henry Harrison, Sr., 56

Coppin, Fanny Jackson: career of, 120; at Institute for Colored Youth, 59; in W.P.M.M., 124; mentioned, 134, 176

Coppin, (Bishop) Levi Jenkins: at Bethel A.M.E., 134, 178; and bishopric, 97–98, 242n.19, 256n.40; on church finances, 51; and Citizens and Southern Bank, 59; editorship of *Review* of, 71–72, 87–97, 237n.8; and hymnology, 92–94, 242nn.14,15; and migration, 94, 171, 196; on Morris Brown A.M.E., 47; political beliefs of, 91–92; rallies of, 53, 54; theology of, 87–91; and women, 107; mentioned, 77, 120

Corrothers, (Rev.) Sylvester L., 55, 189

Coupts, S. R. (migrant), 256n.38

Crawford, Anthony, 169

Creditt, (Rev.) William A., 27, 54–55, 58, 140, 253–54n.6

Crime, 31, 38, 91–92, 111

"Cults." *See* Religious sects

Daley, William D. (migrant), 256n.38

Davis, Clara V., 124

Davis, Lania D., 47–48

Debardeleben, Mary, 165–66

Delaware, 2, 88, 133, 134, 160, 176, 251n.27

Democratic Party, 64–65

Dickerson, Selena C. Gaines, 109

Disease, 31–32, 38, 61, 92, 111, 231nn.36,39

Division of Medical Inspection, 31

Dixon, Randy, 36

Dodson, Jualynne, 119

Dorsey, Thomas A., 70

Downingtown Institute, 58

Downs, (Rev.) R. R., 75, 194–97, 211

Drake, St. Clair, 7

Du Bois, W.E.B.: on churchgoers, 3, 46–47, 254n.14; differentiation of black churches, 1; and education, 83; and role of churches, 45–46; and study of Philadelphia, 21, 45–47; and "Talented Tenth," 81; mentioned, 48, 60, 99, 201

Dunbar, Alice M., 112–13

Eason, (Rev.) James Walker Hood, 63, 160, 189–91

East Calvary M.E. Church: and I.M.A., 59–60; and Maryland migrants, 160, 254n.15; and response to migration, 201–2, 204, 206; mentioned, 56, 177, 211. *See also* Tindley Temple M.E. Church

Eddystone Munition Corporation, 33, 34

Education, 154–55, 230n.11, 249n.3; intelligence tests used in, 230n.11

Edwards, (Col.) Philip H.: and O.E.S., 121; as President of Bethel A.M.E., 178–79, 183, 186–89, 255n.33

Eighth Ward Social Settlement, 100

Elks (Order of), 137, 245n.28

Elmwood, Pa., 23

Emlen, John T., 200

Evangelism, 45, 50, 52–57, 65–66, 140–41; women in, 119

Evans, Orrin C., 56

Exodus (metaphor for migration), 11, 147, 164, 193, 199, 200, 209, 220

Federal Council of the Churches of Christ in America, 80

Ferris, William H., 74

First African Baptist Church: color conflict at, 209; description of congregation of, 46, 209, 233n.6; expansion of, 200; and Great Depression, 62; and I.M.A., 59; mentioned, 54, 201, 253n.6

First African Baptist Church (Germantown), 47

First African Presbyterian Church, 59

First Episcopal District A.M.E. Church (Philadelphia and New York), 5, 96, 142, 177, 187, 247n.4, 259n.23

First World War: as cause of migration, 13–14; impact of, on women, 36; impact of termination of, 35; mentioned, 16, 23–24, 32–33, 59, 63, 71, 94, 219

Florida: African Methodists in, 166–69; farm economy of, 161; as source of migrants, 24, 149, 160–62, 181, 220; mentioned, 251n.33, 260n.43

Fort Mifflin, 33

Fortune, T. Thomas, 194–98, 237n.8

Franklin, Vincent P., 64

Franklin Sugar Refining Co., 34, 35, 200

Fraternal orders, 114–18, 136–37. *See also individual orders*

Frazier, E. Franklin: and critique of black bourgeosie, 195–96, 221; and Elks, 245n.28; and *Negro Church*, 10–12, 226n.31

Frederick Douglass Memorial Hospital, 40, 41

Free and Accepted Masons (Order of), 41, 114–18, 121, 167, 182, 250n.19, 253nn.1,47

Fuller, William D., 149, 213

Gaines, (Rev.) Abraham Lincoln, 76, 139

Gaines, (Rev.) Preston Paul, 52, 200

Gaines, (Bishop) W. J., 242n.19

Garner, A. C., 74, 76–77

Garvey, Marcus, 190

Gender: in A.M.E. Churches, 105–27, 244n.2; and African Methodists, 219; definition of, 243n.1; and ghettoization, 111, 127, 218, 261n.4; and theology, 12, 227n.41; mentioned, 9, 15, 66, 172, 232n.55, 251n.23

George, Henry, 83

Georgia: African Methodists in, during Reconstruction, 3; club at Bethel A.M.E, 215, 251n.33; migrants and Citizens and Southern, 207–8; migrants from, 36, 103, 148–49; as source of migration, 24, 160–66, 181, 220; mentioned, 99, 133

Germantown, 5, 23, 230n.15, 245n.25

Germantown A.M.E. Church, 5

Ghettoization, 6–10, 17, 24–25; critique of, 7–8, 223n.2, 225n.23, 226n.30, 229nn.1,6,7, 230n.18; in Detroit, 229nn.6,7; and established churches, 193; and gender, 111, 127, 218; impact of, on churches, 49–50, 55, 66; and "paradox of the ghetto," 8, 42, 218; and segregation, 219; social divisions and, 7–8, 218–20, 261nn.4,5,6; mentioned, 16, 40–43, 64, 127

Gibson, John T., 41

Glenn, William (migrant), 184

Good Templars (Order of), 137, 167, 245n.27

Gospel Feast Party, 56–57

Gospel hymns and music, 70, 76–77, 177

Grace Union A.M.E. Church, 224n.10

Graham, (Rev.) Wesley F., 59, 63, 200, 208, 235–36n.46

Grant Chapel A.M.E. Church (Wilmington), 176

Great Depression: and African Americans' switch to Democratic Party, 65; 220; and black middle class, 41; employment opportunities during, 35–36; impact of, on churches, 51, 54; response of churches to, 60, 62–63; mentioned, 3, 59

"Great Migration," 13–16, 147–73, 227n.42; causes of, 13–14, 150–52; and changing patterns of migration, 220; and church proliferation, 214; church response to, 126–27, 193–94, 199–205; impact of, on black community, 3, 23–25, 33, 42, 96; impact of, on churches, 66, 81, 85, 94, 96, 98–99, 143; interpretations of, 6; lynching and violence in, 13–14, 165–66, 169; "push" and "pull" factors in, 13, 150; theology and, 12, 85–86

Green, Andrew, 36

Greenwood, S.C., 162, 169–72, 214

Greenwood Baptist Church, 214

Gregg, (Bishop) John, 132

Grossman, James R.: analysis of Southern cities, 157–58; description of migrants by, 15, 249n.2; mentioned, 147, 243n.26, 250n.10, 260n.44

Guile, M. E., 125

Gullins, (Rev.) William Richard, Jr., 134

Hall, Annie M., 119

Hampton Institute, 34, 135, 136, 232n.60

Handy, James A., 82–83

Handy, Mary F., 124–25, 247n.59

Harewood, (Rev.) J. Da Costa, 24

Harper, Frances E.W., 39, 78–79, 97, 112

Harrod, (Rev.) William A.: and Citizens and Southern Bank, 235–36n.45; and C.P.A., 63; during

Great Depression, 62; and I.M.A., 59, 201, 259n.23

Hart, D. A. (migrant), 114, 184, 186–87, 257n.49

Heard, Josephine D., 78, 124

Heard, (Bishop) William Henry: at Allen A.M.E., 120; as bishop, 132, 142, 167, 188, 248n.28, 256n.40; and Citizens and Southern, 59; and I.M.A., 63; mentioned, 171, 245n.27

Hershberg, Theodore, 226n.30, 233n.3

Hilldale Baseball Club, 41

Hine, Darlene Clark, 151, 232n.55

Hog Island, 33

Holiness Church, 16, 49, 64, 157, 212, 220, 235n.32

Holy Trinity Baptist Church, 59, 64, 200–201, 208

Hood, (Rev.) Solomon Porter, 238n.13

Hopkins, Paulene Elizabeth, 227n.41

Hostility toward migrants, 17, 25, 42–43, 193, 194, 205–11

Housing, 24, 58, 158; churches and, 58–60, 200–204; overcrowding in, 29–32. See also Philadelphia Housing Association

Hoxter, S. E., 124

Hoxter, (Rev.) W. H., 132

Hymns and hymnology, 76–77, 87, 92–94, 129, 177, 242nn.14,15. See also Coppin, (Bishop) Levi Jenkins; Gospel hymns and music; Tindley, (Rev.) Charles Albert

Ihlder, John, 200

Imes, (Rev.) William Lloyd, 61, 234–35n.28

Immigrants (European), 4, 13, 33, 37, 195, 215, 226n.29, 256n.44; and immigration models, 221; Irish, 15, 211; Italian, 15, 211; Jewish, 15, 28, 159, 179, 256n.44; and similarity with African American migrations, 220; and slums, 23

Influenza epidemic (1918), 31

Institute for Colored Youth, 59

Institutional churches, 58, 99–100, 201

Interdenominational Ministerial Alliance (I.M.A.), 59, 63–64, 201–3

Jacksonville, Fla., 13, 145, 161–62,
    166–69, 173
Jenifer, (Rev.) John T., 73,
    238nn.12,19, 248n.19
Johnson, Benjamin (migrant), 162
Johnson, C. H., 111–12
Johnson, James H.A., 105, 107–8
Johnson, (Rev.) W. D., 165
Jones, Absalom, 2, 69
Jones, Hannah, 109
Jones, (Rev.) H. P., 235–36n.46
Jones, Jacqueline, 39, 118
Jones, Marjorie Sougher, 136
Jones, Mary, 97, 119
Jones, (Rev.) Matthew H.: and assis-
    tance from wife, 136; and Free-
    masons, 116–17; on gaining
    prestige, 8; influences on, 86; and
    work experiences, 34–35
Jones, Ralph H., on prejudice at East
    Calvary, 206
Jones, Scott B., 76
Jones Tabernacle A.M.E. Church, 102
Jordan, (Rev.) A. B., 214

Kealing, Hightower T.: on church
    building, 234n.19; on incorporation,
    185; at Review, 87, 95–96, 107,
    242n.19; and women, 107, 120
Knights of Pythias (Order of), 114,
    137, 245n.27, 250n.19, 252n.55,
    257n.56
Kusmer, Kenneth L., 7–8, 40, 42,
    223n.2, 225n.23

Laing, Margaret, 170
Layten, S. W., 38
Lee, Gertrude B., 121
Lee, (Rev.) John W., 59; and I.M.A.,
    259n.23
Lee, Mary E., 108, 246n.51
Letters of transmittal: purpose of,
    126–27, 182, 190; representative-
    ness of sample of, 251n.26; restric-
    tion of voting to people with, 183,
    186; role of, in migration, 126–27,
    159–60, 172–73, 190, 204–5; text
    of, 252n.34; mentioned, 147, 164,
    256n.38
Lewis, Preston, 64

Liturgy and styles of service, 69–71,
    72–77, 139–40, 180–81
Lloyd, Henry Demarest, 83
Long, (Rev.) James A., 167

Mackey, (Mayor) Harry W., 48, 62
Marks, Carole, 249n.2
Maryland: churches in, during Recon-
    struction, 3; as a source of migrants,
    24, 37, 149, 160, 219, 232n.57,
    244n.19; mentioned, 88
Mason, D. James, 184
Mason, Margaret (migrant), 162
Mattocks, (Rev.) D. D., 60
Mays, Benjamin (and Joseph W.
    Nicholson): on church proliferation,
    213–14; on migration, 215; on min-
    isters' education, 135; on ministers'
    pay, 248n.18; mentioned, 226n.31
McVey, Wardell and Betty (migrants),
    148–49
Meier, August, 240n.38
Men: in occupations, 32–36; roles of,
    in the church, 105–7, 111–18; and
    uplift, 110, 113, 118; on women in
    the church, 105, 107–10
Mercy Hospital, 40, 101
Methodist Episcopal Church (M.E.),
    2, 73, 136, 165, 176, 233n.1
Metropolitan A.M.E. Zion Church,
    190
Migrants. See Southern migrants
Miller, Fredric, 149–50, 213, 249n.6
Mississippi, 133, 160
Morris, Martha, 120
Morris Brown A.M.E. Church: "caste"
    of, 47, 233n.7; financial troubles of,
    51–52; and response to migration,
    200; mentioned, 238n.13
Morris Chapel Baptist Church, 214
Moseley, Isaac, 255n.33
Mossell, Nathan F., 40–41
Mossell, Sadie Tanner (Alexander):
    on decline of black community, 25;
    on financial support for churches,
    50; on hostility toward migrants,
    206–7; on housing migrants, 29–30;
    on impact of migration, 21, 25; and
    study of migration, 27; mentioned,
    41, 220
Mount Airy, 220

Mt. Olive A.M.E. Church, 62
Mt. Olivet Baptist Church, 27
Mt. Pisgah A.M.E. Church, 47
Mt. Zion A.M.E. Church: and "Black
   Herman," 55–56; and conflict with
   bishop, 249n.28; establishment of,
   188; financial troubles of, 55,
   234n.17; mentioned, 114, 121
Mt. Zion A.M.E. Church (Charles-
   ton), 171
Mt. Zion A.M.E. Church (Jackson-
   ville), 166–67
Mt. Zion Baptist Church, 27
Move, 221, 261n.5
Murphy A.M.E. Church (Chester, Pa.,
   177

National Association for the Advance-
   ment of Colored People, 48, 58, 64
National Association of Colored
   Women, 109–10
New Deal, 65
Newton, G. L., 97
Nichols, (Rev.) Edward Kingston, 53–
   54
Nichols, (Rev.) P. A., 138
Nix, (Judge) Robert N.C., Sr., 41
Norris, (Rev.) John William, 81
North Carolina: churches in, during
   Reconstruction, 3; migrants from, in
   Philadelphia, 23, 148, 149; as source
   for migrants, 160, 189, 251n.27;
   mentioned, 133
North Philadelphia, 25–32, 58, 171

Occupations, 29, 32–41: in barbering
   and catering, 3, 33, 40; in department stores, 39, 232n.60; in domestic service, 9, 33, 37–39, 46, 61–62,
   82, 110, 151–52, 219, 230n.15; in
   farming, 147, 150, 161, 170–71; in
   medicine, 1, 40, 41, 109; middle-
   class and professional, 40–42,
   233n.64; of migrants, 155; in restaurants, 37; skilled and unskilled industrial, 155, 219
Ocean Steamship Co., 166
Odd Fellows (Order of), 41, 245n.27,
   250n.19
Ogden, Robert, 58, 232n.60, 241n.50

Order of the Eastern Star (O.E.S.),
   121, 186
Osofsky, Gilbert, 7

Palmer, Jennie M., 124
Palmquist, (Rev.) E.A.E., 61
Paris, Peter J., 12, 227n.40, 237n.9
Parker, Mary F., 124
Payne, (Bishop) Daniel M., 69, 75, 76,
   95, 171, 242n.15
Payne A.M.E. Church, 176
Pennsylvania Railroad, 33–35, 200–
   201
People's Church, 189
Perry, (Rev.) C. P., 162
Perry, Christopher J., 41, 236n.63
Peterson, Roosevelt, 172
Philadelphia Anti-Tuberculosis Com-
   mittee, 61
Philadelphia Association for the Pro-
   tection of Colored Women, 37–38,
   100–101, 111, 244n.19
Philadelphia district. See First Episco-
   pal District A.M.E. Church
Philadelphia Federation of Churches,
   61
Philadelphia Housing Association, 29,
   59, 147, 148–49; Negro Migrant
   Study of, 148–59, 170, 249nn.3,6,
   250nn.7,9,14,16–19, 251n.22,
   252n.46; and Negro Migration
   Committee, 201
Philadelphia Independent: and color,
   209; and decline of churches, 47–
   49; and Democratic Party, 65
Philadelphia Navy Yard, 33
Philadelphia Preachers' Association,
   97, 112, 119
Philadelphia Tribune: and color, 209;
   criticism of churches of, 139–40,
   204; on disease, 31–32; and Freemasons, 117–18; and incidents at
   Bethel A.M.E., 175, 181–82, 188,
   254n.20, 255n.22; and migration, 85,
   111, 118, 199, 204, 244n.19; and
   Republican Party, 64–65; on work
   of Philadelphia Association for the
   Advancement of Colored Women,
   37; mentioned, 41
Phillips, (Archdeacon) Henry L., 60,
   63, 201, 236n.48

Pierce, (Rev.) Robert H., 47–48
Pinchot, (Gov.) Gifford, 149
Pinn Memorial Baptist Church, 27, 64
Police, 63–64, 187
Population movements in city, 21, 25–29, 49, 179; churches' response to, 27–28, 49
Porter, (Rev.) James, 5, 75–76
Powell, John R., 183, 255n.33
Presbyterian Church, 41, 234–35n.28; and I.M.A., 259n.23. *See also individual churches of denomination*
Progressivism, 70, 80, 111, 210, 216
Proletarianization, 7–10, 226n.29
Protestant Episcopal Church, 2, 24, 41, 63, 201, 236n.48. *See also individual churches of denomination*
Prowell, Dickey B.W., 121, 246n.47
Purnell, Sydney E., 184

Race riots, 27, 63–64, 164, 182
Ramsey, Roy, 64
Ransom, (bishop) Reverdy C.: as editor of *Review*, 95–100, 137–38; influence of, on Wright, Jr., 98–100; and Institutional Church, 243n.28; on length of pastorates, 143; and response to migration, 85, 194–95, 197–98, 205, 211, 241n.52; on ritualism in A.M.E. Church, 85; and Social Gospel, 97; on socialism, 83–84; theology of, 98, 237–38n.9, 242n.23; and "uplift," 87; mentioned, 242nn.19,24
Reeve Memorial Presbyterian Mission, 27
Religious sects ("cults"), 11, 16, 49, 216; in 1930s, 49
Renfro, Herbert, 81–82
Republican Party, 64–65, 167, 171, 236n.63, 252n.35
Reynolds, Charlotta D., 184
Rhinelander, (Bishop), 201, 236n.48
Rhodes, E. Washington, 236n.64
Richard Allen House, 204, 257n.57
Richmond, Va., 13, 24, 210
Ringgold, (Rev.) Isaac Henry, 259n.23
Robinson, (Rev.) Abraham R., 63
Robinson, (Rev.) J. G., 132
Roman, C. V., 96
Roosevelt, Eleanor, 65

Roosevelt, Franklin Delano, 48, 65
Rosha Building and Loan Association, 235n.45
Rucker, Herman ("Black Herman"), 55–56

St. George's M.E. Church, 2, 98
St. Mark A.M.E. Zion, 60–61
St. Matthews A.M.E., 114
St. Michael and All Angels Church (P.E.), 24
St. Paul's A.M.E. Church (Harrington, Del.), 176
St. Phillips A.M.E. Church (Savannah, Ga.), 162–64, 166–67
St. Thomas's Church (P.E.), 2, 46
Sampson, (Rev.) John Patterson, 239n.22
Savannah, Ga., 13, 99, 161–66, 173
Schneider, John, 64
Scott, Emmett J., 31
Segregation, 60, 91–92, 114, 164; in accommodations, 21, 24, 29, 206; and black middle class, 27, 40; church opposition to, 69; and ghettoization, 7; in South, 164
Service (ethic), 78–79, 94, 105–27, 130, 197
Simpson, Lawson and Lydia (migrants), 148–49
Singleton, George A., 88
Singleton, (Rev.) Richard Henry, 162–66, 252n.35
Smith, Amanda Berry, 119
Smith, (Rev.) J. W., 240n.40
Smith, Thomas (Mayor), 64
Social Darwinism, 12
Social Gospel: African Methodists and, 79–81; and development of African Methodism, 70–71; and migration, 85; and minister-editors, 87–88; Ransom and, 97; Wright, Jr. and, 100; mentioned, 5, 12, 92, 237nn.2,3, 240nn.37,38
Socialism, 81, 83–84, 97
Society for Organizing Charity, 59, 201
South Africa (Cape Colony), 94–95, 124, 196, 260n.53
South Carolina: A.M.E. Church in, 96; churches in, during Reconstruction,

South Carolina (*cont.*)
   3; and club at Bethel A.M.E., 215,
   (251n.33; farm economy in, 161;
   migrants from, 148–49, 160–62,
   163, 169–73, 181, 214; and Morris
   Chapel migrants, 214; as source of
   migrants, 24, 220, 260n.47; urbanization in, 161; mentioned, 121, 133,
   260n.53
Southern Christian Recorder, 164, 196–
   97
Southern migrants, 6, 147–73; adjustment of, 11, 117–18; Bethel A.M.E.
   and, 178–82; and businesses, 114;
   churches and, 47, 52, 59–60, 65, 71,
   77, 85–86, 99, 126–27, 130, 132,
   143–44, 193–216; church formation
   by, 211–16; church work on behalf
   of, 199–205; definitions of, 15–17,
   249n.2; and disease, 31; diversity of,
   147–59, 219; hostility toward, 87,
   195, 205–11; housing problems of,
   29, 30, 32; impact of, on Philadelphia, 23–25; "migrants" and "refugees," 219, 222; preparations for,
   193–94, 229n.7; return to South of,
   171; settlements of, in Philadelphia,
   27; Varick Temple and, 189–92;
   women among, 37–38
South Philadelphia, 23, 25–32, 45
Spear, Allan H., 7
Spiritualist Church, 16, 49, 64, 213
Spring Street Social Settlement, 101
Stansberry, J. B., 82
Stepteau, (Rev.) C. H., 138–39
Stevens, Emily Calkin, 119
Steward, T. G., 119–20
Stewart, (Rev.) Charles W., 121,
   235n.46
Storey, Ella May, 61–62
Sun Shipyards, 33
Sunday, Billy, 54–55, 253n.6

Tanner, (Bishop) Benjamin Tucker,
   71, 73, 124, 242n.15
Tanner, (Rev.) Carl M., 53
Teister, W. F., 115
Temperance, 109–10
Terrell, Mary Church, 36–38, 109–10
Texas, 96, 251n.27

Theology, 10–13, 65–66, 69–79, 87–
   104; and the migration, 85–86, 194.
   See also Black Theology; Social
   Gospel
Thomas, C.O.H., 80–81
Thomas, Susie A., 121
Thompson, E. P., 7, 224n.15, 226n.29
Thompson, William H., 184, 186–87,
   256n.48, 257n.49
Thornton, (Rev.) Montrose William,
   185–86, 256n.47
Thrift A.M.E. Church, 188
Tiller, Robert (migrant), 36
Tillman, Katherine Davis, 78–79, 106,
   109–10, 112, 120, 122–23, 246n.53
Tindley, (Rev.) Charles Albert, 160;
   and C.P.A., 63; connection with
   Wanamaker, 232n.60, 241n.50; con-
   nection with Williams, Jr., 177; and
   Gospel hymns, 70, 129, 237n.4; and
   Great Depression, 62; and I.M.A.,
   59–60; later years of, 56; and response to migration, 201–2; men-
   tioned, 206
Tindley Temple M.E. Church: ex-
   pansion of, from migration, 202; fi-
   nancial troubles of, 56–57; work on
   behalf of migrants of, 200, 204;
   mentioned, 223n.3, 232n.60. *See also*
   East Calvary M.E. Church
Travelers Aid, 200–201
Trotter, Joe William, Jr., 7–10,
   226n.29
True Reformers (Order of), 137,
   245n.27
Turner, (Bishop) Henry McNeil: and
   length of pastorates, 142; on raising
   money in churches, 52; in South
   Carolina, 171; and support of
   Southern ministers, 96; and
   W.H.F.M., 123; and women, 119
Turner, Jane, 61
Tyree, (Bishop) Evans, 177, 253n.2
Tyree A.M.E. Church, 177, 253n.2

Unemployment, 30, 32, 35–36, 39, 60
Union A.M.E. Church: advertising for
   migrants by, 260n.46; congregation
   at, 47; denomination of, 2, 223n.3,
   224n.10; rallies at, 53–54; women

in, 119–20; mentioned, 206, 245n.25
Union Baptist Church, 46–47, 61
Unions (American Federation of Labor), 29, 85; and discrimination against African Americans, 220
Universal Negro Improvement Associaton, 190
Uplift, philosophy of, 3–5, 69, 224nn.14,15, 225n.16; and African Methodists, 219, 237n.9; Coppin and, 91–92; importance in aiding migrants, 104, 195, 204, 206–7, 210–11, 216; men and, 110, 113, 118; minister-editors and, 87; service ethic and, 105–6; and Social Gospel, 12; women and, 79, 111–12, 118
Urban League. *See* Armstrong Association

Varick Temple A.M.E. Zion, 55, 61, 160, 189–91
Violence, 64, 151, 165, 172
Virginia: businesses, and migrants, 23; as source of migrants, 37, 46, 65, 149, 160, 207, 219, 232n.57, 244n.19, 251n.27, 260n.47; mentioned, 34, 133, 136

Walker, J. A., 138
Wanamaker, John, 39, 58, 232n.60
Ward, (Bishop) T.M.D., 72
Ward A.M.E. Church, 27
Washington, Booker T., 82–83, 250n.10
Washington, Forrester, 206
Washington, D.C., 24, 54, 124, 133, 251n.27
Waters, (Rev.) Hodson, 132
Waters, Laura C., 124
Wesley, Charles, 92–94
Wesley, John, 93–94
Wesley A.M.E. Zion Church, 27, 46, 254n.18
West Philadelphia, 23, 25–32; "top" and "bottom" in, 221, 261n.6
Weston Chapel A.M.E. Church (Greenwood, S.C.), 171
Wheeler, Edward L., 4, 225n.16, 238n.11

White, Charles Fred, 55
White, (Rev.) J.T.S., 140
Whyte, Clarence, 30–31, 231n.32
Wilbank, Arthur, 55, 253n.6
Wilberforce University, 134, 135, 257n.56
William Cramp & Son, 33, 35
Williams, Delores S., 12, 227n.41
Williams, Millie, 184
Williams, (Rev.) Robert J., Jr., 175–92; background of, 132, 134; and conflict at Bethel A.M.E., 182–89, 255n.30; and Freemasons, 137, 253n.1; at Mt. Zion A.M.E., 188; and preaching style, 179–81, 254nn.18,20; response to migration, 143, 147, 163, 173, 178–82, 193, 198–99, 254n.12; mentioned, 253n.2, 255n.22
Williams, Thomas (migrant), 148–49
Wills, David Wood, 95
Wilson, (Rev.) Amos, 51–52
Wilson, Margaret, 119
Wilson, (Mayor) S. Davis, 65
Women: in A.M.E. Church, 118–27; at Bethel, 175, 184–85, 257n.48; in churches, 61–62, 94, 105–11, 129–30, 136, 244n.2; on homeless and church, 60; and migration, 151–52, 170, 219–20, 249n.2; in occupations, 34, 36–39, 244n.19, 250n.16; and proletarianization, 9; and *Review*, 96; role of, as pastor's wives, 124–25, 136, 247n.1; and separate spheres, 106, 110; and theology, 12, 77–79; and uplift, 111–12, 118
Women's Home and Foreign Missionary Society (W.H.F.M.), 123
Women's Parent Mite Missionary Society (W.P.P.M.), 123–24
Woodson, Carter G., 29–31; on hostility toward migrants, 206
Work, Monroe, 158–59, 251nn.21,23
World War I. *See* First World War
Wright, (Bishop) Richard R., Jr., 98–103, 243n.27; and banking, 59; on centrality of churches, 1, 48; and church funding, 1, 57; on church and migrants, 194; in C.P.A., 63, 255n.28; as editor of *Christian Recorder*, 87, 241n.3; on Great Depres-

Wright, (Bishop) Richard R., Jr. (*cont.*) sion, 62–63; on location of black community in Philadelphia, 21–23, 28, 39, 256n.44; on problems of urban churches, 45; response of, to migration, 65, 98–99, 103–4, 194–96, 198, 205, 211, 258n.4; on *Review*, 237n.6; on social work, 57; and styles of worship, 135, 243n.33, 247n.8; on theology, 101–2; and "uplift," 102; on vote for women, 120; mentioned, 163, 210, 252n.42

Wright, (Major) Richard R., Sr., 59, 163, 191, 207–8, 235n.45

YMCA, YWCA, 41

Zoar M.E. Church, 62